Praise for Jan McCanless' Books:

"In these days of stress we can all use a good laugh! This book is bound to make you smile and laugh. Jan's quirky sense of humor and outlook on life will do just that! So forget your troubles, kick your shoes off, sit back and enjoy this delightful read! "—Marie Norway, author, singer, songwriter, radio and TV personality

"McCanless is a well-known, award-winning humorist yes, but her reflections are insightful and her humor is iconic, contemporary and inspirational. She has a knack for getting us all to laugh at ourselves as we agree with her timeless truths. My go-to read. "—Sherry Rentschler, bestselling author of *Time and Blood*, Book 1, Evening Bower series

"Jan McCanless writes with humor, and Southern flair that makes her mysteries even more fun to read."—Author Marni Graf, writer of the Nora Tierney and Truly Genova Manhattan series

"Jan McCanless has the uncanny ability to spin a yarn that is not only enjoyable, but, a good, easy read, perfect for a lazy day in front of a roaring fire, or a crashing wave at the ocean. I have spent a goodly number of hours at the beach, which I am sure is close to Beryl's Cove, immersed in her delightful stories."—Camille Jones, retired ESL Teacher

"My favorite author, yours too after reading one of her books!" Robert G. Hyers, retired engineer, Scientific Atlanta

Empower

Publishing

Also byJan McCanless

Beryl's Cove Stories

Gold, Frankincense and Murrrder

Murder for the Profit

Who Killed theWeatherman

The Choir Loft Murders

All Aboard for Murder

The Haunted Chapel

Great Scott

The Case of the Doomed Diplomat

Beryl's Cove and the Elvis Man

Brother Jerome Series

The Opera House Murder

Murder in Midair

Murder on the Mississippi

Compilations

The Bizarre Brain Drippings of a noted Sagittarian, and, more Thoughts of Home

Tire Patch Cookies are Good for the Soul

Wyatt Earp, GAP Pickles, and Thoughts of Home—winner of the Mover Vine Award for the best short stories

Manual

The In$ and Out$ of Writing for Money

Bizarre Brain Drippings from a Noted Sagittarian, and More Thoughts of Home

A Compilation by Award Winning, Bestselling Author

Jan McCanless

Empower Publishing
Winston-Salem

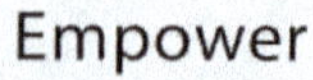

Publishing

Empower Publishing
PO Box 26701
Winston-Salem, NC 27114

First Empower Publishing Books edition published
November, 2019
Empower Publishing, Feather Pen, and all production design are trademarks.

For information regarding bulk purchases of this book, digital purchase and special discounts, please contact the publisher at
empowerpublishing2015@gmail.com

Cover design by Pan Morelli

Manufactured in the United States of America
ISBN 978-1-63066-495-4

Dedication

A compilation takes years to amass, writing for this publication, that venue, and encompasses many, many encounters with numerous people. If you find yourself in this book, it's because I consider you to be a friend, and I think well enough of you to include you in these stories. Believe it or not, the majority of them are true, and, the Chapter entitled ***Brain Drippings*** are my ideas, some of which are whacky and out of kilter, but, what can I say, I'm kind of whacky and out of kilter myself !!!

Special thanks to you, my readers, my kinfolk who just happen to have been born related to me, and most of all, to Genevieve Baker for her expertise in putting it all together for me. She is pure genius, and knowing that there is no way I could do this myself, I am especially grateful.

Enjoy!!!

—Jan

Author's Word

This is my third compilation of my humor columns, amassed from years ago, and, ... last week. They have appeared in newspapers, magazines, and whatever other venue that will print my work. Most of them are funny, but, a few are thoughtful and provocative. There's just no accounting for taste, but, they have been well received, nevertheless.

I love writing about my family, what can I say, they're kin, you gotta love em!!! All the stories about encounters with offbeat, odd characters are true, I seem to attract them, and thankfully, they give me fodder for my cannon. If you don't believe me, I invite you to follow me around one day, and meet some of them. You'll be amazed!!!

This book is dedicated to all those fans out there who just love my work, and can't get thru the day without reading something I have written. God Love ya!!!!! Hope you enjoy these stories, and all I can say is, keep reading me in the funny papers!!!!

—Jan

Table of Contents

Chapter I
Welcome to Geezerland and More Thoughts of Home

Welcome to Geezerland!

Ah, June…puts me in mind of weddings, flowers, and all thing bridal. Last year I was invited to four weddings. I even KNEW some of the people involved! Boy, I can remember my own wedding just as if it were 41 years ago! When our generation married, we'd go to the jewelry store and register china and silver patterns, and, probably, order our invitations at the same time. Nowadays, these brides register at the big department stores, asking for everything from paper towel holders to major appliances. I was so grateful for every tea towel and silver candle snuffer I got, and wouldn't dream of asking for half the stuff today's brides take for granted that they'll get. Well, times change.

Our generation lived through several wars, a depression, presidential assassination, and political scandals. We were born before lava lamps and Medicare.

Kids were different in "our" day as well. Remember the "look" from Mom if we behaved badly or sassed an adult? All moms had to do back then was fix this blistering stare on a youngster, and we straightened up pronto! Boy, try that today, and you are just as likely to be sued!

It was the cars back then that I found so fascinating. Remember the old Packard's? Enough chrome on them to sink a battleship. but when they were all polished up, those Packard's shone like sterling! I loved the huge, white-wall tires on cars, too. To NOT have the white-walls put you in the same class as a farm vehicle, and my dad went out of his way to make certain his cars had the widest white-walls of anyone.

Now, we have fast food, instant messaging, and hybrid cars. I'm not sure I like all these changes, but I know we have to "go with the flow," or be miserable.

I've come up with a really neat idea to feed the old "nostalgia" genes. It's a theme park aptly called "GEEZERLAND." Now, here's the thing, you have to be at least 55 years old, and 5 feet tall to even be admitted to my theme park, and it opens at 7 am and closes at 9 pm so we can all go home and go to bed. "Elevator music" is played throughout, and one is encouraged to sing along. Hamburgers are any way you want them, and only cost a quarter. Soft drinks are the kind we used to get from the fountains at the drugstore. You know, you put a dollop of syrup in the glass, and add seltzer.

Speed limit in my theme park is a mandatory 35 mph, and anyone caught driving in the right-hand lane with their left turn clicker on, is rewarded with a free ride on the vintage cars. Only big, clunky cars are allowed inside the park. No cell phones, and if you want to phone anybody you have to sit in the phone booths. but don't worry – they all have bench seats in them.

The Geezerland Hotel and Convention center has TV sets in all rooms, and the programming ends at 9 pm with the paying of the national anthem, played by the US Marine Band, conducted by the clone of John Philip Sousa. If you get sick while in my theme park, the doctor will make a house call for you, and charge you $5 or a handful of home-grown vegetables – whichever is handiest.

Well, I can dream, can't I? Seems like a plan to me. Maybe I should just go buy my Cheerwine slushy, and think about the good old days while I sit on park bench and people watch!

I'm Where?????

As I've gotten older, I'm happy to say, my sense of direction has gotten considerably better. Time was, however, when I couldn't find my way out of the driveway. Well, I could find my way, I just simply didn't know where I was once I got there. Never lost, just moderately confused.

When I first moved to North Carolina in 1961, I used to love to ride around town and figure out where things were. Usually my Mom was in the car with me – she didn't drive – and depended on me to get here everywhere she wanted to go. Unfortunately, I got lost all the time, or, I would take one of my famous shortcuts, thereby adding a good 45 minutes on to our drive time. She laughed about it all the time, constantly kidding me about my lack of direction.

Of course, all this bragging on myself doesn't count if I'm out of town. All those one-way streets and such. However, lately, I've had to navigate quite a bit for the spouse and me when we go someplace. That may be why we don't travel all that often anymore, too!

My brother, knowing my penchant for getting lost, bought me a sweatshirt you see pictured here. I was up in Wisconsin recently visiting him and he wanted to be sure that, should I get lost, someone would find me and return me to his house. My daughter even bought me a shirt with a dot on it saying "You Are Here." No respect.

Well, like I said, that was then. This is now. I do pretty well, I think, unlike an uncle of mine who, upon being stopped for traversing a one-way street in Atlanta, declared to the officer that he was only going "ONE WAY."

I really think it has something to do with being left-handed. My daughter is left-handed, and when I want her to make a right turn, I tell her to take her "other left." We of the southpaw persuasion have to think twice as hard as other people, due to the fact it's a right-handed world, and we "lefties" have to stick together. Roads are made for right-handers, signs, everything. That may be the reason behind my aversion to maps. They are obviously folded by a right-handed individual, hoping to confuse the rest of us.

Happily, I did not get lost in Wisconsin. I wore my sweatshirt just in case. Good thing, too, as it's mighty cold in Wisconsin. All that Canadian air coming at you. That's one place where, I'm almost positive, one could navigate by the stars. My family lives out in the country where there are no lights or distractions, so the northern lights and the Milky Way are quite visible in the night sky.

Hmmm, if I wear my Door County, Wisconsin, sweatshirt, maybe someone will ship me back up there. So long as they don't ask me to fly the place, I'm pretty sure I would not get lost!

Summer "Matters"

I love to start up conversations with strangers, you'd be surprised how much in common you can find with others, and, make new friends along the way. You want to start a conversation – mention home grown tomatoes, and instantly, you'll have people talking, oftentimes at once!

One of the things I love most about summer is the food. Fresh fruit and produce, just can't be beat, and with so many farms around the area, and farmer markets, produce stands, etc. the selection is outstanding. In cold weather, we enjoy our roasts, and baked items, but come summer, I want salads, watermelon, fruit, all things cool and fresh, and one of the best things of summer is the tomato sandwich. Now, there is a knack to this delicacy for sure. For one thing, it's got to be made on white bread, no other kind, slap on some mayonnaise, my brand of choice is Duke's, and then, slice a big, red, juicy tomato, and place it in the middle of the bread, put the two sides together, and man oh man, that is good eating! It helps if you have a lot of mayonnaise, and the tomato is really juicy. It just doesn't get any better than this!

The other day, at the "Y," a friend of mine was telling me that she didn't have any idea what to fix for supper the night before, so, she made tomato sandwiches, stewed up some corn on the cob, fresh fruit, and apple cake. Made my mouth water just thinking about it!! Now, the spouse, he tells me that he ate a tomato sandwich every day for lunch as long as he was in school. Reckon it stopped when he hit high school, but now he claims, he can take them or leave them, when it comes to tomato sandwiches. I did not enjoy that delicacy as a child, so, I have some catching up to do.

Several years ago, I was writing a "man in the street" sort of thing for a newspaper and decided I would ask passersby about tomato sandwiches. It was, after all, summer, and the crop that year looked especially good, so, out onto the corner I went. Things were going well until I stopped one gentleman, obviously a farmer, and asked him about tomatoes, did he eat them in sandwiches? He scratched his head momentarily, and said he'd rather talk about oatmeal. I'm game for anything and said, "Sure, what do you like in your oatmeal?" "Beans and corn," he declared. To say I was taken aback somewhat was an understatement, as I stared wide eyed at the man, I couldn't believe I heard him right. "Beans and corn? In your oatmeal?"

"Sure," he said, "what d' you eat it in?" "Sugar and cream," I managed to mutter. Lots of folks put brown sugar and cinnamon on it, but I stick with the sugar and cream. Just as he was about to walk away, I grabbed him and asked him if he would mind telling me about the tomatoes he eats. "Never touch 'em," he told me. Well, so much for my roving reporter days.

During post World War II time, back in the late 40's, everybody had a victory garden, as a kid, I attempted one during that time, hoping I could produce enough to feed myself, brother and parents, and taking great pride in what I was hoping to accomplish I set out to hoe, rake, and plant. I mean, I was just a little kid, but I put a lot of love and effort into that garden, it was a neighborhood thing, and each of us had a little plot to call our own. Even told my mom that I would work it and do all the gardening, she was simply to stand by with the basket to collect the produce. Funny thing is, it didn't yield anything but dusty ground and dead plants, seems someone forgot to tell me you had to water them. Remember, I was just a little kid, 5 or 6 years old, and while I enjoyed working the garden, it yielded nothing. I was so embarrassed. Fortunately for our family, we had real gardeners in the family who managed to provide us with all the wonderful summer goods we could eat, and the tomatoes, oh they were glorious! Mama made the best bacon, lettuce, and tomato sandwiches around, and I was usually able to convince her to fry up a couple extra pieces of bacon for me when she did.

Sometimes, today, I will put a slice of cheese on my sandwich, Swiss seems to work really well, and interacts deliciously with the tomato. Anyway, back to my theory, that if you want to start a conversation, just mention summer "matters" to someone you know and see what happens. My only question now is, when fall gets here, what will we talk about that will get people as fired up? I can't see anyone getting excited over pumpkins, but who knows, maybe I'll try it anyway!

If You Really Want to Feel Good About Yourself, Don't Eat Breakfast with This Man!

I love the study of family histories, and I have some interesting characters swinging from my genealogical tree, so to speak. For instance, on my mother's side, if you go back several generations to that Rolf fella in England who married Pocahontas: I'm related to them, and there's supposed to be some distant relationship to that 30's movie actor, William Powell.

Like most southern families, ours is full of eccentrics. Some have even suggested that I am one, and we should parade them out in public so that everyone can enjoy them.

Eccentric or not, we have always taken pride in our most famous member, AP Hill. You know, the civil war guy who had an entire fort named after him. Well, there I was one morning, having breakfast in the church fellowship hall, when I decided to regale a friend with my knowledge of all things "civil war." Now, for those who don't know my friend, he lives in rural North Carolina, and is the definitive authority in these parts on all things and persons pertaining to that particular period in our history. He is a re-enactor, and even has his own museum. I was going to impress him!

I happened to ask him if he had seen my article about Gettysburg that had appeared in the local paper. Casually, I asked him if he had ever been to the Gettysburg Battlefield and cemetery.

"Yes," he replied. "I went there on my honeymoon."

Well, I have always wondered what sort of individual would travel to a cemetery on their honeymoon! Feeling somewhat proud of my AP Hill connection, I mentioned the fact that was related. Then I did the DUMBEST thing I have ever done. I asked him if he knew anything about the Hon. Gen. Hill.

"Only that he had syphilis, and rode his horse right up through the Northern ranks and got shot," he said.

Boy, talk about a defining moment, while everyone was laughing, I lost my appetite! There went my familial pride.

Well, my friend doesn't know EVERYTHING: my mother's maiden name was Gregg. Also involved in the civil war was a Brigadier general, David McGregg, second division, cavalry corps. In fact, there is a street in the Gettysburg cemetery named after General Gregg, as you can see by this photograph. Funny, I didn't notice a POPE AVENUE or LANE or STREET when I was there!

Oh, one small thing, General Gregg fought for the "other" side during the hostilities, just don't say anything to David about it!

Who Are All these Old People?

Now, I know I am getting older, I'll be 34 again next year, but I pride myself on staying in some sort of shape. I am not fond of class reunions, nevertheless, I went to my own couple summers ago in Atlanta.

I made the reservation; it was for dinner, cocktails, and a night of fun, the invite said, Oh, what the heck, I thought, it's been many, many moons since I saw everybody, so, I booked a train ticket, and took off for my old stomping ground of Atlanta, the "jewel of the South."

The venue for our reunion was a place in the Buckhead section of Atlanta, that didn't even exist when I was a teenager. Buckhead at that time had a hardware store, a drugstore, hair salon, and small diner. Period. But I lived there and had only to walk across the street to my high school. Today it's THE place to be.

Well, here I was at the restaurant, the place was jumping, parking lot was full, and my driver let me off right at the front door. A "child," younger than the shoes I was wearing, led me up to the rooftop garden where our reunion was to take place. I looked around, but did not see a single classmate of mine – anywhere. They had all stayed away, and sent their grandparents in their place. Didn't recognize anybody, except Bruce, the guy who was on the planning committee. Couldn't miss Bruce, he was still 7 feet tall, and had been our star basketball player for North Fulton High School.

Who are all these old people, I wondered, surely not the same "kids" I was in school with. Finally found a seat next to an elderly gentleman at the table, who was soon joined by his wife. She greeted me like a long-lost friend, and as I stared at her, I couldn't help asking myself, "Who are you, and what have you done with my classmates?" Eventually, I got up the courage to ask her if I knew her. She replied that yes, we used to chat, every day in the library. Oh really, interesting, soon we were joined by a woman on a walker, who had her boyfriend with her. He had his oxygen tank at the ready and was on crutches.

Now, don't get me wrong, there is nothing wrong with being elderly, and using devices like walkers, it's just that I didn't know these people, and I couldn't imagine going to school with them – after all, I am only 34!!

As we began to eat our meal, and get reacquainted, slide photos from our senior yearbook were flashed on the wall, and wouldn't you know it, there I was. I was going to be polite and stay with my tablemates, they seemed like nice folks. My classmates, of course were nowhere to be found, so, I was simply going to socialize with this group. Then, the photos appeared, and to my astonishment, I began to recognize a few of the individuals there.

Well, it gave me smug satisfaction to see that while I stayed 34, my classmates had been caught up in time. Who knew?

I'm still not fond of my own reunions, but I will say it was interesting to go back in time and see these folks. Not that I wish anyone ill will, but me, and my crowd were not part of the "homecoming queen" set, so, I took small satisfaction in seeing our homecoming queen in the corner holding forth with her girlfriends from the court, then, she stood up, all 300 pounds of her.

Not so bad being 34 after all!

Jan McCanless

Wrong Way Corrigan Ain't Got Nothin on Me!

It used to bring a huge laugh, when Gracie Allen would be on her radio or early TV show and tell George she switched the contents of the sugar bowl and saltshaker, because, she said, "if I'm wrong, then, I'm right." I never could understand the laughter, I mean, what's wrong with that?

I'm one of those people who can screw up a one car funeral procession. Not that I'm addled, you understand, it's just that I have better things to do with my mind than remember stuff! Take the other day, I was conversing electronically with my publisher, and he mentioned the fact that emailing with me was always an "adventure," because he was never sure what would happen. Not sure, but I think I resemble, er, resent that. Can I help it if my computer does not speak the same language I do?

Once, in my capacity as a teacher of high school students, I got in a rush one morning, and put on two different colored shoes. Standing there, monitoring the hall traffic, was, shall we say, challenging? Finally, I gave up, and ignoring the snickers of my students, told them it was a new fashion trend I was trying to set.

Then, there was the time, I drove out in the country to a church circle meeting, and went to the wrong house. Banging on the door, I couldn't understand why no one would answer it, especially since we were all expected. I didn't find out the mistake until I turned around and saw all my circle ladies standing the lawn next door, waving to me. Well?? It was an honest mistake.

Two of my friends are named, Helen, one spelled with an extra "e," but their names are side by side in my contact list, so naturally, every so often one will get the email intended for the other one. That wouldn't be so bad, except now, due to one little slip up they've become friends and are emailing each other about me! If I was really concerned, I'd be embarrassed, but like I said, I have other things on my mind.

A lot of writers are this way, I hope, because we all are so busy with our brains spilling over with words, we get a little bit careless. Well, the only ones it really bothers are the kids, they can't understand why I'm not in some kind of group home somewhere, dribbling my soup. I truly believe they think the group home folks are too smart to accept me, I'd give them all a bad name!

A good friend of mine, another author, writes a bi-weekly blog, and she has asked me to fill in for her a couple times, knowing, she says, she never has any idea what I'll come up with, and therein lies the adventures. She once asked me if I was on social media. I said no, because sure as shootin, I'd hit the wrong key, end up talking to Habib in Bangladesh, and the next thing you know, "poof" my world would explode. I couldn't live with that. No, for the sake of humanity, I stay off social media.

As for all that other stuff, well, isn't it enough I write the world's greatest mystery stories, and can balance my own checkbook? Some of us are talented, and some not. Besides, after you lived to be 34 like me, one should be entitled to a little eccentricity – doncha think?

I'm Not Ready for This

I know that time passes quickly, especially the older one gets, but this is ridiculous!! I was not even over the celebration of Thanksgiving, before Christmas was upon us, and now we are already into 2019! Shouldn't there be some kind of law against this?

Every year I rale against the retailers for beginning the holiday season right after Labor Day, then, before the pumpkins are even old and stale, out comes the Christmas decorations. No sooner is the 26th of December here, when the Valentine's pop up everywhere. I tell you, I am not ready for this! Auld Lang Synge has barely faded into the background, and the stores are already telling us what to give loved ones for Valentine's Day. We gotta quit this.

Remember, as a kid, lying in the grass, pondering the cloud formation as they rolled by? It was usually on a sultry summer day, when the world moved slowly, and most everything came to a halt for a couple hours every afternoon. The idea of Christmas, New Year's and Valentine's Day were not anywhere in our thoughts, we were simply enjoying the moment we were in. What would it hurt to resurrect that train of thought?

Just before Christmas, I was downtown and it looked to me like everyone was moving at warp speed, then, the after Christmas white sales began, and shopping became almost a contact sport.

I love to watch the ***Garfield*** movie with my grandchildren when they visit, and that cat may be on the right track. Anytime you feel like getting up and doing something, lay down till the feeling passes – that's his philosophy. I used to fret at seasoned citizens as they meandered across the street, or took their time ordering from a restaurant menu. You know what? I'm one of them now. I have become my mother! Now my Mama, God rest her soul, she never moved fast for anything, and if she wanted to sleep until noon, she would. She would fumble around in her purse looking for enough coins to pay for an item in the store, and she'd stand and read labels for the l-o-n-g-e-s-t time before she'd put an item in the basket. Well guess what guys, I am now doing the same thing!

My children think I'm nuts, because when I do cross the street, I wave to the cars waiting there are the light. I smile broadly, and take my time. I mean, I'm retired, what's my hurry? Besides, I might know those folks in the car, or they might know me, and I would hate to slight anyone.

I've decided to get off the warp speedway and slow down – enjoy the passing parade, and savor the moment. This summer, I am going to my class reunion in Atlanta. I don't know any of them anymore, wouldn't recognize anyone from my class if I saw them walk up to me, but you know what? I'll go, reminisce, talk about the "old days," lie about my fortune and success, and imagine I'm lying there in the grass once more marveling at the shapes in the clouds.

Racing around is for NASCAR, not me!

The Splendors of Autumn

I'm truly an autumn person, I was born in the fall, married in the fall, and have always thought October and November the best months of the year. It was in the fall when the love of my life came into my world, so, it is no wonder that I truly revel in this season of the year.

The leaves on the trees in my yard are beginning now to turn to their glorious reds, gold and orange, and it's a riot of color that is unsurpassed anywhere. I can't wait to get back up into the mountains and check out the Blue Ridge in all its splendor.

As a kid, I used to love it when my dad would rake up the leaves into a big pile at the curb. That pile of leaves was just made for jumping into, and as much trouble as I put my dad to after raking them up a second and third time, he never stopped me from my fun. The smell of burning leaves to this day, makes me all nostalgic for that leaf pile.

Then, there is Halloween – just saying the word conjures up all kinds of mental memories. I mean, nowadays, you see people out on the street who need no costume or mask. Have you seen some of these folks walking around? If you've missed them, go to any shopping center anywhere, for instances, and there they are, just for the looking! As a kid, it was my favorite time of year, the best night in the world. Me and my cousin, Shari, would often go out together, carrying a large grocery bag, take it home and empty it out, then go back out again! There was this man on our street who always insisted we perform some kind of "trick" before he'd come forth with treats, so, my neighbor buddies and I would end up doing a little dance, or singing some crazy ditty just to cadge a piece of Double Bubble bubblegum from him. We used to think him unbearably cruel, but upon retrospect, I see he was enjoying the evening as much as we were, in his own way.

Aunt Florence made it very special for us though. For days beforehand, she'd be making up popcorn balls and candied apples for us at her door, and while she was not in our neighborhood, I always insisted Mom or Pop drive me and brother over there just to get her homemade treats, which were beyond delicious. As soon as she'd plop them in our bag, we'd go around the corner, wait a few minutes, and go back a 2nd time for more. Naturally, she never let on that it was us coming around once again, she was just that kind of person. You show up at her door, you get something, even if it was the 5th or 6th time she'd seen you that night. Her Collie dog, Wags, always gave us away, as we were his particular favorites and no matter how many times we'd knock on her door for Halloween, Waggy would spot us and frantically wag his tail, while Aunt Florence acted totally surprised. Wonderful memories of a special time and person in my life.

I always dressed my children in Devil costumes or some homemade horror of some kind, and the first place I'd take them was their Dad's office, where they collected a large assortment of things. They seemed to enjoy answering the door and doling out the goodies as much as collecting them for themselves.

With so many churches in the area having a safer, inside festival and Halloween, I miss seeing all the little ghosts and goblins running amok through the neighborhood as they once did. I know it's safer for them, but it seems to have taken some of the fun away from the holiday in the process.

I hope all the little ghosts, monsters, and goblins out there have a safe and happy Halloween this year, and all I can say is Boo! Thank God for memories!

Jan McCanless

Fashion by Hopalong

A TV set was not something my parents were eager to buy, since they didn't think that television would outlast radio.

We did, however, visit a great deal with my Aunt Florence, who owned the first TV set in the family – a Muntz with a 6-inch screen encased in 4 feet of bulky cabinet. Uncle Steve could hardly wait for the evening news and wrestling matches, and Aunt Florence always accommodated my love of Westerns.

The TV serial Westerns were all the rage, and my all-time favorite was ***Hopalong Cassidy***. I was the happiest little girl in the world when, for my birthday in 1950, I received my cowgirl outfit with accompanying six shooter.

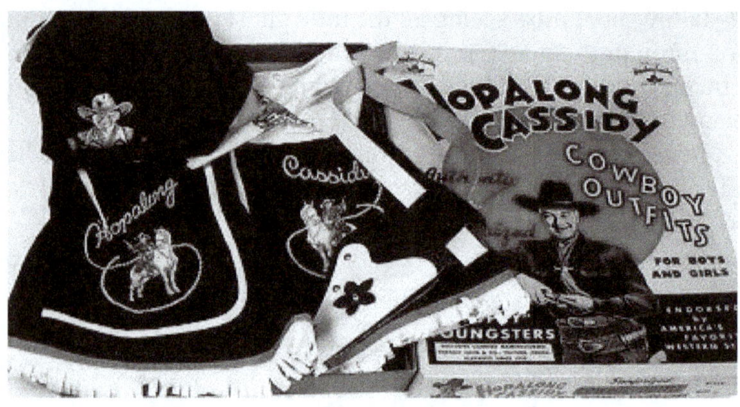

Hurry September

Now I am not one of these folks who wishes their life away by saying I wish it was soon going to be this or that date, but c'mon, this summer has not been the delightful bucket of giggles that the season is meant to bring.

What little grass we have is burned up, my flowers are drooping, the trees are sagging, and the humidity has me dragging. Whenever it has rained this summer, one can almost see the grass turning green under your very eyes, and everything looks so happy and refreshed. Then, a month later, we'll get another 11 drops of water, and on it goes. Now here it is September, and I have not accomplished a whole lot of what I wanted to do this summer. In June, I spent 3 days in Raleigh with a girlfriend for a "girls" only time out, and it was wonderful, we went to movies, we shopped, we ate whatever we wanted, and we talked about our menfolk. Could not have been more fun.

But September, now, that presents a whole 'nother scenario. For one thing, schools start back up, and I am instantly carried back several years (at least 10!) to my school days. I got a new pair of shoes, a couple dresses, a notebook, paper, and new pencil box. What joy filled my heart as I gazed upon my "cache" and loved that new smell all of it had. My pencils were sharpened to a dangerous point, and I was ready. Have you read the list of school supplies the students nowadays are supposed to buy? I'd need to take out a loan to buy all that stuff on there. I mean, really, it boggles the mind.

I was one of those kids who checked off the calendar how many days until our first holiday, which usually occurred on Columbus Day in October, then, I aspired to nothing more than head eraser cleaner. I really didn't care all that much for school, all I looked forward to was getting out. Now, the kids have so many more activities while they learn, and it all looks like fun. Even when I was a teacher, I tried to make it interesting and fun for my students, at least less boring than other classes.

Well, back to my school, elementary school to be specific. With my active imagination, I would come up with all kinds of reasons as to why I should not and could not attend that day. Mother never bought it though, and one day, I told her I was sure the school might catch on fire and I'd have to come home anyway, but still she insisted

I go. Now, bear in mind my school was old, lots of wood in it, and it could happen, the fire, I mean. We also had no cafeteria, so, I walked home for lunch, then, walked back, and if you were a student who lived too far away to walk, you carried a sack lunch and ate it on the playground. Well, this one day, I walked home for lunch, ate my bologna sandwich, and started back, a distance of some 6 blocks or so. As I approached the school yard on my return trip, I saw all kinds of activities, fire trucks, police cars, all the kids lined up on the playground, yep, it had happened, the school had caught on fire, and no, I had not set it. All the teachers came around and told us to go home, there would be no school the rest of the afternoon, or the next day either.

Oh the joy, freedom, a whole afternoon off, and I didn't have to come up with some excuse as to why I was once again walking home. I walked into our kitchen, Mama was surprised to see me, and when I told her the school had been on fire, what did she do? Well, she didn't believe me, I can tell you, she picked up the phone and called some of the mothers of my classmates to find out the "truth" she said. Sure enough, they told her about the fire, and how there would be no school the next day either I had never felt such joy and freedom in my entire life!!! All 7 years of it!!! I could not change my clothes and run outside fast enough. As always, Mama told me to be careful, and to come home when it got dark.

I don't suppose the same thing would play out today, first off, the kids would spend the rest of the day texting one another, no such thing as running outside to play, and if the mothers told them to come home at dark, they more than likely would be arrested for child neglect. I got a flash for you guys, we even drank water from the garden hose!

Well, so much for the good old days, but because of that fire, I've always had a soft spot in my heart for September.

March Madness Made Personal

You see this photo of me holding the fish I had caught up at my Aunt Florence's place in Green Lake, Wisconsin?

It's proof positive that I can and have caught a fish. When the children were small, I took them often, out to the park and we would spend the day fishing together. They would bring up bream, bass, even a good-sized catfish or two, while I would make the most beautiful casts you ever saw and bring up seaweed! On one of my casts, a really good one, I hauled in a boot full of seaweed, much to the children's delight.

One time in particular, I cast my line, it went skyward, hooking a duck as it passed by. It caught the duck on a wing feather, no damage done, but I had to reel the bird in to unhook it and send it on its way. That's when the trouble started. Seems the poor duck didn't enjoy being reeled in and squawked its head off, sending the young'uns into peals of laughter, causing the other fishermen around us to collectively utter a loud "SHHH" in unison, and making the wildlife authorities not too happy in the process. Seems I couldn't get a break, the faster I reeled in, the louder the duck squawked, the more the kids laughed, and the angrier everybody else got. Finally, everything was righted, and the ruffled bird sailed away, to join Mrs. Duck presumably, and whisper about the crazy lady on shore who was a menace to all. Probably told the fish about me too, as I didn't catch anything all day, all the while the children were bringing them in one after another. We continued to fish there, for years…why, I have no idea.

One day, with her children in school, my darling, dumpling daughter suggested just the two of us go back to the park and drown a few worms. It was a warm, sunny March day, so, I thought why not, it will be wonderful to bond with my youngest and maybe once and for all, show her I really could catch a fish. This time, being older, both of us carted along a nice yard chair, a cooler full of soft drinks, and some sandwiches. We were going to make a day of it and really enjoy ourselves. Being the "seasoned" sportswomen we were, we even made small talk with the other fishermen, "hiya, how're they biting?" that sort of thing. There we were, lazily watching our bobbers float, thoroughly enjoying the warm, March day, when she very sweetly said to me, "Mom, don't look now, but there's a snake swimming in front of you, going to get tangled in your line." Have you any idea of how this scene played out? Now, my daughter has never been afraid of snakes, but me, now that's another matter. She very calmly continued to fish, I jumped up, overturning my lawn chair, and in my haste to fold it up and get the heck outta there, I cut my thumb, badly. Bleeding all over the place, screaming in terror, my child laughing at me, all the other fishermen collectively hollering "SHH" at me, and upsetting the wildlife authorities. It was then, I decided we needed some recreational counseling of some sort, and I haven't fished since.

However, come March, my thoughts turn to spring, and all the fun I used to have up at my Aunt's lake place, and I want you to now I caught plenty of fish, just look at that stringer I'm holding!!! Gives new meaning to the term March Madness when it gets personal like this!

You should've seen the one that got away!!

June is Bustin Out all Over, and all that Good Stuff!

I love it when I get a response to one of my columns. Someone will stop me on the street or telephone, and make some comment. Good or bad, I love it. I was, however, quite surprised when someone quite recently gave me a recipe for stewed possum, in response to my springtime article about fricasseeing Punxsutawney Phil because of all the bad weather we've had. Along with the recipe, they also noted that they too had a grandmother skillful about preparing "roadkill." It was heady stuff, and I share the ground hog recipe with you now, only as an addendum to what I'm writing this month. You might also get a laugh from it.

First off, find a ground hog, and take him home. After you have prepared a pot with water, herbs, butter, a brick, and some seasoning, throw in the ground hog. Yes, you heard me right, a brick. Anyway, after all this is mixed up, then lastly, empty a bottle of whiskey into the pot. Stew him for several hours, empty the pot, throw out the ground hog, and eat the brick. Sounds like a plan to me!!

The point of all this being I am preparing for a trip throughout the Midwest in June, and I am concerned about the weather. It seems every day there is another story of a tornado, a severe storm, or even snow, in late May!!! Yet June being the month of weddings, I am even planning on attending a family wedding when I go, and I don't know whether to pack a parka and earmuffs, or Bermuda shorts. To make matters worse, I've asked my brother, with whom, I'm staying, what the weather is like, and all of you know I can't get a straight answer out of him, he's a goofball! One minute he says it's beautiful, warm (warm to him is 45'), and definitely fishing weather. The next minute my sister-in-law tells me she is running the heat because it's only in the low 40's up there where they live, the frozen tundra of northern Wisconsin. Gregg did tell me the ice is beginning to melt in the bay, and that, my friends, is supposed to comfort me.

Why don't you compromise, he said, and wear your fur coat, but wear it with flip flops. That should take care of everything. See, I told you he was a goofball.

A few months back, I was so fed up with continual winter, I decided to begin another mystery book. Even though today, my thermometer is now resting right on 90', I don't trust anyone connected with weather. So, I sit here pondering what sort of wardrobe I should take, and writing on my book. The title? ***"Who Killed the Weatherman!!"***

Was there any doubt?

Anybody Got a Good Recipe…for Ground Hog?

Usually, April is one of my most favorite months, all the flowers, the trees in bloom, the fresh air, church on Easter Sunday, all of it is so special and I look forward to this month all year.

What do we have this year? Cold, threats of snow, rain, threats of ice and sleet, and more cold. Nothing's in bloom, and the air is so fresh with ice, it will burn your lungs. I have a friend in California who is fighting floods and mudslides now, a friend in Las Vegas who is suffering through a semi drought, my brother is buried in snow in Wisconsin, and my niece in Chicago is cross country skiing to her office every day. What we have here is a failure to communicate with the powers that be, and reiterate to him/her/them, that this is supposed to be spring, not an extension of winter!!!!

I remember how happy I was as a child when springtime arrived. It meant a new pair of Mary Janes for me, maybe a new Easter dress, flowers in the yard, fresh air, and most of all, the chance to get outside and play in the sunshine. Seemed to me, seasons were more defined back then, we seldom went from winter into a sliding summer, we actually enjoyed a prolonged spring. Summers were hot and languid, and almost always too short. Autumn was for running through that pile of leaves your dad had just raked up, and Thanksgiving and Christmas came on the heels of Halloween, and a fun time had by all. Every April, I knew that school would soon be out for the summer, and I could go up the street and around the corner to raid that nice man's rhubarb patch. I'd sit there for hours, red juice dripping down my chin, watching the birds fly around. He never caught me, or maybe, he simply let me eat my fill of his rhubarb. Who knows, I only know it was a time for being outside and enjoying myself. If it was a particularly warm spring, that was even better, that meant that many more weeks of nice weather to be outdoors in.

I've done a bit of traveling this winter, and everywhere I've gone, I've had bad weather follow me, heard the locals grumbling about it, the women wondering when on earth they can get the kids back outside. Dodging sleet balls and raindrops for my book signings and other appearances, I have asked myself numerous times what on earth we have done to deserve this awful winter. No answer for that, but I know who started it all, Punxsutawney Phil, that's who!!!! there he was sound asleep in his cave, when all of the sudden he's grabbed from behind, yanked out into the cold, with flashbulbs on TV lights shining in his eyes, heck, I'd be mad too!

Personally, I think he's angry with his handlers for cutting his winter nap too short, and I can't say as I blame him, but honestly, Phil, cut us some slack, and give us some nice weather!!! I find him, I'm gonna make soup out of him – anybody have a good recipe for ground hog?

With my luck, it will clear up the day after I submit this column. Oh well, have a happy Easter and a pretty springtime, y'all!!

Jan McCanless

That's What I Love about Springtime

April showers bring May flowers, everybody knows that. April serves as a sort of introduction to May, warmer and longer days, everything in bloom, and we can at last get outside after a long cold winter.

And then, there's Easter. It almost always comes in April. I have come to realize over the years, that Easter will mean different things to you at different times of your life.

When we are young, all we think about are new clothes, corsages, and, maybe, a new Easter basket filled with goodies. As we age, however, I think we come to appreciate more the spiritual side of this most sacred of holidays.

The passing of winter always seems to me like it ushers in a renewed and refreshed time. Like starting all over again, a new lease on the year.

Easter reminds me of a new pair of shoes, clean, unmarked, without a speck of dirt or grime on them. As we wear them more and more, we break them in and we become more comfortable in these new shoes. Like the grace and comes with the Resurrection, the longer we live in it, the more comfortable we are with it.

Nothing beats the beauty of the spring season, and it reminds us every year that nature has another chance to get it right. We relish in the comfort of the warmth and brightness of each new day.

This spring, as we move towards the holy days of Easter, I hope for each one of us the renewal and exhilaration that this time of year always brings. May the hope and joy of the Resurrection be with you all throughout the year.

As Red Buttons Used to Say, Straaaaaange Things Are Happening

Well, to say that "something strange happened to me the other day" is likened to saying "it's gonna rain soon." Strange things are always happening to me. I seem to attract the odd characters and oddball events like flies to honey. but for me, even THIS incident was weird.

Everyone who knows me knows that I collect giraffes: on clothes, jewelry, stuffed, bronze, any way I can get them. I have written magazine articles about my giraffes, and theirs is the first exhibit I head for at the zoo.

There I was at church meeting, wearing a nice shirt with giraffes all over it, and I was carrying my giraffe handbag that I had purchased at Al Johnson's Gift Shop when I was in Wisconsin visiting my brother last year. A woman approached me, someone I did not know (she was attending another meeting elsewhere in the building), and she wanted to buy my shirt from me, right then and there! It was beautiful she told me. I thanked her, but under the circumstances, I hardly felt I could sell it to her on the spot.

Later that same morning, I was in an area antiques store, when a man looking at my handbag, admired it, and asked if I could possibly sell it to him for his wife. He especially like the material, he said. Again, I had to say no. I was beginning to feel I was living ***"The***

Price is Right," or something quite akin to it.

When I left the antiques store, there at the curb was a man standing looking at my car. It was his car, he declared.

Of course, I couldn't see how it could possibly be his, when we have had it almost a year now. No, he said, he had been to the same dealer, wanted the car; then left to shop around for a good deal, and when he went back to buy it, we had gotten it.

"I'll write you a check for it right now," he offered, pulling his checkbook from his shirt pocket. I must say, I had much to think about on my drive home and I couldn't wait to tell the spouse all about it.

"I could have walked home shirtless, with no handbag." I told him.

"Well," he pondered "why didn't you? Surely someone would have stopped, picked you up, and given you a lift home."

Indeed! Well, these folks were pretty strong about wanting my clothing and car. So, if you should happen to see me in this condition, you'll know what happened.

Someone would have picked me up, honestly!

Tire Patch Cookies Are Good for the Soul

This year marks the 50th anniversary of the assassination of President Kennedy. He's been all over the news lately, in one film clip or another, and I got to thinking the other day, about all the history I have lived through, and it's depressing. There was also Nixon's resignation, the Challenger explosion, some little girl falling down a well, all kinds of things I have lived through. I remember watching the so-called launch of a space capsule early in 1967, and seeing as the entire thing filled with pure oxygen killing the three astronauts aboard. It seem the more we progress, the greater the chances are of these kinds of things. Tragedies such as these make us uneasy, especially if they come on the heels of great triumph.

I've discovered, as I age, that I prefer not to dwell on these things, and would much prefer to remember the good stuff. So, as I sat and relived those Kennedy years in film clips, I turned off the TV, and thought back to one of the funniest things that had ever occurred in my life, and naturally, my nutzoid brother was the instigator. Bless his heart, I could always count on Gregg to come up with some scheme or other that would get us in hot water with our parents, and keep me in stitches.

It happened like this; he was 12, and I was 7, and my folks were going out for the evening and decided to leave him in charge. BIG, MISTAKE! Gregg was bored, so, he phoned Mom at the restaurant they had gone to, and asked if he could make a batch of cookies, because as HE related to her, I was not behaving, and he thought the cookies would calm me down. Uh huh. In her naivety, she thought if she said yes, he could bake 3 cookies, it would be an impossible task for him, he'd quit, and would eventually settle on some activity, like listening to the radio, reading, or watching his Lionel train run around the track. Her mistake was believing in this theory!

Gregg began gathering the ingredients for Toll House cookies (have they been around that long??), and realized that the mixing bowls were on the top shelf of the cupboard, which necessitated him trying to get one down. The only way he could reasonably do this was to push the kitchen table over to the cupboard, climb on top, and opening the door, he could then reach the bowl he needed. Seems he hung on to the cabinet door just a tad too long, and before long, we heard this loud crack as the door separated from the rest of the cupboard. No matter, he had the bowl, and table back in place, the torn door resting on top, and he began to mix up the ingredients. Everything went well until he got to the part where Mom had admonished him to make only 3 cookies, and being the ever-obedient son, he filled 3 cookie sheets with one each, of this humongous cookie. And then, he baked, 3 cookies, each one the size of a cookie sheet. Together we ate one of them, the equivalent I suppose of 8 or 9 cookies apiece, and the rest? Well, he saved them on the table for our parents so they could see that he had made only 3 of them.

Well, despite herself, Mom laughed, because he had done as she asked, and then, we cleaned up the kitchen. Pop wasn't too happy about the broken cupboard door, but it was fixable, and ever after Mother referred to them as tire patch cookies, because she felt they were big enough to patch the tires on a truck.

Gregg and I laugh about this to this day, and when I laugh I feel good, and when I feel good, it's good for my soul. A whole lot happier to think about then all the bad stuff, isn't it. You shoulda been there.

What Do I Look Like, a Bird?

You, my readers, know that a lot of things tick me off, and the older I get, the more things irritate me. For instance, I am forever being asked if I am only on social media, you know, Facebook and all that mess. No, and I'll tell you way; there is quite enough information about me on the Internet, I have no idea who put it here or how it gets added to, but it's there, so why should I do anymore? I don't want to do any more, I think there should be some air of mystery to everyone, don't just lay it all out there, I mean, what would be the point of trying to get to know another person, if you can look on the Internet and find out what they ate for breakfast that day?

I have decided too, that the next person who asks me if I tweet, I will look them in the eye and say no, do I look like a bird?

I've mentioned my genius cousins, Jim and Rick before. They're always ragging on me to come into the 21st Century, and that Rick, he can make a computer stand up and dance, so, just to appease them one day, I attempted to write a blog. Now, I am not the smartest person, electronically speaking, but I thought, how hard could it be? So, I googled the instructions on blogging, and much to my surprise, they were clear and concise – the only problem being, I did not have the buttons, slots or what have you, on my computer to complete the job. Sooooo, I emailed back to my kinfolk that I couldn't do it, and I know, I just know, they are still laughing hysterically at me.

When, as a child, I would attend family dinners, I was always put on the end, by myself, because being left-handed, they didn't want me punching anyone while we ate. For years I longed to sit in the middle of the table, join in the conversation, and be able to pass the mashed potatoes to my left, or right, or across the thing, but no, there I was in dining Siberia, nodding and smiling just as though I knew what was going on! I come from a huge family, lots of aunts, uncles, cousins, and there is just my Uncle al, God rest his soul, me, and two of my grandchildren who are possessed of left handedness, and, I read somewhere that lefties are smarter than the right handed folks, because, we primarily use the right side of our brains, and everybody and their dog know that the right side is dominate. I have taken that knowledge to heart, and sit here secretly smirking that all you computer geeks and electronic wizards are really not as bright as me. Supposedly, we are craftier, play better baseball, write better books (hey, that sounds familiar), sing prettier songs, and dance better than the rest of you! We can also do more tricks with a yoyo than you righties.

Well, I'll take what I can get, and as I sit here smugly pondering my superior intelligence, I will also tell you I don't have a digital camera either – so there! If it ever warms up, I will go out to my patio, gaze upon my gorgeous flowers and feel sorry for all you people sitting in front of a square screen all day. Smarter, indeed!!

Cruisin the Big Muddy

I used to think vacationing in the wintertime was nuts, but now, I'm not so sure. As devotees of the Mississippi river, we had the opportunity to cruise the mighty river this past winter, and it was wonderful.

Our boat was the Mississippi Queen, a new one in the American Cruise Line fleet, our previous cruise had been on the Queen of the Mississippi, now out of commission. We boarded the weekend after Christmas to all kinds of New Orleans Jazz and Dixieland combos, beautiful holiday decorations, and food, food, food, everywhere.

We made numerous port stops, and one of the onboard tours included the ships dining room and galley, surprisingly small considering the meals they turned out in there. Our chef told us he had been the executive chef for the Miami Dolphins, and was hired away by the cruise line, and now cooking for us. That may have explained why all the beef portions were so large, he had been used to preparing food for football players!

The boat made shore stops at Oak Alley, St. Francisville, Baton Rouge, Natchez and Vicksburg, before returning to home base in New Orleans. We had interesting stops at the various ports of call, and our fellow travelers were an interesting mix of very nice folks. One couple flew all the way from Australia for the cruise, another woman on board told us she was the conductor for the University of

Chicago symphony; a very nice gentleman and his wife from Montana were especially friendly. One day, up in the sky lounge, I asked him what part of Montana he was from. "Most of it" was his reply. Turns out his ranch encompassed nearly half the state, and he told me he had a "modest" herd of Black Angus beef cattle. How many head, I asked. Only 12,000 was his reply.

The weather driving to New Orleans was not good, it rained on us all the way, but we did not have a couple nice days on the boat, where we could get out on deck and enjoy the sun. Not exactly warm, but certainly not too chilly either, just what I would call "refreshing."

Cruising the lower river, there is a great deal to see. Although I loved the scenery, it consisted mostly of river and riverbanks full of bare trees. By the time we reached the lower river, all the barge traffic had disappeared, and even the alligators were hiding, so, the cruise director decided we should all go up to the top deck and fly a kite – literally; so, up we trudged, holding our kites in our hands. The air was on the mild side, no wind, and not really much space to run with our kites, so, we all wondered how we could possibly get them airborne. The on-board hotel manager decided then to offer the sangrias to all the kite flyers, and that's when the fun started! By this time, a few our kites were up in the air, trailing the colorful tails on them, and we must have been a pretty sight, the gorgeous boat with all the colors and shapes of those kites soaring above us. By the time the sangrias were consumed, the kites were beginning to look like the passengers, all wrapped around the railings, wobbling as they soared, and just a few falling on the deck as they lost momentum. For all intents and purposes, the kite flying session was over, and while I don't care for sangrias myself, it was more than a little interesting to see this all unfold.

The bridge was also on the top deck, and I can just imagine what the captain thought as these kites flew past his window. After getting to know him somewhat on this cruise, I can well imagine how amused he was.

Well, eventually, what was left of the kites were brought in, wrapped up, and stowed away, and we passengers made our way back down to the sky lounge or various other resting places on board, and hit the afternoon cookie and donut buffet. After all, we needed sustenance for our cocktail party at 5:30, dinner at 6:30, and the ice cream sodas that distributed every night at 9 p.m.

New Year's Eve was filled with music, dancing, a great dinner, and more fun that we would have had at home watching the ball drop in New York. Considering the weather, the flu we fought upon our return, and all the other miseries of winter, we had a great season, thankfully, pretty short, and now, we are ready for spring. All those daffodils blooming in my yard are telling me it's time, and I'm ready.

Rick and Ilsa from Casablanca may have had their Paris, but I had the Mississippi, and glad of it!

Celebrating the Wondrous Joyous June

June is truly the month of celebrations; we have weddings, graduations, church picnics, not to mention Father's Day, it's just a wonderful time of year to celebrate anything. In our family, we also celebrate numerous June birthdays.

This month, I'll be traveling to Atlanta, Georgia to join in celebrating my own high school graduation, and, it is with some trepidation that I go. I have not been to one of my own reunions, and I thought this year, I'd go. Our graduation did not go smoothly, however, when over half my class, myself included, got food poisoning three days before the big event. We had gone to a senior class luncheon, gotten a hold of some bad beef, you know how teenagers eat, so, we ATE! As we marched into the civic auditorium in Atlanta, our vice principal was there with spoon and paregoric to dose all of us. No way we would have made it through the ceremony otherwise.

One of the sweetest June weddings I ever attended was my great niece, Rachel, last year, in Wisconsin. What a beautiful affair, the bridesmaids all in their country dresses and cowboy boots, spring bouquets in their arms. It was held in a barn, wonderfully decorated by my niece, Rachel's mother, for the occasion. A terrific time to celebrate with family and close friends, and it's hard to believe that a whole year has gone by since that day.

God must have known what He was doing when He created June, it's such a happy month. So many lives changed drastically during the month. A new beginning, new experiences, it's hard to fathom them all.

Where we live now, sometimes we can hear the roaring of the crowd at the football games, played from the high school stadium down the road, and graduation night always brings the usual assortment of shouting, horn blowing and laughter. I used to teach at that high school, and how well I remember the joy of the three family graduations I attended. One son and daughter marched into the stadium on a warm, clear night, the other son was relegated to the auditorium as rain pelted the grounds, and just about ruined everything that had already been set up for the outdoor ceremony. Wonderful memories, of a glorious time. I'm thinking now of all the grads this month, all the brides and grooms, and the years yet to come. I wish them well, and God speed. Most of all I wish them God's blessings in their life's adventures. Hold tight and remember kids, that time and euphoria will never come again. As for your dads out there, may you have a happy, happy day.

Who's the Guy in the Skirt?

One of my favorite all time things to do is people watch, whatever I'm doing, or wherever I am, I watch the "passing parade."

I was at a mall in a city near me recently, and if ever there was a place to watch the "natives," it's this mall. For one thing, I must have observed literally a hundred or more people in an hour's time, and not a single one of them was without a cell phone attached to their head. Not one, and I made the observation that I wondered if they were speaking to each other, because all the heads seemed to be nodding in sync, from the oldest to the youngest.

After that observation, I began to pay attention, in earnest to the clothes they were wearing, and that was a revelation! I used to have to pass inspection from my mother each and every minute that I walked through our door to the outside world, and I'm here to tell you, none of these folks would have passed Mama's test!!! I saw torn jeans, literally in tatters on people, I saw flip flops, crazy hats, dangling jewelry, low cut blouses, I mean, really low-cut blouses. I would have been afraid to sneeze wearing something like that out in public! Every so often, I would see an elegantly dressed, obviously successful Businesswoman, loping along wearing these extremely high stiletto heels, and I couldn't help but wonder how on earth they walked in those things, and on concrete floors yet.

A lot of women are taking a pretty scarf and attaching it to their purse and as they walk along, it will flutter. An elegant fashion statement, and I noticed you can change the look of any outfit by dangling a scarf. Years ago, there was a similar fad going around, where one would have a scarf at the shoulder of a coat, suit coat or overcoat, and it was considered very high fashion for the time. Well, one day, I decided to try it. I'm always wanting to be in style after all, so I found a very pretty scarf in the drawer, flung it over my shoulder and set out. Before the day was out, I had 4 people stop me to tell me I had a scarf hanging from my coat, did I know that? Now, why don't these fads ever work for me, I wonder. I tried once, flinging a pashmina around in a really neat way, like I knew what I was doing, and, of course, it didn't work for me either. It completely covered my head, and I couldn't see where I was going! Maybe I ought to join the military and walk around in loose fitting camouflage, not only would it be comfortable, but that particular style would work I'm pretty sure!

Well, back to the mall. In addition to the cell phones, most everyone was walking along sipping from a Starbucks cup too, looking at their watch, and carrying huge shopping bags full of merchandise. How do they do that, and what is preventing them from crashing into a concrete pillar, or falling down the escalator?

It's entertaining, to say the least watching folks go about their day, especially when they have no idea they are being observed. You can learn a lot about humankind that way. It takes all kinds to make up this crazy quilt world we inhabit, and the older I get, the more I think diversity may not be such bad thing.

My favorite on this particular day was the man with the orange Mohawk, and I have no idea who that man was wearing a dark skirt with his hair in a ponytail. Just as well, I really didn't want to get that familiar with him, but I gotta tell ya, he made my day!

Is It Spring Yet?

Isn't there some law that says it's illegal to be this cold out? Why isn't it being enforced? The weatherman is not making brownie points with me (see my book, ***Who Killed the Weatherman***!).

Anyone who knows me, knows I am strictly a fair-weather person, cold and I do not get along. When my northern cousins email me and tell me WE should not be complaining about the cold, I want to hit someone!!! Maybe they think 18 feet of snow is exciting, I find it repugnant, and no way will allow that, not down here.

I used to brag to people that at any given time in North Carolina, we are only 30 days from spring, but this year, I am not so sure, and, if you are going to the Valentine's dance this year, wear your long snugglies.

Valentine's Day, can you believe it? I marvel all the time about how fast all these holidays come and go, it would seem that time is moving at warp speed. As I sit and put my feet up, fix myself a cup of tea, and grab a good book. I leave you with this Valentine to you, my readers. A bit of happy nostalgia for your afternoon pleasure.

Rest assured though, I still intend to take matters into hand concerning the weather, surely there must be something we can do about it, and I am going to find the solution to this misery…trust me.

As Bob Hope would say "Thanks for the memories."

Heavens to Murgatroyd!

Would you believe the email spell checker did not recognize the word, Murgatroyd? Lost words from our childhood: Words gone as fast as the buggy whip! Sad, really!

The other day a not so elderly (65) lady said something to her son about driving a jalopy and he looked at her quizzically and said, "What the heck is a jalopy?" He never heard of the word jalopy!...or rattle trap? She knew she was old but not that old.

Well, I hope you are Hunky Dory after you read this.

About a month ago, I illuminated some old expressions that have become obsolete because of the inexorable march of technology. These phrases included "Don't touch that dial," "carbon copy," "You sound like a broken record" and "Hung out to dry." Back in the olden days we had a lot of moxie. We'd put on our best bib and tucker to straighten up and fly right.

Heavens to Betsy!...Gee whilikers! Jumping Jehoshaphat!...Holy Moley!

We were in like Flynn and living the life of Riley, and even a regular guy couldn't accuse us of being a knucklehead, a nincompoop or a pill. Not for all the tea in China!

Back in the olden days, life used to be swell, but when's the last time anything was swell? Swell has gone the way of beehives, pageboys, and the DA; of spats, knickers, fedoras, poodle skirts, saddle shoes and pedal pushers.

Oh, my aching back. Kilroy was here, but he isn't anymore.

We wake up from what surely has been just a short nap, and before we can say, well I'll be a monkey's uncle!

Or, "This is a fine kettle of fish!" We discover that the words we grew up with, the words that seemed omnipresent, as oxygen, have vanished with scarcely a notice from our tongues and our pens and our keyboards. Poof, go the words of our youth, the words we've left behind. We blink, and they're gone. Where have all those phrases gone?

Long gone: Pshaw, the milkman did it.

Hey! It's your nickel…Don't forget to pull the chain. Knee high to a grasshopper. Well, Fiddlesticks! Going like sixty…I'll see you in the funny papers. Don't take any wooden nickels.

It turns out there are more of these lost words and expressions than Carter has liver pills. This can be disturbing stuff!

We of a certain age have been blessed to live in changeable times. For a child, each new word is like a shiny toy, a toy that has no age. We at the other end of the chronological arc have the advantage of remembering there are words that once did not exist and there were words that once strutted their hour upon the earthly stage and now are heard no more, except in our collective memory. It's one of the greatest advantages of aging.

Happy Valentine's Day, Ya'll See ya later, Alligator!...After a while, Crocodile!

Bad Weather and Lizards Scare Me

Lots of severe weather in the headlines recently, makes you wonder what's going on, doesn't it.

After experiencing Hugo back in '89, I figured I could like through anything. Coming from Florida, as a child, I have seen many hurricanes, but never saw a backyard shed float uphill as I did during Hugo. That was a first!

I can recall one such storm while in Jacksonville. Can't remember the name, but I know my mom got all nervous about it. The wind picked up, the waters rose, we were just blocks from the ocean, and I had my first experience with really high tide, I mean, REALLY high tide. After all the huffing and puffing was over, I walked outside our little house, and saw the strangest sight I had ever beheld. We had a screened porch on the side of the house, and the entire screen was covered in lizards that had blown up there during the storm. Some were those little green chameleons, some were brown, but all were lizards, and as far as I'm concerned, all lizards can go to some other continent to live, I hate them. One of them chases me around the yard here, but that's another story entirely.

Eventually, the horrid things found their way off our screens, but what a terrifying sight is was.

Tornados are another thing I am leery of. My one experience with getting close up and personal with a tornado happened while we were on the road one time. My dad was driving, and Gregg and I were in the back seat, playing games, always trying to think up ways to get into mischief – we were experts at that.

At some point, I looked out the back window and saw this huge funnel shaped thing bearing down on us, right on the same road we were traveling. Now back then, a lot of cars didn't have very generous rear windows, so, you often couldn't see a whole lot, but I knew a funnel cloud when I saw one. I hollered to my dad that we were going to be swallowed up by a tornado, and he just shook his head and said not to bother him while he was driving. Then my brother chimed, and said, the same thing.

We kept driving, not many cars on the back-country roads, where we were. Gregg tapped my mom on the shoulder and told her to turn around and look, she did, and she screamed at my dad that there was a tornado bearing down on us. Finally, he took his eyes off the front of the road and looked. Suddenly, he turned left, and drove a right angle to the cloud, across a field, picking up weeks, mud, wildflowers, whatever else was in the way, the car mowed them down or threw them up onto the radiator. The car was a mess. Pops brand new Desoto, and it looked awful. Pop had managed to drive a little ways into the woods, and now, we were stuck. The storm had missed us by several feet, and all we got was a huge wind, which blew more trash onto the car.

All of us helped to clean up that car, and my dad and brother pushed it out of the wooded area, almost to the road. After several chugs and sputters, the engine turned over, and we continued on our way, stopping at the nearest gas station to get it cleaned up. Back in those days, a full-service gas station meant just that, you could get most anything for your car there, and the proprietor let us borrow his hose to wash the Desoto off. It wasn't good as new, but prit'ner.

Well, hurricane season is in full swing now, and I watch each weather report, hoping to see what's next on the horizon for us. I find it all terribly fascinating, and after each weather disaster, I have to ask myself, "is someone trying to tell us something?"

Jan McCanless

Keep the Dark Spots at Bay

Someone sent me a fascinating email the other day, about a college professor who passed out exam papers, and on the page, was one big, dark spot. He then asked his students to explain what they saw.

Nearly all the class members wrote elaborate descriptions of the dark spot, how it stood out against the white paper, how it got so much attention, there was not enough space for thoughts of anything else. They went on to make up elaborate stories of how the dark spot came into existence, and how, we can't really think of anything else, but the disturbing presence of that dark spot. It obliterates everything else.

One student, however, took another route, about how insignificant the spot was in comparison to all the brightness around it. It could even be compared to the minuteness of planted earth, in the grand scheme of things. This student went on to point out how little that dark spot was when compared to all the brightness and whiteness surrounding it, how truly insignificant it was. The professor was impressed.

The meaning of the lesson was, he pointed out, that the dark spot represented all that was negative in our lives: bills, illness, dissension, negative thoughts, what is holding you back from happiness and peace of mind, and how we can oftentimes see nothing but the dark spot, as opposed to seeing the brightness around it. We quite often miss the good, by concentrating only on the bad.

Excellent lesson, I thought, and one we all badly need. In this stressful time, we need to concentrate our efforts on the positive, the good, and changing that which we can, so, that our dark spots are completely overshadowed by all the brightness and good in our lives. Heaven knows we need this in today's world.

Starting today, right now, I am going to begin to emphasize the positive, the good, the excellent in today's world, and hopefully, little by little, change my world. Attitude and action both begin with the same letter "A." Capitalize it and go for it!!

I hope you'll join me.

And Along Comes Pretty Little May…

It is May, is it not? As the old Rogers and Hammerstein song says and, along comes pretty little May. Hah!! I'm freezing to death! What happened to warmth, flowers, outdoor cooking, nice little Mother's Day? This is not fair, we toil all winter, just so we can enjoy some sunshine, warm temperatures, and a little outdoor living comes the last of April, on into May.

Some of my fondest memories are of a warm May day, watching as the kids make me third base for their ball games, or have me climbing fences to retrieve their baseballs that wandered off. I'll never forget the Mother's Day when our when our backyard neighbor knocked on the door and handed me a handful of eggs our wayward chickens deposited on his garage floor. He was not exactly thrilled about it either. Whatever happened to those days?

May has always been one of my favorite months of the year, so much happens that month and the weather is so nice, you can enjoy every day outside. You hear that, weatherman? Maybe I should send him a copy of my ***"Who Killed the Weatherman"*** book, just to drive home the point.

My oldest son and his wife have a wedding anniversary that month, so does my niece, ditto my brother and his wife, I remember, as if yesterday, my high school graduation that fell on the 25th of May, there are birthdays galore during the month. It's one of the happiest months of the year.

I recall one very fond memory of a Mother's Day, when my little daughter brought me a handful of crushed dandelions so I would have flowers to put in a vase. I put them in there too, you betcha. Then, my oldest came home and said, “Get in the truck Mom, it’s Mother’s Day, I’m taking you 4-wheeling.” Now there’s an experience for you, especially when you do it while being blasted by the latest acid rock group, Brains of Concrete, or some such. Truly an unforgettable occasion.

Sigh, well, I love May, and all its splendor, be it flowers, raindrops, sunshine, bad weather, good weather, whatever, because it’s the introduction to summer, and all that it brings. Every pretty, warm day, brings another aha moment in this glorious world of ours. The miracle of rejuvenation occurs every year at this time. The earth and all her splendor is renewed for yet another season, giving hope to all us mortals for yet another chance at whatever it is we hope to accomplish. As for Mother’s Day, I enjoyed each and every one of them, there were no bad ones, only “different.” The kids are all scattered now, I can’t be with them all the time, but I hope the daughter and the daughters-in-law have the wonderful, funny and warm ones I had. For those of us who no longer have our moms with us, I know I speak for all of us when I say, what I wouldn’t give to have her back…just for a day.

Ladies, enjoy your day, enjoy the month, and see ya around the bar-b-que grill!

Motoring Memories

This photo, from Easter Sunday 1963, shows me with my first car, an Oldsmobile F85, which was 2 or 3 years old when my dad got it for me.

The car was sporty and economical but had a stick shift, which I never could master. Every time I got behind the wheel, I either had to have someone shift for me or had to drive backward, as I could manage that.

At the time of the picture, the car had been mine just a few short weeks. Due to my shifting trouble, I had to trade it in for a sedate sedan with automatic transmission. It was a terrible blow to my ego, not to mention my image, but the roads were much safer for other drivers and me!

Celebrate the Wondrous, Joyous June

June is truly the month of celebrations; we have weddings, graduations, church picnics, not to mention Father's Day, it's just a wonderful time of year to celebrate anything. In our family, we also celebrate numerous June birthdays.

This month, I'll be traveling to Atlanta, Georgia to join in celebrating my own high school graduation, and, it is with some trepidation that I go. I have not been to one of own reunions, and I thought this year, I'd go. Our graduation did not go smoothly, however, when over half my class, myself included, got food poisoning 3 days before the big event. We had gone to a senior class luncheon, gotten a hold of some bad beef, you know how teenagers eat, so, we ATE!! As we marched into the civic auditorium in Atlanta, our vice principal was there with spoon and paregoric to dose all of us. No way we would have made it through the ceremony otherwise.

One of the sweetest June weddings I ever attended was for the daughter of a neighbor. Her groom was especially nervous, and you could see his knees shaking through the movement of the fabric in his trousers. Well, sir, came the time in the service when he had to repeat his vows to sweet little Vicky, and instead of taking her for his lawful wedded wife, he took her for his lawful bedded wife. Poor guy was so upset, he began to cry, then, he ended up sobbing, but somehow, they made it through, and, I'm happy to say, they continue in their wedded bliss to this day, 40 years later.

God must have known what He was doing when He created June, it's such a happy month. So many lives change drastically during the month. A new beginning, new experience, it's hard to fathom them all.

Where we live now, sometimes we can hear the roaring crowd as the football games, played from the high school stadium down the road and graduation night always brings the usual assortment of shouting, horn blowing and laughter. I used to teach at that high school, and how well I remember the joy of the three family graduations I attended. One son and daughter marched into the stadium on a warm, clear night, the other son was relegated to the auditorium as rain pelted the grounds, and just about ruined everything that had already been set up for the outdoor ceremony.

Wonderful memories, of a glorious time. I'm thinking now of all the grads this month, all the brides and grooms, and the years yet to come. I wish them well, and God speed. Most of all. I wish them God's blessing in their life's adventures. Hold tight and remember kids, that time and euphoria will never come again. As for you dads out there, may you have a happy, happy day.

Jan McCanless

The NC Patchwork of Fall Colors

How can anyone look upon our carpet of beautiful autumn colors and not see God's handiwork? I'm drawn to fall because of the warm and vibrant colors that surround me.

Think about bright, perky red, and notice how it enlivens everything around it. It's the brightest, the most outstanding of the autumns colors, and drive along somewhere, and every time you see bright red, you smile and think "ahh."

I love orange, and think of it as the consummate autumn color. Orange leave, orange pumpkins, it's such a bright and cheerful color, you can't look at orange and not smile. Surely God intended that when he created the blaze of orange that graces our countryside this time of year. Orange is a happy color for sure.

Yellow is an interesting color, and it's usually the first autumn color to make the scene, all the poplar trees turn yellow about mid-August, and then, I know, fall is soon to follow. Yellow is another happy color, and I smile every time I see a yellow leaf catch the sunlight and shimmer on a cool, autumn day.

To balance it all out, we even need some brown in there, it makes us appreciate all the sparkling reds and oranges, but brown is a necessary fall color. It tells us the leaves are dying and falling off, getting ready for the foliage to hibernate, and create new life come spring. I've heard so many folks talk about the "dead of winter," but to me, it's simply a reminder that God is in His heaven, sending us this panoply of gorgeous colors and letting us know that in another season, we will again burst forth into glorious spring, with new colors to add to our list of favorites. It's a reminder that life goes on, we are not in charge, but told to sit back, let God do it, and revel in the beautiful changes to our scenery that He provides for us.

The changing seasons bring life and renewal, they let us experience life and all of it changes. They usher in the glories of autumn, and the hope that we appreciate all that the season has to give us. Smell the air, savor the aroma of burning leaves, and smile at the funny pumpkin faces that we'll see adorning our neighborhood porches.

Sit back, enjoy the fall foliage, praise it, and give thanks for it, it's all part of this blessed world that our Creator made just for us.

My August Blues

I had to check my calendar twice the other day, I couldn't believe my eyes, August? Already? Really? I've always thought of August as a transitional month, we transition to autumn, never mind that we still have most of September to go yet before fall arrives, I still think of August as the tail end of summer, much like March being the tail end of winter. It's one of those months that enables us to ease from one season to the next. This last full month of summer always makes me a little nostalgic. I remember, as a child, mentally preparing myself for the next school year during the month, and contemplating all the great new school supplies, not to mention the new shoes, I would receive before the first bell tolled. With great sadness, we always wound down our summers at our Michigan cabin, where the fishing, swimming and lollygagging were never ending, and our thoughts turned to the coming autumn months. How many days until Halloween, how many until Christmas? It was just what we did, as kids.

This August seems to have arrived after the shortest year of my life. Why is it the longer we live, the faster time flies? earlier this year, my good friend Camille and I had our girls week R & R we try to take every year, I had a busy and successful book tour, we all lived through some health problems, I attended my 55th high school reunion in Atlanta and here we are again, into August.

Try as I might, I cannot get overly concerned about the passage of time, I'm having too much fun living in the moment. I may be getting old, I may be slower of step, and can't run with the big dogs anymore, but by golly, I can still have fun!!! This month has two of my precious grandsons having birthdays, putting them ever closer to the day they leave for college, my aforementioned friend Camille, just got a clean bill of health after a scare, and I just received another bionic part for this old carcass. Woo hoo!!! I'm on a roll. Autumn may be just around the corner, but my life is definitely blessed, in so many ways. No matter the time of year, I am thankful and grateful for my many dear friends, my church family, my personal relationships, all those darling grandkids.

Every month brings more blessings, more wonderful surprises, and more reasons to get out of bed each day. A week ago, we were so dry and parched, my flowers were wilting, and then…it rained two days ago. Now, the flowers in my yard are big, bright, and flourishing once again. The earth around us is vibrant and green.

Life is wonderful, and God is good.

Jan McCanless

The Beautiful Colors of Fall

As I write this, it's raining catfish and hushpuppies outside, and we are expecting some affects from the hurricane now churning up the Atlantic. We have really experienced some quixotic weather this summer have we not? As I've aged, I've learned a thing or two, and this much I know. Weather will always straighten itself out. If it's too dry, sooner or later, it will rain, too wet, and eventually it will dry out. If it just works that way I do concern myself with the farmers at times, because I know their livelihood depends on the weather, but there is nothing any of us can do about it, so, why worry?

Autumn is my very favorite time of the year, so much happens in our family then, birthdays, anniversaries, Thanksgiving, Halloween, it's really busy. In college, the spouse and I dated all fall at the football games, and dances afterward. Very economical for struggling college students. What I enjoy the most are the colors of fall, the glorious, deep reds, the blazing oranges, and majestic purples. They splash across the landscape in riotous shades, reminding me of those wonderful farmers who grew them, and the marvelous God who lays them all out for us to enjoy.

Beautiful flowers in gorgeous colors spread their cheer and warmth far and wide this time of year. They are everywhere, in stores, garden shops, and adorning lawns every place you look. My own yard is at this moment, abounding in pots of the happy, yellow blooms. They make me smile to see them, and they add so much joy to the already blazing trees we have. The wonderful reds of the dogwood trees and the pretty oranges of the maple trees. Just looking at them fills me with such thankfulness that we live in this world, this country, and can enjoy natures wonder with no restraints.

We are blessed in America to be able to enjoy all of fall bounty, not just the colors, but the smells, the pumpkins, the little ghosts and goblins as they trick or treat in their adorable costumes.

I try to be thankful to God for each and every day, and to appreciate every season that he gives us, but this one, - ah, this one is special. Come on out and enjoy it with me!

Beautiful August

Some folks refer to them as the dog days of summer, and I've heard a lot of people complain that once the 4th of July comes and goes, summer is over. Not according to me, I've had some of my fondest summer memories from August. My dad could never take much heat, so, every summer, we would pack up the car, and head out for a cabin in Michigan, where it's a lot cooler than it is down in the South. We'd spend all of July and August up there, fishing and just generally having a languid, lazy summer. Mostly fishing, as we were big on that. My brother and I were never at a loss for something to do, and August being the height of the season, we loved every minute of it.

As I've gotten older, I realize that I too, am not all that crazy about the really high temperatures and humidity, however, I still love summer, and try to squeeze as much out of it as I possibly can.

We have a beautiful county park here, and one of the things we most enjoy is going over there in the early morning, sitting at the lake, and simply soaking it in. The other day I was over there, I looked at the gorgeous, stately trees, listened to the birds sing, watched a squirrel grab a carrot off a picnic table, and laughed at the antics of all the ducks and geese that floated by my line of vision. I was almost overcome with emotion over the beauty and tranquility of it all. It got me to thinking about nature and our world.

The quiet, meditative times can be so meaningful, if we just sit and listen, and absorb it all. In the hurry up rush experience we all live in now, it's a wonderfully refreshing and powerful to simply sit and enjoy the view. Our world is marvelous, who can look at a tree, or a pond, or a duck for that matter, and not feel insignificant when compared to all of nature and her wonders.

God has blessed us with our beautiful country, and how fortunate we are to live in the unique and splendid America. No wonder so many folks come over here, we have it all; mountains, sea, prairie, desert, it's all here, all ours for the taking. Enjoy it, cherish it, and give thanks for the wonders of this great nation.

Dog days of summer? I don't think so, I think they are just another spin of the old earth, another vantage point for us to see and appreciate. When it gets so awfully warm and muggy, take your shoes off, curl up on a porch swing, and just look around. So much to see, we can scarce take it all in!

Just When I Get it all Figured Out, They Change the Rules on Me

Boy, I remember the first time I ever saw a vending machine, I thought it was the greatest thing in the world. The first supermarket I ever went to was the old A&P, not far from our house. We had to put our food on the counter, and the clerk would grab each item, ring it up, then, put it aside for the bagger. There was no sliding belt to convey your food over to the checker, and the grocery carts were big and cumbersome, and never worked quite right.

That was then, this is now. Now, just when I get accustomed to using those individual customer cards, they come along with the automated self-checkout counter. Well, that's all well and good, for anybody else but me. I'm from the on/off switch generation, and I don't do machines well. Like that aforementioned vending machine, they frustrate me because I can never work them, and how I hate those horrible newspaper vending machines. I have lost more money than I care to remember in those things.

In theory, those self-checkout places are a good idea in reality, I can't manage it. I insist on talking to the blasted contraption. My children refuse to accompany me anywhere anymore because they say I embarrass them talking to these machines. The electronic thing can't hear me, they tell me, so why do I stand there and argue with it?

I like the old timey stores where one could speak personally with all the employees, that includes whatever device was used to check out one's groceries.

It had not been a good day for me the first time I encountered one of these machines. It kept telling me I had not put enough money into it, and I stood there arguing that I had. Finally, I threw my money at it, whereupon a clerk appeared and told me it was not nice to treat their machine that way. Well, if they can come out of nowhere to reprimand you, why can't these clerks stand there and check out your food?

Finally getting my order straight, AND, checked out, I went in search of my daughter, who was hiding from me. Silly girl, did she really think she could hide from me?

As I was searching for her, a very sweet lady approached me wondering if we had met somewhere. Assuring her I didn't know her, she persisted in telling me she had seen me someplace before, she simply could not remember where or when. Maybe, I suggest to her, she had seen my picture in the paper with my column. "No," she said, she had seen that picture, and it wasn't me.

Like I said, it had not been a good day. In one of the area chain stores, there are employees who will walk you through the process of the self-checkout. I tried it, and getting braver, I can now put my own groceries up on the counter!

Who said an old dog can't learn a new trick!

Jan McCanless

Where's Matt Dillon When You need Him???

I don't know about the rest of you, but some of the news headlines today are really scary. One has to wonder where all the manners went, what happened to neighborliness, and, I guess the Golden Rule went out the door!!!! When I was a kid, we just simply did not have all this violence and destruction. For one thing, it was right after World War II, and it seemed everyone was so happy just to get that over with, and see what all they could do to help their neighbor, that "love thy neighbor" and friendliness just went hand in hand. The exception of course, seems to be the folks out in the Midwest who have suffered through these tornadoes, they are being given a helping hand, and when our town experiences some tragedy, like the local funeral home burning down, the good folks of our town always reach out to them.

My children are always the first to slap hand to forehead and roll those big brown eyes, every time I get on a reminiscing jag, but there's a reason why they call them the good old days! I have really enjoyed reading the articles about the early days of our local theater group for instance. I was a part of those days, and the first play I worked on was ***"The Glass Menagerie;"*** we performed it at a local school, and I think my friend was the director. It was done without benefit of curtain, and I was in charge of the props, so, every time the stage went dark, we would scoot out there wearing all black, and move the props around for the next scene. Man, it was a great time!

Another thing I enjoyed was reading about Sidney Blackmer. I was a lab technician at the local hospital back when Sidney used to come in for his checkups of whatever he was having done at the time. Sidney liked to be "on," so we had to call his room and notify him when we were headed up to do blood work on him, give him time to prepare himself for our "visit."

There was a lot of interesting things going on in the so-called "good old days," but what I used to love was listening to the radio. I remember the Christmas I got a nice radio, and I would be in my room at night or on the weekends listening to all the good shows. We used our imagination and if we closed our eyes, we could really visualize all the action taking place in that small, square box next to the bed. My favorites were always the westerns, ***"The Lone Ranger, Hopalong Cassidy"*** and the like. Years later these programs transferred to black and white television, and for 15 minutes, I was carried away to the old Wild West, where men like Wyatt Earp and Matt Dillon held sway on his show, ***Gunsmoke***. Occasionally I still catch one of the ***Gunsmoke*** shows on TV Land, and I realize all over again, why it has been my favorite all these years. It's a classic, the violence was minimal, nobody blowing up anything, no weird, really far out characters from outer space or some such, they were simply good shows.

I got to thinking the other day, that we have no heroes anymore. No men on white horses come to save the whole town from a gang of blood thirsty outlaws, and no true action shows where your imagination has to do most of the work for you. What a shame that is too, the best part of childhood was following these characters. Men like Superman and Batman, The Green Hornet and others were simply the most wonderful folks in the world, who would not admire their altruistic lifestyle, and their bravery in the face of real danger? Well, time moves on, and we now have to look for new heroes, I guess.

Television and movies have come a long way since then, I know, but I still have fun remembering the past, AND, those old TV sets. TV came late to our house, so, I used to watch it at my aunt's house a lot. My Aunt Florence had one of the first console sets, and old Muntz. It had a 6" screen, set into 4 feet of cabinet! You could get the news on it, Milton Berle of course, every Tuesday night, maybe a drama or two, and wrestling, which my uncle simply loved. He'd eat a bowl of cornflakes, drink a soft drink and watch the wrestlers, men like ***"Gorgeous George"*** and others. When the match went off, the star-spangled banner was played, and we went to bed. Don't recall as many folks getting into trouble back then either keeping those hours.

Oh I know, I have slipped from reminiscing to old fogeydom, but who cares. The memories are almost as good as the real thing was! Just wish we had a real-life Matt Dillon out there now, we could really use him!!!

Chapter II
Holidays I've Known and Loved

Day by Day...

Yep, it's January already, the start of a New Year, almost a new decade, and the first day of the rest of your life.

There is something so refreshing about January, not just the bracing cold weather, it's a way to begin anew, start over, wipe the slate clean, and have a brand-new year. Yesterday is forgotten, and tomorrow is out of sight. We all have an opportunity to have a do over, start anew, and make the New Year, the best ever.

This country, and we, as its citizens, have had a busy year. A lot of disturbing headlines this year, and some, maybe not so bad. But today, ah, that is new, we can start over, maybe make better headlines this year, and put forth the effort to try and make this a better world for our friends, family, and mother earth.

Several years ago, there was a play that opened on Broadway, called ***Jesus Christ, Superstar***, and some of the music from that play is not only beautiful, but prophetic and haunting. One of my favorite songs from the show is entitled ***Day by Day***, and the lyrics say that *Day by Day, I will see thee more Clearly, love Thee more Dearly, and follow Thee more nearly, day by day*. Think about that for a moment, what if we all did that, in all our relationships, and most especially, with the relationships we enjoy with our Lord and Savior. Can you possibly fathom how we could literally change the world with this philosophy?

Now, we can, it's January, a new start to a new day and New Year. What if we applied this Day by Day mind set to everything we do for 2019, and everyone we come into contact with throughout the year. The possibilities are endless, and truly thrilling to anticipate.

My fervent wish for you is to have a wonderful and prosperous and healthy New Year. Day by Day, I want us to meet the New Year headlong, one day at a time, and with the mindset that we will love our neighbors, ourselves and our world more dearly, see everything more clearly, and follow our new "mantra" more nearly.

I am *so* looking forward to an exciting and beautiful New Year!

I'm My Father's Fault

My dad was a prankster. My mom had a good sense of humor, but Pop's bordered on the hilarious – at time. I understand he got it from HIS father, whom I never met, my paternal grandfather died when Pop was a teenager.

Being a publisher of some pretty big names, my father entertained a lot at our house, and it was not unlike my dad to serve drinks in one of those dribble glasses, thinking it was hilarious. I wonder how many suits and evening gowns were ruined due to this prank.

I guess it's no wonder why Gregg and I pulled so many pranks during our growing up years, we had a good role model. My dad would laugh at us short sheeting his bed or doing whatever else came into our demented minds. Mother was not amused.

He had friends who were on the same wavelength as he, like the Hollywood producer, who shall remain nameless; who threw a party and invited all the movie glitterati he could safely get into his house. Before hand, he hung an out of order sign on the bathroom door, instructing people to go outside to the portable booney he had installed just for the occasion. In the meanwhile, he had it wired for sound, so that whenever anyone went inside and shut the door, a booming voice from inside the house would utter something totally ridiculous; thus, causing gales of laughter from all. That was the sort of mischief my dad really enjoyed. Mother was not amused.

My dad was very tall, dark, and in his younger days, could be termed handsome. He resembled guy Lombardo a lot when he was young. As he aged and his features sagged a little he bore a strong resemblance to Raymond Burr.

He was in New York one day, tending to business at the "big" office, when he was approached on the street by a star struck middle aged lady, giggling and fawning over my dad. She called him Mr. Lombardo repeatedly, and just gushed about how she loved his music. Finally, she asked him for an autograph.

Years later, when he told me this story, I asked him, "What did you do?" "Wrote best wishes, Guy Lombardo," he said. "What else?"

Father's Days have been quiet since he's been gone. To him and all dads everywhere, Happy Dad's Day!

Jan McCanless

To All the Mothers in My Life

I know you may find this hard to believe, but I drove my mother nuts. Yeah, I did. I was always asking her questions, like, why isn't cough spelled coff, or why do lemons grow on trees? Made her crazy. Then, there was my brother Gregg. He had more plots coming out of his brain than Steven Spielberg, and for some reason, they always involved me. Like the time my parents went out for the evening, on April 1st, and HE decided that the two of us would play the proverbial April fools' prank on them. Naturally, he had to say it was my idea, but we swapped closets with my mom and dad, switching them around so her things were in his closet, and vice versa. Then, Gregg reasoned, why not fix it so a scatter rug would fall on their heads when they opened their bedroom door that night? Done. Next came the toothbrush mangling, when we put garlic powder, pepper and onion salt on what we thought was my dad's toothbrush. Uh uh, guess who's it was? All this and more, and she still didn't put us up for adoption.

Honestly, we were good kids, and while we vexed our mother considerably, we also did a lot for her, and Mother's Day was always special for her, we made it so.

I had some favorite aunts with whom I spent a great deal of time, and I looked on them as my secondary moms. On my mom's side, there was my Aunt Florence, who really mothered me, and spoiled me rotten, but then, certainly I deserved it!

On my dad's side, there was…um, well, they were all my favorites; a sweeter group of women never existed. Pop had 4 sisters, and they were all my very favorites.

His older sister, my Aunt Alda, was a spinster schoolteacher, who lived with and supported my grandmother, and she was absolutely the best storyteller in the world. With each niece and nephew, she'd sit us on her knee, and make up a story, starring us, and simply mesmerize us with the details. With 9 of us first cousins, there always seemed to be a little one around she could cuddle.

My dad's other sisters, all younger, were very special as well. My Aunt Melva, a former beauty queen was extremely kind, sweet, and loving; 5 minutes in her presence, and you were devoted to her for the rest of your life. My Aunt Leah was gracious, sweet, and hospitable, and boy, could she cook!

Then, there was my grandmother, Nonna to us. She loved us all, and we took turns spending the weekend with her; she said she couldn't handle but one of us at a time. Sometimes, I was with my cousin Shari, but I was always trying to do something nefarious to my little cousin, so, eventually, it was just me or her alone. Loved it, because on Saturday morning, Aunt Alda would fix pancakes for breakfast, and Sunday mornings, it was waffles, my favorite, so, spending our weekends playing Chinese checkers with Nonna, was a treat. Except she cheated, but I won't tell if you won't.

Mama's sisters, 4 of them, were all great cooks as well, and dinners at any one of their homes was a delicious experience.

My Aunt Florence bore the brunt of our pranks though, and brother and I were forever calling her on the phone with some scheme or other. Like the time we phoned and asked if her refrigerator was running. She said yes, so, we giggled and told her she'd better go catch it. Silly stuff, which, at the time, we thought terrific fun.

How we ever got through childhood pulling some of the stuff we did, is amazing to me. No, it's downright miraculous!

Through the years, I tried to remember all these great women on Mother's Day. I was close to my Aunt Gladys, my dad's baby sister, and spent as much time with her as I did my own mother. She was very artistic, and creative. To this day, I have many of her paintings hanging in my home, and I think of her every time I look at them.

Always there for me, supportive and loving, all my "mothers" deserve the tributes given on Mother's Day. They supplied me with cousins, and helped me keep the growing up years, lively. I loved them all, miss them all, and give them honor on Mother's Day.

Wish you were here, ladies.

For the Love of a Grandmother

So much is made of Mother's Day, and rightly so, we are, after all, what makes the world spin!! I am a mother and a grandmother, nine times over, so, I can speak with some authority – there is no finer, more satisfying job in the world than this.

My little six-year-old grandson knows all the right buttons to push, and once he gazes at me with those huge brown eyes, gets that lip to quivering, there is nothing in the world I would not get for him. Trouble is, he knows it too!!!

I had two very interesting grandmothers, both now gone. My maternal grandmother was a British lady, all very proper and how I loved to hear her talk, in that clipped, very correct way the Brits have. She was a little tiny thing, and loved me dearly, always ready with a hug whenever I saw her. She used to have to compete with Grandpa though, for my attention, as he had one of those bristly, scrub brush mustaches, which he would rub against my face every opportunity he had. Rubbed my face raw, he did, then, he'd put me off his lap, laugh, and aim for the spittoon across the room. No wonder grandma though him a nuisance, but I did love the attention.

Pop's mother stuck around until almost my teen years, and I did spend a lot of time with her as a youngster. She lived with a spinster daughter, and would rather have had a grandchild with her, than eat when she was hungry. She was a very lovable, and grandmotherly grandparent.

She and my aunt had this huge, wind up alarm clock, that had the loudest tick to it I ever heard. My brother and I called it the bomb alarm clock, because it was so loud, it sounded like any moment the thing would explode. One of those that had 2 bells on the top of it. I couldn't get away with saying "bomb alarm clock" in this day and age, but that's what we called it.

On any given weekend, Nonna and aunt Alda would have one of her nine grandchildren spending the weekend with them. I can remember, as if yesterday, that every Saturday, Aunt Alda would mix up pancakes for us, and they had one of the most real old timey toasters, where both sides would come down, you'd turn the toast around, put the side back up, and toast that side. I was fascinated with it.

Sunday mornings always meant waffles, the old fashioned kind, you put the batter in the waffle iron, then, when it was done, you plopped it on your plate. Delicious, and waffles have not tasted the same since!

When my children were all at home, we'd get out the monopoly game, set it up on the kitchen table and play for hours. I had to make extra play money for it, because none of my children wanted to be out of cash, so, I'd make up more, just so we could keep the game going. Then, we'd buy up everything we could get our hands on! Now, with the grands, we play cards, only, they have to refresh my memory of how to play. They think it's great fun to teach grandmom how to play. Naturally, they whip my shorts off!!!

Now, Nonna, she liked to play as well. We'd either play Chinese checkers, or regular checkers, but there is one thing though…um…she cheated. We'd be engaged in a rousing game of Chinese checkers, and she'd be jumping all over the board, here, there, sideways, front, back, didn't matter. So long as Nonna was doing it, she was happy. We were, however, told to stick to the rules.

It's these little, seemingly simple things that stick in our minds about grandmothers. God made them very special, and there's not one of them that is not convinced that her grandchild is the best, most special, smartest, prettiest, handsomest, most wonderful child in the word, and how in the world did that marvelous creature come out of my kid???

Well, Happy Mother's Day all you awesome grandmas out there, and know this, mine really are the most special, smartest, prettiest, handsomest, most wonderful children in the world. As for me??? Awesome, indeed!

Jan McCanless

You Know It's Gonna Be A Bad Day, When the Buzzards Start Circling

Ever have one of "those" days? I have weeks at a time like that. Well, for instance, the other day, it started out kinda strange, as all my days do. I was outside, and all I could see when I looked up was a flock of buzzards circling overhead. That can give a person pause, trust me. After I went inside, I find out I had put too much detergent in with the laundry, and my utility room was awash in bubbles. Soooo, I thought I'd put my shoes on and get it all mopped up pretty quick, and I would have too, except my shoelace broke in mid stride. Now already I'm thinking I may have done something really terrible to warrant all this, then, I remembered the buzzards, they must know something I don't, I thought.

There were a few things on my grocery list I forgot at the super market as well that morning, so, as I was driving back to the grocery store, the buzzards began circling the car, one even flew level with my passenger side window, and I want to tell you, that is one unnerving sight, to say the least.

Eventually, all things got sorted out, but I was wrung out. I want to tell you, so, I did the best thing I could have done, I got in my car, and took a drive out in the country. We live out in the country, so, doing this was not a huge undertaking, but occasionally I enjoy looking at cows, flowers, breathing in the fresh air, which isn't easy when there are cows around! Nothing fills up the senses like a drive through the countryside. If you don't believe me, ask John Denver, he wrote a song about it, and he was right.

My dad taught me this lesson, and he was good at stress relief, he went fishing, or he descended into the basement with my brother to tie fishing flies, they enjoyed that. He knew what was good for the soul, and when I was a kid, a chocolate milkshake, would do it for me. I can't have those anymore, so, I look elsewhere.

A drive through the countryside was exactly what I needed that day, and when I get home, I felt I could handle anything, even the buzzards!!

Thanks, Pop and Happy Father's Day to all!

The Greatest Generation Remembers

Boy, nothing gets the old memory juices going like discussing World War II. The other day I was on email with my brother and our mutual friend in England. She was telling us about the wonderful celebration in honor of VE Day that England was enjoying. Even Vera Lynn, the famous 40o's era singer had come out for it, and made an appearance in London to mark the occasion.

I told our friend of our uncles' war exploits while under the command of General Omar Bradley, and my brother added the story of one of his friends having a mother who was a driver for one of the officers in France during the war. When she wasn't on duty, she was singing at the USO Clubs and for Radio Free Europe.

Age brings with it an appreciation for these kinds of connections. Ties that bind us to one another, or join one family to another. The three of us truly felt a wonderful sense of "belonging" as we conversed electronically.

There is a marvelous book out now that talks about the five people one encounters in heaven, and it illustrates to the reader the fact that none of us is an island unto ourselves. We are all connected in some way, however small, to our fellow man. In great measure, we are all responsible of our quality of life here on earth.

We have just celebrated the anniversaries of VE Day, of Memorial Day, and we are coming up on the remembrance of D Day, PLUS, Father's Day. That's quite a triune of date when you think about it.

I don't think anyone can denigrate the contribution that women have made to our armed forces, and to the fiber of this rich country, but it is the men who have borne the brunt of wars fought by the United States.

I have uncles, cousins, sons, a husband, and a brother who all have served their country, and they are all fathers. They are all fathers of freedom and democracy, of honor and valor. I can't think of a more fitting way to honor our fathers of soldiers in this country, than by honoring those who have served this country.

Fatherhood, like motherhood, is not always easy. It has its highs and lows. We are grateful to the men – the veterans, the soldiers, and the fathers of this nation who have given so valiantly of their time, their strengths, often times their all, for those of us who remain behind, supporting them through all of life.

If you are a veteran, a father, one or both, we salute you. You have "stepped up to the plate" when called, and you have done us proud. I've always heard it said one never forgets the day you enter the service, the day you leave the military, or the day you become a parent.

Whichever one you are, whenever your "unforgettable" day occurred, we thank you. And we appreciate you!

Valentine's Day

I guess Valentine's Day is a good thing, kinda give us something to do between New Year's and Lent!

The Valentine's Day of my youth were efforts in futility, trying to get the cute boy I liked to notice me, while discouraging the "geek" in the front row who did.

Our teacher used to insist that everyone make a Valentine for everyone else in the class, and I remember getting one from a girl I didn't particularly care for. She didn't like me either, and always wrote some disgusting poem like, "Roses are red, violets are blue, I don't stink, but you do too." You know how it goes.

When I gold older, and actually HAD a Valentine, they got considerably mushier. Lace, hearts, and flowers all over them, they could be really embarrassing. I remember the first year the spouse and I were married, he came into the house with a HUGE, I mean HUGE box of candy, must have weighted ten pounds. Telling my boss about it the next day, she said if her husband did that to her, she'd kill him!

One never knows what to get as a gift for the male Valentine's in one's life. Candy and flowers just don't seem to mean much to men. They certainly don't want poems written about them, and those mushy Valentine's just seem to embarrass then no end.

After having two children in two years, one year I thought I'd be real practical, and get the spouse something really nice that would keep him busy outdoors for a change. So I went in search of the perfect outdoor Valentine gift.

My search took me to the garden center of the nearest store, where I told the clerk my intent to buy something nice and outdoorsy for my husband. Naturally, the clerk thought I was a little "off kilter," to put it nicely. But he showed me all the power tools and extension cords he had in stock.

Eventually, I settled on a new wheelbarrow for him, so I took it home, where I proceeded to wrap it up for Valentine's Day.

These kinds of stories are what make the best memories for me. The children laugh every time I tell it. But I explain to them that you don't need hearts and flowers to show your appreciation for the Valentine in your life. Poems and candy are nice too, but nothing lasts like the gift that can be used for years to come. Of course, an occasional hug and "I love you" does wonders, or just treating someone you love the way you want to be treated. Make this Valentine's Day special for ALL you loved ones!

The wheelbarrow? Well, I used it to give my kids a ride in, all over the yard. All three of them!!!

Fun on the 4th

One can't think about the 4th of July without it bringing a smile to your face. Like Thanksgiving, it's a uniquely America holiday that nobody but an American can really understand, or truly appreciate.

I can remember some wonderful 4th's from my past – like the time I rode in the parade in my white strapless evening gown – blistering hot, and our float was directly behind our TV's Wyatt Earp, Hugh O'Brien. We were in awe of him and the magnificent horse he rode, and none of us dared to sweat in the heart. Somehow, it just wasn't seemly to perspire in front of a movie star! As a Boy Scout Leader, I used to ride sometimes with my troop in parades, one year commandeering the infant brother of one of our scouts, to ride in my lap. Seems the poor child fell asleep, and I rode the entire parade route with this lovely toddler on my lap.

The very first Faith 4th of July that I enjoyed was way back in 1962. We only had been in North Carolina six months or so, and all I had been hearing was the big, explosive celebration in our neighboring town of Faith. I had a boyfriend come to town that week, so we took it in. I do recall having to walk about a mile outside of town, as that was the nearest parking space. The parade was noisy, hot, and just a lot of fun. I never knew that many fire engines existed, quite frankly, and I got my first taste of North Carolina bar-b-que that day. Once married with children, the Faith parade and fireworks became a part of our yearly celebration.

Fireworks, now that conjures up some tremendous memories. I love fireworks, and have seen some wonderful displays – even put on a few of them within the family. I'll always remember the wide coverage of the tall ships and various parades and fireworks displays during American's bicentennial. That was truly about the best 4th of July I've ever seen. Even the queen of England had to come over and take it all in.

For years, my brother has been telling me about the nice parade and various 4th activities up in his neck of the woods. Northern Wisconsin doesn't get the heat that we do, but their heart is just as big. Seems every year he drives his truck in it, all spiffed out in red, white, and blue, and he rides escort for all the Peninsula Players actors and actresses.

The Peninsula Playhouse is a large summer stock, outdoor theater where many of our more noteworthy personalities have gotten their show business start. You may not have heard it, but it's really quite well known. Seems the actors and actresses who are currently interning there get all dolled up, and cavort around the truck as it moves through the parade route in Door County, Wisconsin. "Only thing is," my brother informed me, "they dance and move about in mime, nobody talks."

I'll be in the front seat of Gregg's truck, silent, with the mimes. That couldn't possibly be why he asked me to ride with him could it – not saying a word???

Nah!!!!!

Trumpet Heralded Great Christmas

Somebody told me once that the best part of Christmas would always be the memories you make of it. I'm inclined to agree with them, as I have some outstanding remembrances of Christmas' past.

The first Christmas I can recall is the one when my brother got his trumpet. We were just kids, and our parents made a big deal out of escorting us from our rooms into the "front room" where the tree and all the gifts were. That year, I believe, I got a Toni doll.

If you remember, the Toni doll was a really hot item in its day, because she was the forerunner to Barbie, and you could actually give her a Toni permanent. In fact, the doll came with a Toni kit that enabled you to perm her hair and do all sorts of exotic things with it. Naturally, I tried it, but the solution turned my doll purple. I loved it anyhow and played with it for years.

Back to brother, for some strange reason, he was born with the ability to play the trumpet, and he must have been 9 or so when he asked for one. Well, there we were in our jammies and robes, pulling out gifts from under the tree one Christmas morning, and he unwrapped his trumpet, pulled some sheet music out from his bathrobe, declaring he just happened to have some on him, and proceeded to play the horn. That really stands out in my memory.

Of course my children have given us some terrific memories. Knowing how children are, it should have come as no surprise to the spouse and me that after having been up half the night preparing for Santa Claus, apparently our little dumplings outlasted us; when we arose bright and early at 4 a.m. Christmas morning, we found that many of the toys had already been played with, rearranged, and in a few instances, even swapped around between the three of them.

Christmas Eve's at my grandmother's house have garnered some wonderful memories, as well as the time my father decided we would brave the cold and spend the holidays at our cabin in northern Michigan, ice fishing.

Whoa! There weren't enough adjectives around to adequately describe the cold *that* holiday brought with it!

We come now to just one of the most wonderful times of Christmas, and that is the grandchildren! Besides attending my church, my greatest Christmas' have been spent making the grandchildren happy. I read once that grandkids were God's reward to us for having raised teenagers, and I believe it.

Nothing is so sweet as a small child sitting in your lap, eyes full of wonder, as he or she unwraps a new toy or book, maybe a shirt or pretty dress. How you smile as they hug and kiss their cousins and play with each other's toys. How marvelous it is when they wrap their arms around you and declare your cookies the "bestest" ever!

There isn't enough money in the world to compensate for such wonderful memories!

This is what I would wish for all of you this holiday season; enough joy to fill your heart, enough peace to elate your soul, enough love to make you the most important person in someone else's world.

Merry Christmas to all and God bless us, everyone.

Serendipity

The old-timers had a word for it, “serendipity” – that one momentous, wonderful occasion, when everything comes together at the right time and place, into an event so wonderful, it may never come again. That’s what happened on Christmas Day, many years ago.

After a lifetime of big, noisy Christmases, with assorted children, their significant others, huge 10 foot Christmas trees piled high with gifts, and a buffet that made my dining room table groan, we had a complete change of pace. It came about as the offspring gradually married and moved away, or opted to spend the holidays with the other set of parents. The spouse and I found ourselves one year with no holiday guests, no huge tree or groaning buffet table. We had, in fact, moved into our downsized retirement age new home facing the fact that only our daughter remained near enough to us to spend the holiday with us. She wanted to stay home and cook for her own family, and I put our few packages into the car and set out across the back roads in our county, now barren in winter, to a new sort of celebration.

As we slowly drove along a very quiet and still country road one Christmas morning, we suddenly spied a trio of deer feeding in a field, not too many yards out to the side of the car. We stopped and rolled down the window to watch, as the deer, snorting their frozen breath, bent their heads to the field.

It was so quiet, one could have heard a pin drop as we watched in awe as these beautiful creatures moved soundlessly around in the field, eating at their leisure. A pickup truck approached slowly from the other direction, it was a young dad, out with his small son. They, too, stopped and watched. The child, wide eyed with wonder, was just speechless.

The four of us sat there observing one of Nature's most elegant and graceful creatures, and the little boy was simply awe struck. Finally, his father quietly explained that they were Santa's reindeer, resting after a long night of pulling Santa's heavy toy-laden sleigh. Finally a very soft "WOW" came from the little boy, and wrapped his small arms around his father's neck, he whispered, "Thanks, Daddy."

It was a moment that defied description, and such a simple thing, but it brought home the meaning of Christmas to us, as nothing else quite could.

It comes to us in the small things, as it did over 2,000 years ago, when it came in the form of a small baby. It comes in the simple, quiet things, like a child's eyes, or a pristine winter's day. It comes in with wonder and awe as you observe nature at her finest and humblest. It comes in the peace and serenity one finds in the quietude of the season. It comes in joy and love.

We may never experience another Christmas like that again. But we had that one, and it was enough.

Ode to Thanksgiving

November is upon us, and I'm just not ready yet.
It seems the hurrier I go, the behinder I get!
So much to do, turkeys to buy, cookies to bake,
I'm so frazzled, boy, do I need a break!
The great philosophers once said, slow down, take time to smell the roses
How can I do that, when everyone says to stay on your toeses?
Thanksgiving, anniversaries and birthdays to come,
I'm so busy stuffing and wrapping, I'm coming undone!
Should I, could I, would I slow down if I tried?
Don't know, can't do it, I'm baking a pie!
Thanksgiving is a most blessed day –
We need to savor it, and maybe pray
Turkeys and stuffing, pie and gifts –
All are part of our holiday riff.
For this I am grateful and proud to say it –
Wouldn't change a minute of it – or trade it!
My wish for all of you is this:
Handouts of love, spoonful of bliss, and blessings galore,
Just don't rush it; the holidays come in with a roar
So much fun, never a bore.
Happiness abound, gifts piled in a mound.
Happy Thanksgiving to all, enjoy your meal.
All this, and the US of A to boot – what a deal!
HAPPY THANKSGIVING!

Jan McCanless

The Spirit of Christmas

It seems that Christmas means different things to different people. Some folks like to think of it as a family time, others see it as a time for partying, still others see in it all the glitz and commercialism they can.

Christmas makes me nostalgic, and I vividly recall almost every Christmas I've ever spent: some good, some not so good, some – just simply great. Coming at the end of the year as it does, the holiday always puts me in a mood for giving thanks. For one thing, I'm eternally grateful that I have made through another year, and, of course, I am always grateful to be able to celebrate the birth of our Lord and Savior, Jesus Christ. To me, all the plastic Santa's and blow up snowmen can't dim that reality. And I find great comfort and peace in church on Christmas Eve. Knowing that Christmas leads to another year, one for which I am so happy to be experiencing, you might say that Christmas Day is the best day of my life.

Some time ago, I ran across an essay written by GK Marshall Perry, entitled, ***"The Best Day of My Life,"*** and it speaks to that gratefulness. I want to share it with you now, even though it is not particularly seasonal, it's a good reminder of our blessings; this, or any other, time of year.

"Today, when I awoke, I suddenly realized that this is the best day of my life, ever! There were times when I wondered if I would make it to today, but I did! And, because I did, I'm going to celebrate.

Today I'm going to celebrate what an unbelievable life I have had so far: the accomplishments, the many blessings, and yes, even the hardships because they have served to make me stronger.

I will go through the day with my head held high and a happy heart. I will marvel at God's seemingly simple fits: the morning dew, the sun, the clouds, the trees, the flowers, the birds, and the SON. Today, none of these miraculous creations will escape my notice.

Today is the day I quit worrying about what I don't have, and start being grateful for all the wonderful things God has already given me. I'll remember that to worry is just a waste of time, because my faith in God, and His Divine Plan ensures everything will be just fine."

May you have the best, most grateful Christmas you have ever had!

Christmas Comes, Sometimes, When You Least Expect It

Like all kids growing up 50 years ago, not every Christmas was a gift feast. My dad, like a lot of them back then, had fortunes go up and down, and during the down times, you "dug in," and did the best you could.

It was just such a time that Christmas snuck up on me one year, and, made a lasting impression.

Dad, Mother, and I made up our family that year, my brother having moved out of the house, on his own, in another part of the country. We lived in Atlanta, and at this particular time our fortunes were slim. My mother had to work six days a week while my dad continued to travel for a living. I had already been told not to expect Christmas that year. My mom was too busy and tired to try and do any baking or decorating. My dad, on the road had said he would be home for Christmas, but it would be very late in the day on Christmas Eve before we were to expect him.

While my friends were enjoying their big trees with mounds of gifts under them, our house looked much as it had the other 364 days of the year. No tree, no decorations, not even a wreath on the door, no special food being prepared, not even a carol being sung from our record player.

I don't know when it hit me, but suddenly I realized that to have no holiday spirit at all was just not working for me. So, I went in search of pine branches that I could tie a ribbon on to and hang on our front door. Once found, I took the cards we had received and hung them on the wall in the shape of a tree. I was only 13, but I realized that if my parents could not provide Christmas for me, I would provide it for them. Loving to cook even then, I struggled with making a nice dinner, even setting out a plate of store-bought cookies on the table, so they would be ready when my mother got home from work.

My parents arrived almost simultaneously – Mama from her job at the WT Grant & Co. Store and Pop from his long drive off the road. It was already dark out, but I was ready for them.

Much to my surprise and delight, Mama came in carrying a small, artificial tree that the store manager had given her so we proudly placed it on the table in front of the front room window. Not many decorations on it, and no lights, but it looked good to me. My father had stopped at a drugstore on the way home and bought some very small gifts for us that year – some gum, a little perfume, a pen and pencil set. All gaily wrapped by the store personnel. It was then that Mama brought a box out from under the bed in their room. One of her sisters had decided that year to mail a gift to me, something she had never done before.

We had few gifts, spare decorations, a hastily put together meal done by a child; but we had Christmas. We did attend church that Christmas Eve, and I realized that Christmas is not always wrapped up in a big, red bow. It doesn't always arrive amid a lot of fanfare. Sometimes it sneaks up on you. Barely there, but a reminder, nevertheless, of the greatest event in history. Over 2,000 years ago, a small baby arrived with no fanfare, no decorations, and spare gifts, yet He brought the greatest gift of all in His presence.

If you can keep that spirit alive in you throughout the year. If you can remember the simple gifts, the spare decorations, and the greatest, most wonderful event in the history of man, then, my friend, you are rich beyond dreams.

Oftentimes, it is the Christmas that sneaks up on you that leaves the most lasting impression. I wish you peace, grace, and love, this holiday season.

Stuff a Turkey with Candles and Blow Out the Pumpkin…It's that Time of Year Again!

It isn't hard for me to get sentimental this time of year, my favorite. At the risk of repeating myself, I do love the Thanksgiving season. Mostly I love the weather; the beauty of the changing season; and, the wonderful atmosphere that Thanksgiving brings to the home.

I was thinking the other day of some of the really fun times my family has had during this most special of times. There was the year the spouse and I were courting and we drove up to Hickory to see the Catawba/Lenoir-Rhyne Football game. It began to snow right after half-time, and naturally, the game went into overtime this particular year. My mother was expecting us back home about 3 pm for Thanksgiving dinner, but we missed it by several hours. Not only because of the longer than usual game, but because the roads were so hazardous on the trip back home. She was not a happy camper, I can tell you. But at least we didn't have to tell her we ran out of gas. She would never have believed us.

There were numerous Thanksgiving dinners my parents hosted for other family members. I was always wanting to pull some kind of prank, so one year I told my grandmother that Mama had dropped the turkey as she was getting it out of the oven. Mama wasn't amused that year, either, if I remember.

It was after I had married that we began our own Thanksgiving tradition by hosting as many family and friends as we could possibly get in our dining room. It was always such an interesting mix. And, happily, many of those same couples became fast friends and stayed in touch long after the November celebration was over. That has been very gratifying. Even today, as scattered as we all have become, we manage to stay in touch and keep one another up to date on our activities.

My niece, Wizzy, came for Thanksgiving one year. Our most raucous dinner yet. We were expecting more than 15 people, some relatives, mostly friends, all dearly loved and cherished. I had put two dining room tables together in a "T" formation, with side tables holding desserts and coffee. Before we knew it, the day had slipped into evening, and we were still all together having a marvelous time. We marked a Silver Anniversary that year as well, so it was a double celebration.

I asked my three-year-old grandson the other day what Thanksgiving meant to him. His answer? "It's when we stuff candles in the turkey, blow out the pumpkin, and everybody brings presents." We-e-l-l-l-l-l, close.

I remember what I like; and, I like this time of year. I remember the wonderful dinners, the fun-filled time were loved ones, the marvelous warm feelings that smelling that delicious aroma of our turkey dinner evoked in all of us. I even remember that handsome, dark-haired boy that almost got us stranded in Hickory that day as we cheered on our Catawba Indians. As I gaze upon him now, asleep on our sofa, supposedly watching two TV sets, both were football games on, I remember the "dream-boat" he used to be.

Well, maybe not.

There isn't one amongst us who doesn't have much to be thankful and grateful for. I only hope we can keep this warm appreciative feeling going throughout the year. Whatever your circumstances, be glad you are here to share another Thanksgiving Day with us. And, above all, enjoy it!

Our Country Red, White and Blue

There is absolutely nothing that warms the soul quite like an old fashioned 4th of July celebration Independence Day is uniquely American, and how we celebrate it seem to be as well. I have European friends, all of whom would rather come to this country for our celebration, than witness their own low-keyed attempt.

The 4th's that we celebrated when I was a kid remain in my memory as positively the best time in the entire year. It's Christmas, birthdays, and Halloween all rolled into one. We'd always get up early, earlier, than on any other day, and head over to a fellow parishioner's home, where our church families put the finishing touches on the parade float we always entered. Most of the time, our youth group would ride on them, and what a treat that was, I waved to everybody, whether I knew them or not, I waved. One year, Hugh O'Brien, TV's Wyatt Earp was the grand marshal, and we were right behind him and that beautifully decked out horse of his. I would swear he had a 1,000 pounds of silver on that horse, and woven into his clothing. What a sight he was, and I became an instant fan when he trotted over to our church float and chatted up all us girls. We swooned appropriately, and rode with stars in our eyes the entire parade route.

After the parade, there was the picnic, I can't remember who all was there, but it seemed at the time like the entire community turned out for it, and probably they did. The hot dogs, hamburgers and assorted side dishes were without equal, and the fact that we would eventually drop a hot dog on the ground, made no difference to us. We'd pick it up, brush it off, resmear the mustard on it, plop it back in the bun, and have at it!! The only things better were the watermelon and homemade ice cream for dessert.

Evening brought the fireworks. On the fireworks! What joy they brought to old and young alike. Stars, shooting sparkling things, fireworks that went boom, and others that set the night aglow with every patriotic theme one could think of. The colors were always red, white, and blue, although an occasional green would sneak in there. We'd ooh, and aah, and gasp at the sight of it all. It would oftentimes, take a week or more for the patriotic lump to leave our throats after witnessing these spectacular shows. What a day!

I have always been a patriot, and I hope I have appreciated fully what the Good Lord has blessed us with here in America. No country on earth is anything like ours, and no country on earth has the freedoms we so take for granted here in the United States.

One of my sons served in Desert Storm, long before cell phones and computers were available for the soldiers to use. He was gone a year, with no contact of him at all, and yes, I worried, every day, I prayed God would protect him and bring him home to us. Well, he did come home to us, all in one piece too, and since that time, I've tried not to take anything for granted, especially this glorious Red, White, and Blue America.

I read somewhere in one of my daily prayer books the following. *"What would you have with you if you died today with only the things you thanked God for yesterday."* My answer would be simple. America, my family, and this wonderful celebration we call the 4th of July.

Go out and make it a good one, a joyful one, a noisy one, and a thankful one.

A Simple Piece of Wood

During our snowstorm towards the end of January, I looked out my window one day and noticed the lack of color everywhere. The sky was gray; bare, gray trees, and some dirty snow on the ground. Very monochromatic. Until that is, a bright red, male Cardinal landed on a tree branch right outside my window. His coloring was brilliant and beautiful, and he stood out so well in such a bland background. Wow, I thought.

Then, moving to another window in a different part of the house, I looked out and saw a half dozen daffodils in full bloom, amidst all the snow and gray. Another wow, for sure. When we look hard enough, and really "see" what we're looking at, there's color all around us, and glory in this world we have. You have to look on these things as positive signs that spring will soon be with us. 2 days later, I heard birds singing. The wonders just never stop.

Spring is the happiest of seasons, I think. Here we are digging out from cold and uncomfortable winter, and looking around us, we see renewal all over the place. Spring conjures up all sort of visuals for me, flowers, warm air, sunshine, longer days, a real sense of the earth awakening from slumber. The best part of all this, is the knowledge that we are on the cusp of Easter.

Easter, even the word is beautiful, peaceful, quiet. As a child, I always thought Christmas was the end all to be all, until I aged, and realized what Easter truly meant to me. Now, it's my favorite holiday, and as a former pastor once told me, "now I have grown up." When you stop to think that the very basis our Christianity is based on the Resurrection, it becomes the most precious story in the Bible. The crucifixion of Jesus was based on a lot of lies told about him. He was marched to his death, carrying a simple piece of wood, upon which they would nail Him to another piece of wood. Awesome. That piece of wood brought the crucifixion home to all who were there, to us, and made us realize what this man Jesus really meant to the world. Where would we be if He had decided that no, He was not going to die for our sin, no He would not be nailed to the cross, and no, there would be no redemption? All because of that piece of wood. How could such a simple thing carry so much significance for us? How could such an event change the course of history, and lead us to the movement known as Christianity?

Perhaps, in this day and time, with so much going on in the world, we need to pause a little longer, see a little bit deeper, and really understand what the Easter season brings to us, it's more flowers, warm air, and jasmine; new shoes and pretty hats. 2,000 years ago, a prophet walked up the hill to Golgotha, to be nailed on a cross, so, we might have eternal life. So that we who came after Him would benefit by spending eternity with the Father. We who lived and walked the earth centuries later would see the beauty in a drab field, we would have our wow moment in the colors of a bird, and the glory in some bent, snow laden flowers. We would have eternal life, because of Him, and the simple piece of wood He carried.

He is risen – He is risen, indeed!!

February Is for Lovers

I am once again marveling at how fast this year is going. Valentine's Day already! February's here, and one of the best days of the year. It's an interesting holiday, don't you think?

The first-year spouse and I were married, he came in with a 10lb box of candy for me, and all kinds of mushy cards. Do you know how big 10lbs of candy is? Trust me, it's huge. He meant well, I'm sure, but for a lady who is watching her diet, 10lbs of candy is a tremendous temptation. Ended up I would secrete 5 or 6 pieces a day in a napkin and take them to the break room at work to share. No way I could eat that much candy, nor would I want to.

Second year we were married he improved somewhat. He only gave me a 5lbs of candy, and I was expecting our first child by then, and didn't need 5lbs of candy. He did it anyway.

Well, fortunately, over the years, the candy stopped, the mushy cards stopped, and soon we were exchanging gifts like a new wheelbarrow or hair dryer. Great fun of course, but nothing compares with the old-fashioned way we did it as kids.

Remember those big, lacy heart covered boxes our teacher would put in the front of the room? We were supposed to put our Valentine's to fellow students in this box sometime the week of Valentine's Day. We girls were rather bold, dropping in bunches of them at a time. The boys, however, would surreptitiously sneak them in when they thought no one was watching them. Our teachers encouraged us all to include every student in our class with a Valentine card. We did, but still agonized over the fact that maybe that cute boy in the front row would not send one to us. We all were hoping for one from him, and he didn't seemed inclined to do that sort of thing, he was too "cool."

When my own children were in school, my daughter was all in favor of the Valentine's, and took great pains to address them herself and scrawl a name on the front of the envelope. She was such a little social butterfly though, she not only included her own roommates, she would want them for kids in other classes as well. I was so proud!

Her brothers though, now that's another story altogether. They wanted no part of giving Valentine's to other kids, especially girls!! So, Mom would get the cards laid out, place an envelope beside each one, and order them to sit down and begin to fill in names. They were not happy, and when I explained to them that one day they would meet a girl and would not be able to wait to give them a Valentine, or flowers, or chocolates, or "gasp" a kiss. That would send them to their rooms with their head under a pillow. It would not be too many years before I was proved right, and, in fact, the oldest one had many, many Valentine's one year. I often wondered if each knew about the other ones. I can only hope he gave each girl a different card.

Well times change, and while Valentine's Day remains a romantic holiday, just made for lovers, it no longer holds the magic it once did. What a shame, romance should never go out of style!

Couple months ago, I spoke to a men's group one evening, and, at the end of my talk, I opened the floor to questions. One man raised his hand and sheepishly asked me how to understand and deal with a woman. He claimed we are the most fascinating, frustrating, but delightful creatures in the world. His question drew a laugh, but my answer was serious.

Years ago there was a wonderful musical on Broadway called ***Camelot***, and one of my favorite songs from the show is entitled, ***"How to Handle a Woman."***

How to handle a Woman,
you love her,
merely love her,
simply love her,
love her, love her!

Surprisingly, that philosophy works for everybody…everybody.

Time for Renewal

I remember as a child, being so jealous of all the adults who got to stay up on New Year's Eve. Just couldn't wait until I got enough to do so, but as I aged, I realized that New Year's Eve is not just about parties and celebrations. It's a time for renewal, reflection, resolutions, and some serious, deep thinking.

Just think about it for a while, the start to a brand-new year, new beginnings, turning over a new leaf, reflecting on the past year, and maybe some different resolutions this year. There are always going to be the usual promises made to ourselves, lose weight, clean out the hall closet, re-arrange the stuff in the garage. Out with the old, we shout, and in with the new!

It would be wonderful if we really could start over – maybe be a little kinder to ourselves, nicer and more patient to our family members, a little bit more attentive in church perhaps, and a tad more active in the community, and a great deal more passionate with those less fortunate.

Remember all the buzz about Y2K? Some naysayers were proclaiming the end of civilization as we know it, the electric grids would go kaput, banks would have to close, computers would crash, it was a regular frenzy, and, all the while folks were stockpiling provisions and guns, yes, guns, to get them thru the end times. Reminded me of all the brouhaha back in the 50's over the bomb shelters, and the "atomic drills" we suffered through at school. Sure, if an atomic bomb drops on us, curling ourselves up against a wall will surely save us!!! A whole lot of nonsense, if you ask me, and that is not where it's at.

At some point in time, we have to have faith. Faith that our elected leaders will not engage us in some fractious, catastrophic war, faith that the everyday citizen will stop and think before they act. Faith that the good people of this glorious land of ours will begin to obey the laws that have been put in place for their own safety and protection. We can't rely on the doomsayers and negative aspects of our society, we have to be actively engaged ourselves in making this a better world for us all. January is the time to do it. The first day of the first month of a brand-new year. Now is the time, and now, we have the opportunity.

Go ahead, promise yourself that you will be a better person, lose the weight, clean out the garage, do whatever it takes to renew and re-energize yourself. The slate is clean, we are starting fresh with a brand-new year. The past is over and done with, let's concentrate on making our own and everything else's future all that it can be.

Oh, and there is one more thing. We were told, eons ago, that the greatest commandment of all was to love one another. If we really do that, then, all the worry we have over high prices, fractured families, terrorists, whatever befalls us, would be entirely unnecessary. That's all we need, to love one another.

We need to work on that. In the meantime, Happy New Year, each and every month of 2019, may it be the best ever for you and yours.

Thanksgiving with the Home Folk

Ok I get it, it's Thanksgiving time once again, although I just bought my Halloween pumpkins, I have come to the realization that the year is almost over. If you find out where it went, let me know.

We always had big Thanksgiving, my mother would put on a spread, and buy the biggest turkey she could find to feed us all. I can't recall specifically who all was at our table, but I know it was a bunch, aunts, uncles, cousins, whoever was around, dropped in. My parents had a lot of friends they saw socially, so, I know some of them were dining with us as well.

I continued the tradition in my new home, every year inviting more than the previous year. Sometimes I had 2 or 3 tables set up in addition to the dining room table for all the overflow. Since I was born on Thanksgiving, the years my birthday fell on the holiday always made me feel a little cheated, as it got lost in the celebration of thanks, plus I did the cooking too!!! Somewhere in the mix is a wedding anniversary as well, so, my birthday has always been put on the back burner. No parties as a kid, because Mama was always getting ready for the "big day." Don't worry, I got over it, really, I have.

One of my favorite sitcoms was ***Everybody Loves Raymond***. Ray's mother Marie was a piece of work, a "real" mother-in-law, but I can relate to her protestations that everything she made was so good because it was done with love. I think love is what makes every holiday great for us, and memorable for years to come. Like my Grandmothers' Christmas, my Aunt's Halloween, I tried to make Thanksgiving memorable for my family, and after all the kids married, at least until they had children of their own, they continued to come home for the holiday. Marie Barrone is right, when you put on your best, and do your finest meal preparations, the love shown thru. I've often wondered how the folks who don't cook, celebrate this wonderful national holiday of ours, I mean, we can't all go home to mother's place and yet how do you cook love into a boiling hot dog!

Ya'll remember the first Thanksgiving meal you prepared? We went home to Mama's for our first Thanksgiving after the spouse and I married (remember we were newlyweds, and took the opportunity to pick up our wedding gifts), so, for the 2nd one, we had been transferred to Boston, had just barely been able to move into our home in time and going to the grocery store the day before the big day, all I was able to find in time for a meal were the ingredients for a meat loaf. Well, I made my meat loaf, quickly baked a pumpkin pie, and it was darned good, I'll have you know. It was also the last time we had meat loaf for Thanksgiving.

I don't think it matters so much what you have to eat on the day, as much as what the day represents – Thanksgiving. The dictionary defines thanksgiving as a feeling of gratefulness, of being grateful for what we have.

We're having some problems in this country now, some of which are pretty scary, but it's still the best system of government anywhere. If it weren't there wouldn't be so many folks trying to get here at the risk of life and limb!

Whatever your meal plan for the day might be, I truly hope it's memorable for you, and that you are surrounded by people you love, and love "doing" for. Giving thanks.

Couldn't have said it better myself.

The Home of the Free Because of the Brave

For 69 years and counting the City of Faith, North Carolina, has provided a 4th of July Celebration that is one of the best events to celebrate our nations' freedom and heritage. It has been a part of many peoples' memories as kids, as families, first dates for younger couples. As we grow older, it is a great evening to spend with our grandchildren and our families. For 69 years, the Faith 4th of July, has supported charities now well over 10000 of them providing help for those in need, throughout the year.

I have always loved the 4th of July, well, who wouldn't…I mean it's in the middle of summertime, that great season of warmth, and everybody seems to have such a good time doing it all!!

It's all about history, really, those first soldiers who laid it all on the line to form a new Republic with her own laws and statutes. Think of those revolutionary soldiers, many with no shoes on their feet, slogging thru the harsh winters, the unbearable summers, carrying primitive weaponry, eating mostly whatever food they could catch, grab or beg, all in order to form a more perfect union, guided by God and existing on pure adrenaline. WOW, boggles the mind! Makes you wonder how many of our youngsters alive today could endure half of what these early soldiers did, and would they? I have my doubts.

My own darling, Charlie, was a part of America's finest for 26 years, serving in wars overseas, inspired mainly by the same things these ancients were. We are extremely proud of our Charlie, and he as a Purple Heart, Navy Cross and numerous other medals and "badges" of honor to show for it. So, when you see him and other veterans, thank them for their service, won't you?

As a kid, I remember the 4th of July lasting all day and half the night, that was the fun of it. We'd get up in the morning, prepare for the parade, and oft times I would be riding in one, or brother marching in one. So, off we'd go, and following the parade, there was always a picnic, oh what fun! The fireworks at night were nothing less than spectacular, and the lump in my throat as I watched them would get bigger every year. Just the memory of it still send chills down my back!

One of my best 4ths was spent up in Wisconsin, visiting my brother Gregg and his family. Our friends, Helene and Brian were visiting from England, that's them in a photo with me, as we lined up for the parade thru Door County. I was riding, they were watching. My brother, sister-in-law and I were in the truck, all the actors from the local little theater were in the back, in costume, singing patriotic songs.

Well, there we were riding, along ever so slowly, when we rounded a corner, and there stood Helene and Brian, each waving an American flag as hard as they could. What a beautiful sight to see, British citizens joining in, smiling, reveling in the celebration that had ultimately separated us from their homeland. It was gratifying to see. English blood runs deep within Brother and I, and it was so wonderful to see these dear friends taking so much pleasure in a uniquely American celebration.

Despite what you may read in the paper, or see on the evening news, there is still much to be grateful about in this country. My theory is, if this country and her government are so bad, why do so many try to get here??? Every government, every country can stand some improvement, and I know ours will come, it always does.

In the meantime, we have 4th of July to come, and those marvelous memories, man, what a day!

Easter, And All Its Glory

For the past 30 days or so, I've had my computer set on a website that has allowed me to view an Eagles nest high in a tree, on the campus of Berry College in Georgia. I have watched as the Mama bird sat on her eggs to incubate them, saw the Daddy Eagle as he flew back and forth with food for her, then, would take his turn on the nest, and have delighted to see now, the 2 hatchlings, as they grow and thrive.

Currently, the mother bird is feeding them several times a day, she then, will move the sticks and twigs around in the nest to make a resting spot for them, as she settles down on top of them to keep them warm, and free from harm. Papa continues to check on his family periodically, and to relieve his spouse so she can have a little free "flight time" for herself. It's fascinating to watch, and gives one terrific insight into family life in the avian society.

You have to wonder, don't you, at how attentive and tender something like a bird can be to her offspring, as she sets an example of wonderful mothering. They lack human traits, but just watch for a while, and you see spousal fidelity, parental responsibility, and unconditional love. Some of the most beautiful expressions of love on the face of the planet, and they are all manifested in one Eagles nest on the campus of a small college in Georgia. Mother Nature at her finest.

As I watched them this morning, the idea struck me of its corollary to Easter. We are God's fledglings, struggling to be fed, warmed and protected, and God is our parent, taking care of us. He feeds us, warm us, and guards us from harm, but unlike the birds, we have more free will, and can reject or accept His goodness.

Think of it in terms of Easter – Easter is God's promise to us of redemption, and love, and through the gift of resurrection, He has granted us eternal life. Wow! It just doesn't get any better than this! God is our Mama Eagle, there to watch over us, feed us, guide us, and even when we leave the so-called nest, and enter into this world as adults, He is still there nurturing us and loving us. Through the resurrection, He always will be.

May you all have the most beautiful and blessed of Easters!

How Can You Have the Winter Blahs with a Valentine in Your Heart?

As I write this, I am wearing a sling on my right arm, recovering from shoulder replacement surgery before Christmas. Now, I don't do winter well, or forced confinement, and, once my imagination takes flight during all this, no telling where it will lead. They say an idle mind is the devil's workshop, but I've written some pretty good stuff this time of year.

With the holidays and New Year's over with, and the white sales un-accessible for me, the next thing I have to look forward to is the day they yank that poor ground hog out of his nest to see if we're in for more winter. Poor guy, I've always felt sorry for him, all snug and warm, then some yahoo in a tuxedo jerks him out into the cold. It's a wonder he doesn't bite the hand that pulls on him. I would. Personally, I think it would be a whole lot more fun if we pulled a politician out of his office, or dropped him down from a building. Just think about it for a minute, you'll see I'm right.

So, I'm sitting here wondering what would keep me out of the doldrums and save me from the mid-winter blahs. Of course, Valentine's Day!

When I was a child, I used to look forward to it so much. We'd make that fancy Valentine Box for the classroom, remember? It was covered in red hearts, lots of lace, and sat right in the middle of the room, where we would surreptitiously sneak in an occasional card. Wanting everyone to give us one, but not wanting to be caught stuffing ours into the box. Oh how I hoped that cute boy who sat at the front of my row would put a card in there for me, it's all I thought about for days before hand. Invariably he would, but it would one of those kiddie cards, with a picture of a skunk on the front of it and the verse saying something like, "Hey, Stinky, by my Valentine." Oh boys could be soooo tedious at times!

The party we'd have after the distribution of our cards was always fund and we'd play some goofy, silly, boy/girl games too, working off some of that chocolate we ate during the party. I hate to brag, but I always managed to get a tall pile of cards, not that anyone was counting, you understand.

Valentine's, when I got older, now, that's when we got serious about it all. I used to love it when a boyfriend would buy me a truly beautiful, romantic card, and maybe some flowers along with it. Oh how my heart would swoon, and some guys, well, they never outgrew the card with the skunk on it. The first year I was married, spouse came in the door with a 5lb box of chocolates for me, which he proceeded to eat himself. What a guy! Knowing him, I'm surprised it wasn't a new ironing board or laundry basket!! I got him good though, one year, I bought him a brand-new wheelbarrow, it was however, the most "romantic" one I could find.

Well, all in all, the holiday can still be a lot of fun, and keeping love in your heart all year long, ah, that's the trick! Cards, hearts and flowers are all nice, but telling someone you love that you really love them is so much better. When we declare our love for one another, it not only makes them feel good, it does wonders for ourselves as well. That's what's it's all about, what makes our wheels spin, and engine rev.

This Valentine's Day, I hope you have love in your life, love in your heart, and feel, oh so good. If you don't have a Valentine now, then I truly hope you have one soon, I do!

Too Soon Already

As I sit here writing, I'm finding it difficult to wrap my mind around the fact that we are into a new year again. 365 days gone by once more, and soon, we'll be pulling that poor ground hog outta his hole, sending Valentine's, and stocking up on our Easter eggs! I mean, where does the time go anyway?

It seems like only yesterday I was on vacation in Midwest, or finishing up another book. Knowing me, you surely are aware that I have a plan to slow things down a bit. Here it is.

The first part of my plan calls for one to be continually crossing the international dateline, that way we can always be a day behind ourselves. That may help. If that doesn't work, then stir things up a bit by arguing all the time, with everyone you meet. I've read that argumentative, unhappy people say that for them, time stands still, and days are very long. That too may help. Lastly buy one of those artificial sun lamps where you can retain the daytime for as long as you like, that way, you can stretch out the daylight hours indefinitely, making the day seem interminable. The only problem with that is, you still have to deal with the nighttime darkness, and we all need our sleep, so, that may not be the best plan after all. Well, I never said it was a good plan only that I had one.

As a kid, the longest day in the world for me was two-fold, the first and last days of school, I thought they'd never end. Then before you know it, I was graduating and throwing myself at the world. Who knew?

Not too many days ago, I celebrated a birthday, and while I would love to stay perpetually young, I know it just ain't gonna happen. It helps if I tell people how old I am in dog years. Somehow saying I'm 10 doesn't sound as bad as saying I'm pushing 40. Yeah, uh huh.

Centuries ago, old Ponce de Leon searched for the fountain of youth, thought he'd found it in Florida, but alas, he too grew old and died, never realizing, like so many of us, that youth and time are all relevant. I like the adage that one of our residence homes has, "putting life into our years."

One of the "youngest" persons I ever knew told me on her 100th birthday that she was somewhat saddened to know that her life was at that time, half over. Imagine, half over at 100! What a wonderful outlook to have. Well, being only 10, I have a long ways to go, there are things I want to do yet, places I would like to go, and people I want to be with, so, I think I'll hang on a little while longer, taking my time to do anything. I got news for you, if you slow down, then time will also. Old age isn't so bad, if you think young, and in that respect, I am definitely younger than my oldest child! As a matter of fact, the other day one of mine asked me I was ever going to grow up. Why should I, I replied, I'm having too much fun being 10!

Happy New Year to All!

Well, another year has come and gone, and I am still in shock over it. I mean, why does it have to go so fast? I'm at the age now where I take things kinda slow, and I expect everything else to slow down as well. Honestly, now how hard could it be?

As a kid, I always wanted to stay up late and watch the New Year come in, and was always resentful that I had to have a babysitter while my parents went out to parties on that night, and I could never manage to stay up late and see it. I thought something magical happened, like the earth tilting on its axis or some kind of revolutionary occurrence and we would never be the same. It seems to me, I used to wake up on New Year's Day and nothing had changed but the date. I never felt any different, almost never looked any different, so, why the big deal?

Finally, I got old enough to stay up late and see the New Year in. I can't remember going to but one New Year's Eve party, and I was an adult then, and us women sat around the kitchen table talking while the menfolk either watched a football game or talked about one. Finally, we all gathered around the TV set in the living room and watched the ball drop, then, we all went back to doing what it was we had been doing. That's it? A ball dropping? I couldn't even find my date when it came time for the midnight kiss, he had gone out to the car to get something to show the other men there. Well, so much for romance!!!

When we hit the year 2,000, I did stay up nearly all night and watched the various celebrations around the world. Peter Jennings was the man of the hour, if I remember, and he hosted this round the world show, and it was nice. Well, I couldn't do much else that year, spouse and I had reservations to attend a nice dinner dance at the downtown hotel, then, he got sick, and we had to cancel, so, while he rolled around in the bed moaning that he was not going to make it January 2 (he had a cold, mind you), everyone else was expecting the world to end. Remember those people? They kept telling us to stockpile bullets and canned beans for the millennium because of major rioting in the streets and massive shutdowns that would wreak global destruction on us all. What ever happened to those people anyway? Well, there I sat in front of the tube all night, the spouse sneezing and moaning in the bedroom, me, sipping my eggnog, as I watched the ball drop once again. So much for the history of my New Year's excitement.

As for resolutions, I never make them, but instead much prefer to make resolutions of what I WILL NOT do in the coming year. More realistic and certainly more interesting. So, for 2019, here's my list of do nots for the year, and I know you are just dying to learn what they are.

1. I will not, definitely not, listen to any more robo calls, but instead will blow a deafening whistle into the phone, to teach them a lesson.

2. I will not, definitely not, punch in any more numbers on an automated menu phone call. If I can't speak to a live person, well, then, I won't speak at all. So there1

3. I will not say something "smart" to the next clerk who asks me if "that will be all" when I purchase an item. Oh I know it's annoying because, if it wasn't all, there would be more merchandise on the counter, wouldn't there. But they have a job to do, and part of it is asking me if that will be all every time I buy something.

4. I will not use one of those automatic check out machines either, I don't like them, and when I yell at it, it never says anything to me. Do they know how irritating that can be??

5. I will not let another day go by without telling my loved ones and friends how much they mean to me, and that I love them, and I will definitely not stop hugging my grandchildren until either they begin to bleed, or they cry "uncle!"

Well, there you have it, my plans for the New Year. 2019 hmm? If I'd known I would live this long, I definitely would have done things differently, and yes, taken better care of myself. Heck, I'm an optimistic person, I might even start buying the green bananas now!

Ya'll have a wonderful New Year!!

The Smallest Christmas Tree

As holiday traditions go, ours were fairly simple. The day the tree went up, I always enjoyed watching my children as they hooped and hollered and danced around. Then, I would bring out the Santa figure that always sat on my mantle, behind his sleigh and reindeer. Quite often, I would later find this same roly poly figure sitting on one of their dressers or laying in their bed, they really loved it, and knew that as soon as it appeared, Christmas would not be far away.

Usually about two weeks before December 25th, I would get out all the baking trays, and ingredients, and mix up several different kinds of cookies. Sometimes, I would simply mix up the batter, then, put it in the refrigerator until I needed to bake them, but oftentimes, I would simply start in baking, and hopefully, save some of the batter to cook up a later date. I liked those times, because I rarely had to fix anything or supper, my clan enjoyed the cookies fresh out of the oven, and it was not unusual to find each child, plus spouse, eating up to a dozen cookies each. They never had any appetite after that, and I could sit by myself at the kitchen table and enjoy a salad, -quietly.

Back in 1987, the whole bunch was home, one son from college, another on leave from the Navy, and daughter Carol still living at home and attending high school. I was scheduled for some surgery that I knew would take a very long time to recover from, so, I decided not to decorate that year. Nothing doing, my offspring shouted, they would do the decorating for me, wrap the gifts, put up the tree, the whole nine yards. Not wanting to bother with a live, very big tree, I went to the local big box store and bought a small, 3' tall artificial tree, and placed it on a table in the living room. I told the young'uns to have at it, and they dragged out all the ornaments, the lights, whatever they could find, and boy, did they decorate! I had lights all over the house, tinsel on every lampshade, gifts piled up, haphazardly wrapped and sitting underneath everything in sight. Carol had made certain that her gifts were prominently placed near our small tree, and the boys, well, she scattered them about too. I had already made up my cookie dough, all they had to do was plop a dollop on the baking sheet, and shove it in the oven. This, they did quite well! Oh, one other thing, they promised to put it all back after the holidays, for sure. Christmas came and went, boxes and tissue, bows and paper all over the house that day, and the three of them soon retreated to their rooms to talk on the phone, or otherwise amuse themselves. There I was, using a walker, with a broken arm to boot, spouse was asleep, and I couldn't even see my shoes for the mess! I went to one after another, asking that they return to the living room and make some sort of order of it, and maybe get all the tinsel off the lamps, before they began to heat up, and maybe smoke a little.

Several days later, the tree was still there, the mess had not been sorted, all the cookies were baked and eaten, and there I sat, wallowing in it all. One thing about it all, we did enjoy the holidays, at least, as much as we could.

A week later, Charlie went back to the Navy, Bob returned to college, and Carol was back in her classes in high school. I was there with the smallest Christmas tree I had ever had, tinsel on my lamps, and lights all over the house. It turned out all right though, I guess, eventually, I got off the walker, my broken arm knitted, and sometime, just before Easter, I got the stuff all put away. Do you know, I used that little tree for almost 20 years after that? We moved soon into a larger home, and I would place that little tree in one of the other rooms, away from the gigantic one we put under the arch between the living and dining rooms. It added a lot to the overall décor of Christmas, and I left the miniature lights on it, and all would enjoy it as we sat in the den watching our holiday shows. The big tree in the front rooms stood as a beacon of the season, but that little tree reminded me of that one Christmas when things were rather a kilter at our house. I do recall the spouse telling me sometime in late March when I was finally able to pack it away, that he would miss that little tree.

You know, sometimes the best things do come in little packages! Have a wonderful holiday!

The Eagle Versus the Turkey

It's a known fact that Benjamin Franklin was our first modern age hippy. He had some wild ideas about things, including women. You've heard his little ditty about them haven't you? He was asked once why he always loved older women and he replied that "they don't tell, they don't swell, and they're grateful as…," well, you get the picture.

He was the one who came up with the idea of the lending library, the fire department, all kinds of good stuff, and then, there were the bifocals. I mean, who would not appreciate this man's genius. So, it stands to reason that we might give serious thought to his theory that the Turkey should be the national symbol, instead of the Eagle. Eagles, he reasoned were majestic, regal, free spirited, soaring, and quite beautiful. Not all that common either, since they do not usually congregate among a lot of people.

Now, turkeys on the other hand, make a lot of noise, waddle around insufferably gobbling about their own importance. They don't fly more than 10-20 feet off the ground, and not only are they stupid looking, and, they can be pretty stubborn. Driving along the Blue Ridge parkway up in the mountains, the spouse and I run into flocks of them quite often. They look at you as if they owned the road, and are slow to move out of your way. Not only that, but they are ugly creatures, not really in keeping with the spirit of the greatest country on the face of the earth, are they? However, they are delicious when cooked, and their very size just screams "thanksgiving" do they not? Best part is, they are abundant, not so the rare Eagle.

Something tells me too that eagles just would not be all that tasty, I mean, they are very strong birds, so, probably would not be all that good to eat. I just can't picture myself asking for a wing off an Eagle. Turkeys now, they have some fat on them, are juicy and tender, and seem born to be devoured, and if they were on all our seals and symbols, I'm afraid I would simply chuckle every time I saw it. Can't help it, they remind me too much of Congress!

Happy Thanksgiving ya'll and bon appetite!

Jan McCanless

Moms are People, Too!

I don't remember when it happened, but somewhere along the way of my growing up, I figured out that Moms were regular people, not magicians, not somebody with eyes in the back of their head, not anyone with super human strength, just regular people.

I'm convinced my own children looked at me as some pathetic, helpless creature who didn't have a clue as to what real music was, had never been to school, therefore, I had no idea of what went on in school; someone so totally bereft of intelligence that I was incapable of independent thought, word and action. I guess they reasoned that their meals just miraculously appeared on the table, the house automatically cleaned itself, and the "doctoring" and "ministering" I gave to them magically worked, in spite of me. Well, gee, thanks, kids!

My own mother, I thought was pretty funny, she had a way with words that could bring a laugh, and sometimes her nonsensical sayings could make me smile – although never in her presence. I remember one time when I was playing with a cousin, and she brought me a sweater and told me to put it on because SHE was cold. One time, she even became good buddies with a teacher, which I considered complete treason, and another time she invited one of my teachers to dinner. THAT was the final straw, I thought.

One of the things my mom did, used to irritate both my brother and I. We'd be on our way to visit someone and she'd tell us to stick out our tongue. She'd swipe it with a handkerchief and literally was our faces with our own spit. Ooh, it used to gross me out, and I never could see the problem with having a little dirt on my face. Not my mom, she was clean a freak, and anything not found in it's a proper place at the end of the day, got thrown out. Her children were going to be neat and clean, by George, or she was not a good mother!

As she aged, my mother could easily get confused, and many's the day I tried to explain to her that the building she saw off in the distance was her own apartment building. That somehow, never worked, and I would have to get her back in the car, drive to her apartment, and show her that yes, that was where she lived. Those were the heartbreaking times.

One humorous incident really sticks out in my mind and it happened in Atlanta. She was asked, as a member of the auxiliary, to model in an Elks' Fashion Show for the ladies of the community. She was given a very beautiful and expensive dress to model, it came from one of Atlanta's pricier establishments and told to be at the Elks' Club on a certain day, at a certain time. Now, my mother had very poor eyesight, and wore some fairly thick corrective lenses, but nevertheless, she wanted to model without her glasses. She felt this would be more glamorous. So, just before she went out on the stage, she handed them to me, then, she sailed forth. Well, she did ok walking a straight line on the runway, but then, she was supposed to turn around slowly, and walk back. Well, she turned all right, ever so slowly, and as she did so, she edged ever closer to the edge of the stage, and a fall of approximately 4'. I jumped up, took her by the hand and directed her to the appropriate spot, and headed her in the right direction back, towards the beginning. She bumped into another lady who was just beginning her parade on the walkway, but she made it safely back and I was Johnnie on the Spot with her spectacles, so, she could find her way back to the dressing room. It was with a sigh of relief I went back to my chair and sat down to enjoy the remainder of the show. I don't know if she ever appreciated my efficiency in saving her from a bad fall, but she did claim that she knew where she was going the whole time. Uh huh.

About the time myself and all my girlfriends were getting married, we all received some pretty funny advice from our mothers. One girlfriend said her mom told her to never let her husband see her in the curlers. You all remember curlers, don't you? Having natural curly hair, I never used them, but I sure do remember them. Another friend of mine said her mother told her to treat her husband like a dog – that is, feed him well, and pet him regularly.

My own Mom's advice before the big day?? She suggested I not freeze bread. True, so help me!! Well, it was funny, and it was typical of my mother. My son got her back one day though. She was over at my house, and got on my stationary bicycle to exercise a while, and my son piped up with. "Grandma, I didn't know you knew how to work that thing."

Moms, God bless'em, young, old, living or departed, they made us what we are today. Here's to moms everywhere, may you have a wonderful day!

Mothers Are People Too...Yeah, They Are

I was at a meeting the other day, and someone waved to me and asked if I had found that recipe yet. I smiled back, laughed, and had no clue what they were talking about – that is, until several minutes later, when I realized they were referencing my April column where I asked if anyone had a good recipe for ground hog. Of course, I was delighted that they had read my article. Like Sally Field exclaimed when she was given the Oscar for best actress, "you like me, you really like me!!!"

Getting back to the ground hog story, it jogged a memory I have of my Mom telling me how good her own mother was with what I lovingly refer to as "roadkill." My maternal grandmother was a sweet, very tiny lady, from England. Birmingham, England, to be exact, and she was of course, very British, and very proper. She also had 9 children with my grandfather, the youngest being my mother. Mama would tell me a lot of times of her coming home from work to find her mother stirring a big pot of "something" or other, and every time Mom asked what it was, Grandma would reply, chicken, but Mama, being the wise person she was, knew better. She said with the war on, we're talking World War I here, the Depression, and 11 mouths to feed, Grandma would cook what she had, and often times it was squirrel or something worse, and it was many years before my mother found out that what she ate was very often, not chicken. Well, mothers are like that, they do what they have to in order to keep hearth and home together.

Daddy's mother, my Nonna, had 5 children herself, and was widowed long before I came on the scene, and she too could stretch a sack of potatoes to feed a houseful. My greatest memory of her food was her macaroni and cheese, one of those comforting dishes that was like glue in consistency, a real "stick in the ribs" kind of dish, but boy, was it good! I used to love to spend the weekends with her and my Aunt Alda, because Saturday morning, Aunt Alda would prepare pancakes for us, and Sunday mornings, brought real, homemade waffles. My Aunt Alda was Nonna's eldest, an unmarried daughter with whom she lived, and on weekends, Alda did the breakfast, and it was always good, very good.

I can remember, as a child, during the days right after the Second World War, and people were just beginning to restock the pantries following all the rationing that had gone on during wartime, and very often, we had milk toast for breakfast. Mom would spread her oleo margarine on the toast, making it good and gooey, then, she'd break it up and pour milk on it. It was good to me, but having tried it once myself, I could never get it quite the same consistency that my mother had.

Mother's Day always found me trying to buy something really nice for my Mother, a beautiful plant or something nice to wear. My own children, now there's a story for you. My oldest, bless him, used to insist on taking me for a ride in his truck for Mother's Day. Sometimes we'd end up at a movie house, often times buying a pizza before hand – with me paying, naturally. But it was the truck ride that was memorable, because he had to demonstrate to me how his truck, with those huge, off road tires would go up over a curb or plow through a field, or take a large pothole at a running gallop. As I was tossed about in that thing, he would grin at me and declare that this was a wonderful adventure for us. The last year that he had that truck, I hid from him, but he came in search of me. "C'mon Mom, its Mother's Day, get in the truck," he'd say. I felt like a brood mare going to the breeding barn!!! It didn't make it any easier when he had to grab me by the "behind," and push me up and onto the seat, due to those high tires. Well, that's what makes Mother's Days memorable, I guess.

We all have our memories and special stories of our mothers, and no matter how long they have been gone from us, we still think about them, linger over our thoughts of them, and know we take a piece of them with us everywhere we go. Our moms permeate every fiber of our being, and good, bad, or indifferent, they belong to us, and we are forever tied to them.

I'm a grandmother now, and I am very much aware of the fact, that one day my children and their children will look back at me and say to themselves, "wow, I can't believe she did that!" I want their memories to be good, and full of love for me and my crazy efforts to be the best mom and grandma I can be. Remember the laughter, I tell them. So, to all you moms, grandmoms, favorite aunts, and surrogate moms out there, a very happy and memorable Mother's Day, and please, remember the laughter.

Jingle the Halls, and Deck the Bells… It's Christmas Time Again!

I hate to sound scrooge like, but didn't we just have Christmas? Has it been a whole year since the last one?

It just seems to me that here we have the 4th of July, and next thing we know, boom! Christmas is upon us.

Maybe it's because it seems to start earlier and earlier every year. I was in a store, the day after Halloween, and so help me, Christmas carols were being played over the PA system. That ain't right!

When children, anticipation was half the fun of the season for us, remember? We never got to sit on the department store Santa's lap until well after Thanksgiving, and decorations and carols were not in place nearly as early as they are now. Go to any large drug store chain after Labor Day, and they are, all lined up in a row – artificial Christmas trees, and just below them, the shelf containing assortments of Christmas cards. There oughtta be a law!!

There are some advantages to being a senior citizen this time of year. One is that we can give a check to the kids and ask them to buy the grands something from us for the holiday. One way to avoid the crowds and traffic of doing our shopping, unless we wish to begin in August! Another one is we don't have to entertain anymore, all those business associates of the spouse, we always have activity centers and meal sites to go to for our social outlets. Cooking? No thanks, there's the cafeteria and other places to dine, and we can even not put up a tree if we so wish, after all, nobody expects us to make a fuss anymore!

I think, in a couple weeks, I'll dig out the Christmas cards and maybe while I look at a rerun of Lawrence Welk, I'll get them addressed. I've already gotten my first card, from my British friend Helene, she mailed hers in October, thinking the mail rush would delay us getting them until after Thanksgiving. It arrived in 4 days. Oh well, it looks very nice sitting on my mantel, and I know, another several days, and I'll be getting a lot more in the mail.

I still love Christmas, I just don't think of it in the same way as when we were kids. There is nothing material anyone could give me that I need, so, I'm not anticipating any gifts. Just hugs and kisses from the grandchildren to make my holiday complete. It's still nice to visit the malls this time of year, only now, I go to look at the decorations, and watch the people. I'm a writer, and writers do a lot of people watching, that's how we get our inspiration for the things we write!

I'll tell you what I do miss a lot this time of year, the Christmas variety shows. Entertainers like Bob Hope, Andy Williams, and my all-time favorite, Perry Como. They would always do such nice, family oriented, song laden shows that would really make my heart sing. We looked forward to them every year, and thank goodness I taped them all, because now, all I do is take one out, pop it in machine, and I am instantly transported back in time, when the holiday season was not so commercial, there was more peace on earth and good will to all. Early in December I could begin to think about putting up a real, live tree, one that smelled as fresh as that wonderful woodsy aroma that permeated the house until well past New Year's. A time when the sight and the sounds and smells of the season filled us with awe and inspiration. When Christmas Eve meant walking to church in the snow and hearing the carols, seeing the lights and watching the glow on the faces of all the little angelic "cherubs" as they took their places in the Christmas pageant.

Who could not love a holiday like that? Well, pardon me while I wipe my eyes, blow my nose and pull out an old Perry Como tape for the recorder. I'm in the mood for Christmas, and I sure don't need a plastic tree or a blow-up Santa to put me there. Thank God for memories, right?

Have a wonderful, Merry Christmas, ya'll, and may the joys of the season be yours a thousand-fold!

Turkey Most Fowl

I'm one of the few people I know who just loves turkey, any way that I can get it, and, I especially love it left over. Nothing gives me more satisfaction than to grab a cold turkey leg, some dressing and gravy, and warm it all up and plop down in front of a good movie, and have at it! The founding fathers had it right when they said turkeys were too prevalent and too stupid to be the national bird, that's why they chose the eagle.

Driving along the Blue Ridge Parkway on any given day, one can see flocks of the turkeys as they forage alongside the road. They don't appear to be afraid of cars, but while fearless, they are smart enough to move to the side as we drive by. They can even fly, somewhat…at least as high as tree level, where they sit until one of two things occurs, they fall off, or the branch breaks. Mostly, they nest on the ground, and pretty much stay there.

My mom used to take great care in selecting her holiday birds, and always, she would buy the biggest one she could find, because, every year, we entertained a houseful of relatives of Thanksgiving. She'd clean it well, stuff it with her good, homemade dressing, and cook it, sometimes overnight, so, it'd be ready for dinner when all the aunts, uncles, and cousins piled in around three in the afternoon. There always seemed to be plenty of people around to eat it. I think that is how I always got stuck with the drumstick, now that I think about it. Everybody else was served all the choice parts, and the only thing left were the drums, so, I got one. Probably that's when I learned to love turkey drumsticks.

One year, we were all sitting around the table, my dad ready to carve, and I was sitting next to Nana, our grandmother, and trying to be funny, I piped up that the turkey didn't look at all like Mama had dropped it. Then I told her she had done a terrific job of putting it back together. My brother was the only one who laughed, I can tell you quite honestly, that my mom was not amused, and neither was grandma!

Thanksgiving remains to this day, my favorite holiday, and I enjoy telling folks that I was born on Thanksgiving, and my mom said I was the biggest turkey she'd ever seen! Well, she didn't laugh at my prank, so, I'm not gonna laugh at that!

Well, despite all the rhetoric and nasty campaigning we've had to witness over the past several months, we still have the best country and system of government in the world. If we didn't why would so many people risk life and limb to come here? My own maternal grandparents among them.

Perhaps the best part of the recent campaign is, by the time you read this, it will be over, and we can go back to enjoying whatever it is that we enjoy!

Whatever you do on this holiday, and if you are like us now, and prefer the quiet of a nice lunch at the cafeteria, or you entertain legions of people, I sincerely hope it's the best, most thankful holiday for you and yours.

Show your gratitude, and eat a drumstick for me!

Dear God,

I'm writing about some concerns I have as a turkey. It seems that in your infinite wisdom, you decided to make us fat, flightless, and evidently delicious.

Did we say something to make you mad?

Sincerely Yours, Mr. Turkey

Jan McCanless

A Happy, Warm Fuzzy to You All

It's interesting, the images we conjure up in our minds about holidays. Say Thanksgiving, and instantly, you picture a roasted turkey. Say Christmas, and the answers will vary. Some folks think of a special gift they received, some picture with Santa Claus, others a tree, it varies from person to person. Say Christmas to me, and I immediately think of my grandmother's Christmas tree village, that she and my Aunt Alda put every year under their tree.

It was a glorious, fascinating village, complete with ice skaters, dogs out for a walk, lit up in houses, and quaint churches and other structures. As soon as I hit the front door of Nonna's place, I'd head for that village, moving the skaters around, the miniature people, I'd play with that village all day, and every time I went over there during the holidays, there it would be, everything its place, ready for me to play once again.

Now, there were nine of us cousins on my dad's side of the family, and I don't know how the older ones felt about it, I fell somewhere in the middle of them, but to me, and the younger ones, that village was magic!

Christmas Eve brought all of us together, cousins, aunts, uncles, grandma, and Aunt Alda. After a dinner at the groaning dining room table, including some of Nonna's legendary macaroni and cheese, and maybe some chocolate cake for dessert, we'd all go into the living room, and open gifts. Everybody there got something, nothing elaborate, and maybe not even expensive, but it was a remembrance, and we had a wonderful time. All in sight of that wonderful, glorious village she had. Paper, ribbons everywhere, a lot of laughter, full tummies, it was marvelous, and what I always thought Christmas should be.

I never had a sister, and, my brother Gregg was always into "guy" things, but I have a cousin, Shari, 3 years younger than me, and, the closest thing to a sister I have, and she too enjoyed that village. We sometimes would spend the weekend together, at Nonna's, and we lived fairly close to one another, so, it seemed natural that we would pair up. Between Shari and I, that village was well played with.

After my grandmother's death, I wondered whatever happened to all those figurines, the skaters, the houses and churches, I hated to think they were collecting dust in someone's attic, or worse yet, given away to someone outside the family. What a tragedy, I though!

Years went by, and finally I was able to find out that Shari had gotten the village, and I was overjoyed. To think her young grandchildren are now enjoying it, makes me smile. Memories like this are priceless, and it brings home the message to me that Christmas need not be about a lot of gifts, expensive catered meals, but it is about family, love, being together to celebrate a wonderful and meaningful day.

Thinking about Christmas should give you a warm, fuzzy all over, and that's my special wish for you this holiday. May you have love, family, and a warm, fuzzy!!!

Jan McCanless

New Year, Same Old Face

Here it is, a brand-new year, and you know the old saw, “if I’d known I would live this long, I’d have taken better care of myself.” Well, it’s true.

As a kid, there were two times during the year, I wanted to stay up late, one was Christmas Eve, hoping to catch Santa at work, and the other was New Year’s Eve. No matter how hard I tried, I never made it to midnight either time. No matter where I fell asleep, I always wound up in my bed the next morning. The only time I made it to midnight on New Year’s, was at the turn of the century. I sat up watching TV until the wee small hours of the morning, playing solitaire, the spouse had conked out about 9.

Even as an energetic teenager, I was always home by midnight, just couldn’t make it any later. Obviously, I am not a party girl, rather dull, I’d say.

New Year’s Day always seems cathartic to me, a New Year, a new start, time to wipe the slate clean, and start over, if need be. The naysayers are always harping every year about this being the end times, prepare for doom, etc. and I just laugh about it all. Even if it were the end times, and we are all going to be zapped up to paradise, somebody tell me what the downside of this is.

New Year’s is our gift, our new day, available for us to use any way we can. It would be nice if all peoples everywhere, all nations on the globe, could and would get along. If all our blessing were shared and passed along to others, if every person we saw during the day, greeted us with a smile. Hugs, smiles, and a warm greeting, are free, some of the few things in this world that are, we should spread them around more, I think. Tell someone we love how much they mean to us. What a wonderful, glorious New Year it would be.

I’m going to do my part, every day that I can, every way that I can, to everyone I can, how ‘bout you?

Happy New Year to Our Unsung Heroes

January always seems like a good time for reflection to me. The old year has passed, we are off to a brand-new start. Kinda like a "do over" we're given every year.

We, as a nation, have had some rough times this past year, with lots of scary headlines along the way. Some, maybe, not so scary. At some point in time, I got to thinking about all of the people in our world who do things without any thanks or acknowledgement at all.

For instance, the police have had a very tough year, and it seems that they are not all that appreciated at the moment. Well, I for one, do appreciate them and give thanks every day for all our law enforcement and fire protection personnel, where in the world would we be without them? How about the poor guys up in bucket trucks fixing wires and lines on cold or steaming hot days? Any time our power goes out, and we call the repair line, we are back in business in a short time. Think about the poor people in underdeveloped nations who have no access to electricity or refrigeration, or phone service. Remember that the next time you see a lineman dangling 50 feet above you.

I hate worse than anything going to a hospital or emergency room, but when I do, those "angels" in uniform one sees, look so good to me! And, they are there, no matter the day or time.

Ever driven a garbage truck? Me neither, and I wouldn't want to. I hear ours, 5 a.m. every Wednesday morning, without fail, no matter the weather, and I think what a wonderful service they provide.

Well, I think you get my drift. SO much that happens in our society does so out of the public eye, yet, they are all vitally necessary to the smooth running of our cities and towns. I've made a pledge to be more appreciative of these good folks this year, and to tell them so. We can get mighty complacent in our day to day existence, and now, in these times especially, I think we need to show our gratitude more.

Every January we are given a chance to wipe the slate clean, start over, begin again, so, let's do it. Along the way, have yourself a very Happy New Year!

God Bless the USA

I don't know of any holiday that gets the old "juice" flowing like the 4th of July. It's purely American and filled with so many wonderful memories for me.

Summer wasn't the same without the 4th of July parade through town, hotdogs in the parks, and the marvelous fireworks display at night. It sends goose bumps down my goose bumps!

So much criticism and rancor now, about everything it seems, we need to stop and think a minute about all that is good in our country. Starting with freedom of speech, which seems to have taken a different connotation of late. Freedom of religion is a real "biggy," and just freedom in general. For all you critics out there, this may not be the most satisfactory system to you, but would you rather have the alternative?

God has truly blessed this country of America and her citizens, we need to remember that. We have everything we need – in abundance. Much of it owed to the good folks who have served the country through the military. If it were not for them we wouldn't be here today, in what is arguably the greatest nation on earth.

Our son has recently retired from 26 years with the Air Force, and he told me that engaging in Desert Storm, the rallying cry was the song so popular at the time, you know the one that said "I'm proud to say I'm an American, where at least I know I'm free, and I'd gladly stand beside her and defend her to this day, God bless the USA!!!"

Couldn't have said it better myself.

It Didn't Used to be This Way

Used to be, I would anticipate Christmas with all the excitement I could muster for such things. That was the holiday of all holidays, and when you're a kid, you look forward to it for all the wrong reasons. Then, I grew up.

I don't recall being very enamored of the Easter bunny the way some children are. The idea of some large rabbit hopping along, hiding eggs (eggs, from a rabbit?) and candy just seemed so ludicrous to me. Now, new clothes and a pair of Mary Janes, I could understand. My, how times change!

As I aged, and grew in my faith, the idea of Easter took on a whole new meaning for me, and how appropriate that it comes on the heels of spring now, sorta like a new beginning for the earth, and all her people. Almost like it was preordained, isn't it. Now, when I think of Easter, I look forward to it as my favorite holiday of the year, not just for its religious significance, but the fact that it usually heralds spring, and it brings with its own sense of awe and inspiration.

I no longer worry about getting new clothes, or new shoes, I look forward to the solemnity of the day, the church rituals, the delightful church youth who prepare breakfast for the congregation, the flowers, music, and everything that goes with the Easter service. I've learned, over the years, that the crucifixion and resurrection of Jesus Christ is the very basis of our Christian faith, and, without those two events, we absolutely would not have any Christianity. It ushers in a renewal, new life and energy from the earth's awakening, and gives a new meaning and depth to our religious faith.

Easter fascinates me, just think about it! Has there ever been any other event in the history of the world that could equal it? I can't think of anything. Because of Easter, I look at spring, flowers, new growth and even green grass in a different light, and have now for many, many years.

Easter is our opportunity to start over, for renewal, and for thanksgiving. You may buy new clothes and shoes, but don't forget the real reason for this holiday. Whatever you do Easter Sunday, wherever you go, I wish for you a renewed and deeper faith, new energy, and an appreciation for this wonderful, glorious world we can enjoy, because a young man once went to his death on your behalf – and mine.

The Scrawniest Christmas Tree

As a child, I felt that Christmas should be celebrated year round, in every room of the house, forever! I think every child feels that way, until we learn better.

When in Junior High School, we lived in a big, two story house with lots and lots of rooms, brother and I had bedrooms' upstairs, with a sun room between us. I loved that place, and spent a great deal of time up there.

One year, I got the bright idea I wanted my own Christmas Tree, with lights and decorations, and I wanted it front and center in my bedroom, which was a generous size. So I went to the Christmas Tree seller at the corner, and begged a tall, scrawny looking, spindly tree from him, dragged it home and up to my room for set up. It already had a couple wooden slats for a stand, so, all I had to do was stand it in the corner, which I did, with, the scrawniest side to the wall. Then I grabbed a string of lights from my parent's cache, and proceeded to string them along my tree. Next, I needed ornaments, and not having any of my own, I also "borrowed" some off our big tree in the downstairs sunroom. What I lacked, I made myself.

As I stood back and admired that tree, I saw that it leaned a little one side, and didn't look particularly full or pretty, but it was mine, and I loved it, as if I had planted, grown and cut it down myself. Well, I did get it home, up the stairs, and set up all by myself! Christmas came and went, New Year's, Valentine's Day, and we were charging towards Easter, and that tree was still up in my room. I was proud of that tree, to me it was beautiful, and it reminded me of Christmas and the joy of the season. Mama, however, was afraid it was becoming a fire hazard, as it had turned a lovely shade of brown, and was pretty dry by that time. In fact, needles were piled on the floor where they had dropped off. It was unfortunately, the scrawniest looking things you ever saw, but I continued to take pleasure in looking at my own Christmas tree.

All things must come to an end, as did the life of this tree, and it was a sad day in early spring when I eventually took it down, dropping dry, brown needles all the way out the door. I don't know why I needed that tree so much that year, but I did, and it gave me comfort and pleasure every time I looked at it. As I've gotten older, like the Grinch, I too have learned that Christmas trees, ornaments, and bright lights do not make Christmas, and the lack of them doesn't stop Christmas from coming. Christmas is a warm, fuzzy feeling brought about by love in the heart; not for all the present you'll receive, or all the cookies and fruitcake you can consume, it's love in your heart, and a feeling of great joy over the Christ child, and the true meaning of the holiday.

I'll never forget that pretty little tree of mine, but Christmas has an entirely different meaning to me now. My wish for you this season is a heart full of love and happiness, as you celebrate the birth of our Lord, and forge onward towards a bright new year.

Two Little Words

Webster's dictionary defines thanksgiving as an "act of being grateful, of giving thanks." Couldn't have said it better myself. We are so accustomed, especially this time of year, of asking for things, praying that something will work out for us, or asking God for something specific. It's always nice I think, to simply say, "thank you" for all that we have, and are given.

I love catalogs, do a good bit of my shopping from them consequently, we are showered with catalogs on a daily basis. One came the other day, and one of the things it offers, is a plaque for the home, and, under the heading, "attitude of gratitude," this is what it says: "Dear God wanna take a minute, not to ask for anything from you, but simply to say thank you for all I have." It's a beautiful thought, being grateful is the most humbling, loving thing we can do for ourselves. Even the not so good things. We should be grateful for those as well as all the stressful times, because when you think about it, every experience in life teaches us something. We can learn a lot from our adversity and our mistakes. Life teaches us lessons, we need to be open to receive them, learn from them, be grateful for the opportunity it offers, and move on.

No matter what our everyday challenges, it's amazing and awesome to see how the load lightens when we stop and take stock of all of God's gifts. With the approach of Thanksgiving, let's pause a moment and take the time to be truly grateful.

Thank you, two little words that carry such impact, and pack such a wallop to our lives. We need to say them more often and mean it!

Mothers, the Eighth Wonder of the World

It's been said that Mother's Day is either the happiest day of the year, or the saddest…depending. For me, it has always brought great joy, I have 3 dumplings, who have blessed me with nine delightful grandchildren, and I cherish each and every one of them. I can't recall how many of the funny, handmade cards I have received, or the numerous macaroni laden cigar boxes that have held hankies or jewelry, and one particular Mother's Day, my oldest decided he would take me for a ride in his truck – as a treat. Now, his truck had those big, bad boy tires on it, so it was difficult for me to just hop right in. Grabbing me by the behind, he pushed me up and onto the seat. Then, we went 4-wheeling. A Mother's Day I'll never forget!!! Well, such is the life of a mom.

For my own mother, I always tried to give her something nice for her day, and one year I bought her a beautiful flowered dress, in her favorite color of lavender, and I smiled each time I saw her wear it. I was so proud of that dress, and it took all my babysitting money to buy it, but if she was happy, I was happy. Later in life, as she became more sedentary, I would buy her a large hanging basket, as she loved flowers. Usually Begonias, and she seemed to take such delight in watering and nurturing those flowers. The year she died, her hanging Begonia was still thriving, so, I brought it home and hung in where I could see it every day, and it absolutely flourished – big, beautiful blossoms on it, and it was big and bushy, I'd look at that plant and I just knew she was ok, and happy.

So, we come to grandchildren. Oh what a blessing they are, and what fun!!!! I'd be a mother ten times over if I could enjoy those grands for a lifetime, and one of them, 15 year old Trevor, thinks I am awesomely awesome!! It doesn't get any better than that!!! Well, he has awesome parents, so, I guess it runs in the family.

There is a beautiful saying, framed and on my bedroom wall that says it all:

"MOTHER
To One Who Bears the Sweetest Name
And Adds a Luster to the Same
Long Life to Her: For There's no Other
Who Takes the Place of One's dear Mother"

I couldn't have said it better. God bless all the mothers, and have a wonderful day…you deserve it!!!

What Would Mom Do?

Spouse has always called me a "free spirit," my college professors called me a free thinker, the kids just think of me as nuts, and mom, well, Mom would call me her "difficult" child.

Now, I pride myself on being someone who always does the right, sane thing; certainly a "free spirit," but not someone who goes outside the law, until now!

Here's what happened. My BFF Camille and I had our "girls' week out" recently, and this year, we went to Wilmington, to partake of all the things the coast has to offer; great shopping, the beach, terrific food, and wonderful entertainment. Well, let me tell you about the night at the theater we enjoyed while down there. Seems my friend Camille had procured some seats for us at the world famous Thalian Hall Theater. A beautiful place, lavishly appointed, with top entertainment. We bought tickets to a play that, unbeknownst to us, was being performed in the little theater portion of the Hall, not the big, plush theater the place is noted for. We donned our glad rags, and headed out for an evening's entertainment.

Once at the hall, we were directed upstairs to the little theater, where we took semi comfortable chairs, and then watched as the audience came in. The first person was a young woman of college age, tattoos all down both arms. She was followed by a man, barefoot, with several holes in his face where his pierced jewelry protruded. They were followed by people in various stages of undress or "questionable" dress. No one in the audience was over 25, or anywhere close to our age. I leaned over and asked Camille if she was sure about the play, it didn't look like "our" crowd. Oh yeah, she said, the play was highly recommended to her, and we were lucky to have tickets.

Being the happy-go-lucky being that I am, I gave her the benefit of a doubt, and settled in for what I hoped was a wonderful theatrical experience. Boy, was I wrong!! We were only 3 rows up from the stage/floor area, and the actors were all over us, so, we sat there listening to lousy music, I forgot to mention that it was a musical, the name of which shall remain only with us, terrible acting, awful singing, and nasty words my mother would never have allowed me to hear, much less utter. I knew when the male actors began to take their pants off that we were in trouble.

Mercifully, intermission arrived, and I suggested we ask for our money back, the play was absolutely the worst thing I had ever witnessed. She felt the same. We left the little theater, and discovered that the play in the "big room" was also on intermission, so Camille wanted to show me this beautiful theater and how handsomely appointed it was. While the patrons were in the lobby drinking champagne, we ducked into the theater to look around. It surpassed our greatest expectations, and yes, it was gorgeous. Just before we left to find the box office and our refund, I asked her what did she think would happen if we just sat down and watched the 2nd half of the opening night of "Gypsy," a wonderful presentation of one of Broadway's biggest hits. The theater looked pretty full to me, but as the audience began filing back in for the 2nd half, suddenly, I found myself in a seat, and motioned for Camille to join me.

This marvelous production was terrific, with great songs, accomplished acting by semi pros, and fabulous sets. The cost was double what we paid for our seats in the little theater, but we sat there mesmerized as the story continued. When it was over, we walked out the door, elegantly dressed, just as if we belonged there; what an adventure, and once we got back to my car, we collapsed in laughter.

Now, for the big question, what would mama do? Well, she'd probably tell me I was wrong, advise Camille and I to go for recreational therapy of some kind, remember, Camille is the friend who cheated at Scrabble last year during our "girls week out," then she'd go into another room, shut the door, and laugh her head off! I had a very understanding mama, and Camille did also. So, I considered our little escapade as a tribute to these 2 fine women who had the good sense to give birth to us. Did I tell spouse or my children? Absolutely not, why spoil a good thing!

So, to all you free spirit out there, I wish many exciting adventures, and a Happy Mother's Day to boot!

April and the Great Reprieve

Well, I never thought it would get here. It's been said that April is Mother Nature's apology for March. I believe it. Quite frankly, I never thought it would get here.

What a winter, just when we got used to enjoying all the unseasonably warm days, we would get a freeze. My daffodils all bloomed, then, got zapped with cold, and my azaleas were thoroughly confused. They weren't the only ones!

One of the things I love about April, is the fact that everything is so new and fresh looking. The green of the leaves and grass is such a brilliant green, so unlike the tired shades of late summer, it's like God has painted a picture postcard for us to enjoy.

When Easter arrives in April, we get a bonus, not only do we get a renewal of the earth, but we get a renewal of our spirit, and the knowledge that we are once again given a "reprieve" – a second chance if you will, to maybe get it right this time!

As a child, I thought of Easter as a time for new shoes, chocolate bunnies, and prettily decorated baskets. It took me a while to grow up and realize the true meaning of Easter, and the Resurrection. It's a time when God pats us on the shoulder and says, "You're covered, don't worry about it."

What joy to know that we are saved children of God, that our debt has been paid, our death has been died – on the cross – for us. The greatest miracle of all, Jesus' resurrection, was accomplished for us. It's probably the most comforting event in history!

The loveliest time of the year is upon us, the birds are back building their nests, the trees are in bloom, the flowers are literally standing at attention, and we have the Easter season, and all its wonder to bask in.

I'll never look at the cross the same way again, and please, get out and enjoy this glorious gift we have, and by all means, have a Happy Easter!!

Want to Do Something Different for Christmas? Try Cruising

Wanting to do something really different for Christmas this year, we fulfilled a lifelong dream by booking a four-day cruise on the Mississippi Queen going along the mighty Mississippi River.

We drove first to Biloxi, which gave us the opportunity to tour the magnificent Jefferson Davis mansion, "Beauvoir." Then on to Gulfport and the lovely mansions along the "gold coast." The ornate casinos were an addition since our last visit and many take up an entire block.

The waters of the Gulf of Mexico were calm the day we were there, with sea birds abounding and lots of sunshine.

When we pulled up to the Delta Steamship Co. Wharf in New Orleans, the porter opened the car door, helped me out and welcomed us to the Mississippi Queen, and our lives were changed forever.

There is nothing more tranquil than cruising down the Mississippi river on a quiet afternoon. The weather was beautiful, around 75 degrees, and the pristine beauty of the more remote areas of the river is breathtaking.

At dinner, we ran into some women from Asheboro and Greensboro. The married son of one of our dinnertime tablemates lives in Concord. It seems that everywhere you find a Carolina connection.

Seeing the homes of the French Quarter and the Garden District decorated for Christmas was nothing compared to the wonderfully colored holiday décor of the Mississippi Queen. Lovely Christmas trees, garlands, angels and gaily wrapped packages were all around the boat. It seemed as if every mirror reflected the lights and bows that greeted us at every turn.

One of the most memorable things about our cruise was food. More food than I have ever seen in my life was everywhere you looked. More than once, I caught the spouse sneaking gingerbread cookies as we waited in line for our table at dinner. When it's there, you have a tendency to eat it, and upon disembarking, we swore we would never eat again.

A shore excursion to the fabulous Oak Alley estate was especially memorable. As hard as it is to believe, the original house and hundreds of acres of land sold for less than $35,000. The Roman Family, original builders of the home, although loyal Southerners, were not sympathetic to slavery so they freed them and encouraged them to stay on as hired servants. Many of them stayed. It's interesting to note that big house with ornate mantels, all the moulding, some of the furniture and everything needed to sustain life was manufactured right there on the mansion grounds. It took two years to accomplish the finished product, but it's a real testimony to American ingenuity and spirit.

When you walk that quarter mile from the levee to the mansion through an oak-lined alley, you are taken back in history to a genteel, luxurious way of life that will never come again. The view from the second floor balcony towards the river is a genuine Kodak moment the docent told us. And she was right.

Back on board the boat, we cruised to our next destination of St. Francisville, LA, home to Cajun Country. We stayed on board while many others took shore excursions to various points of interest, but we found the serenity of the bayou country most relaxing.

The huge calliope of the Queen is a one of a kind instrument, and it was played loudly each time we left a port of call.

Christmas carols, good Dixieland jazz, lots of food, exciting adventures and wonderful new friends made this a marvelous holiday celebration as we cruised from one spot to the other on the American treasure, the Mississippi river.

As we disembarked in our home port of New Orleans, we
wished one and all a safe journey home and a happy holiday
season. It's truly a Christmas we will never forget.

Christmas Remembered

I'm at the age now, where my memories of holidays, sometimes equal or surpass the real deal. Retirees just don't have the same, magical feeling toward them, unless, of course, they have a lot of grandchildren around them. Well, mine are all practically grown, so we don't look at holidays in quite the same way anymore. Visions of dolls and toy trucks have been replaced with cars, girlfriend and expensive jewelry for the girls. What we do have, are a lot of terrific memories.

Christmas Eve at my grandmother's will always hold a special place in my heart for me. All the aunts, uncles, cousins, grandma and Aunt Alda. It was hectic, wonderful, delicious, and exciting. I remember the dinner table groaning with food, ribbon, wrapping paper, and empty boxes all over the living and dining rooms. Adults trying to talk, us cousins running all over the place. It was a dream come true, and forever and a day, I will miss it.

The first Christmas my son was home from Desert Storm was pretty wonderful too. Unfortunately, he had caught a "bug" and was not at his best, but I didn't care, he was home in one piece, and I was one happy mom.

On our second Christmas together, spouse and I had just been transferred to the Boston area, and we were barely in our house in time for Christmas. No time or money to go and buy a tree, I lined the fireplace with greenery, hung our cards in the shape of a tree, and I cooked. Christmas day we woke to a white wonderland from all the snow. So much, in fact, we could not get out the door, so, we lit a fire in the fireplace, exchanged a very few gifts, and enjoyed being alone for the first time.

The year we saw some deer grazing in a field near our home on Christmas morning was indescribably magical. There they were, in a field, the ground covered in glistening frost, and three large deer quietly grazing, I suppose after a hard night of pulling Santa's sleigh all over the world.

One holiday I'll *never* forget, is the year my parents decided to go up to our northern Michigan cabin and do some ice fishing for Christmas. We had a large tree in the middle of the big room of our cabin, the only decorations were popcorn and berries. Very pretty, if not sparse. With no central heat, we could see our breath with every exhale, and my dad's idea of a good time was to put as many clothes on as possible, waddle out on a frozen lake with a saw and a stool. He cut a hole in the ice and dropped a line. Pure heaven, he thought. I have never been so cold in my life, and quite frankly, I didn't think anything could survive at that temperature. I could hardly see around all the scarves and hats I was wearing, and wondered how Eskimos lived that way.

It didn't take me long to realize I was not cut out to be a snow bunny, and longed for my Florida home, where I could roller skate and wear just a sweater on Christmas Day. That to me, seemed a lot more civilized than sliding around on a frozen lake. Even the fish shivered!!

The Christmas a girl gets engaged is always memorable, as it was for me. I have friends and relatives who married at that time of year, but I wasn't that brave to crave all of that "hecticness" during the holidays, I married at Thanksgiving! Yeah, right!

Well, anyway, when I sit in church on Christmas Eve, enjoying the music, the lights, the beautiful Chrismon Tree, and all my church friends around me I will sit there and remember and it will be wonderful!

Merry Christmas my friends!

My Funky Valentine

When I was a kid, all I looked forward to was getting as many Valentines as I could, placed in that big red box the teachers always put at the head of the class. Remember those? Draped in lace, they were large enough to hold everyone's cards, addressed to every student in class. No exceptions, everyone had to contribute, and we did.

The mean old boys always sent ones that said something on the order of: You stink, but be my Valentine. It was us girls who sent the mushy, lovey dovey ones. When my own sons were in grade school, they balked high and loud at having to do it, but I'd go buy those large boxes of generic cards that seem custom made for the Valentine boxes, and then I'd sit them down with pencil and a box of cards and say, write! Invariably they'd forget someone, someone they didn't care for much, and I'd fill in for them. Boys! Honestly, you'd think they were facing open brain surgery the way they carried on.

It's different though, when we meet "the one" isn't it? Couldn't wait to get it home and write our love note to them. Ah, love! It was in our second year of marriage, I was pregnant with our first child, when spouse came home with a five-pound box of candy for me. I haven't forgiven him yet! I was certain that by the time I "hatched," I'd give birth to a 26 pounder, thanks to that box of Candy!

The funniest Valentine's gift I ever gave him came when I was expecting our second little boy, some three years into our marriage. I was quite obviously with child when I walked into the hardware store near our house, pushing number one son in a stroller, and said I wanted to purchase a Valentine's gift for my husband. The clerk though I was nuts, but I explained that he liked to work outside and needed a new wheelbarrow, so I thought I'd get him one. The young clerk looked at me and remarked that maybe he didn't work outside enough, and I said yes, that's why I wanted to the wheelbarrow.

Well, all's well that ends well. He got the wheelbarrow, and I went on to have another child after number two son. Wouldn't you know?

All my life, my big brother was my hero, champion, my friend. When he went into the service after high school I missed him. He had gotten his draft notice a few weeks before, and didn't much care for the Army, when the Air force was playing its siren song to him, so, he enlisted before the draft came. Mama cried, and I thought it would be lonesome up there on that second floor without him. Our bedrooms were the only things up there separated by a nice sunroom, and now, it would be just be me up there. Darn right I missed him!

Gregg was not gone long, only a year or two, due to the fact he got seriously injured jumping out of an airplane, so, after months and months in rehab, he was finally discharged and sent home. He hitchhiked all the way from Texas, and not knowing when to expect him exactly, we simply waited and watched. I was at the dining room windows every day looking for him to come up the driveway. One day I saw him, limping up towards the house, looking so handsome in his uniform, and carrying a big duffle bag across his shoulders. Never had I seen a more wonderful sight in my life, and I ran to the door and opened it to get a big, brotherly hug from the best guy I knew! Even the dog got excited and jumped and spun around in circles. Mama of course, was delirious. I know the feeling, I had it when My own hunk of a son returned home from service. No feeling like in in the world!

It was little before Valentine's Day, but we were so happy to see him. His true love, who is now my darling sister-in-law, was also delighted to see him. They were married a year later, but I can remember that after 2 years without my brother, that Valentine's Day was the best in the world!

I hope you have one as nice!

It's Goosebump Time Again on Main Street!!!

As I write this, it is about mid-June, but already the goosebumps are forming for the 4th of July. I'm a real holiday gal, and July 4th, I think is my all-time favorite. While the British may do pageantry better than anyone else on earth, we Americans do the 4th of July the best – but then, why shouldn't we, it's *our* holiday, our very own, and no other country on earth can celebrate it.

I had some great 4th holidays as a kid, they always involved a parade somewhere, a fireworks display, lots of patriotic music and a grand time had by all. My own children were always treated to the Faith 4th celebration, and as empty nesters, the spouse and I have wandered through old Salem for years now, enjoying their version of it, which is quite good actually.

One of the best ever July 4th's was the year the spouse and I went down to Savannah, Georgia, to watch the parade of Tall ships. Every few years these magnificent sailing vessels make the rounds of various ports of call around the world, and this particular year, they were in Savannah. Now, there is no place on this earth hotter than Georgia in the summertime, but nevertheless, we braved the heat and made our way down to the river several hours prior to their scheduled arrival, we didn't want to miss a thing.

The beautiful parks of Savannah were in full bloom this day, gorgeous, old, gnarly trees, all with so much character, street musicians, carriage rides, we did it all. We even went through Bonaventure Cemetery that week, and shopped till we dropped. Ah, but the ships, that's what we had come to see! When we got down to the riverbank, we found out there was a charter boat going out into the bay to be one of the flotilla of boats that were to escort the tall ships into port. They had 2 seats left, and we got them!!!

Off we sailed, under bright sunshine, or, as the naval military say, "Fair weather and following seas." Thirty minutes or so out, we ran into the armada of ships and they were beautiful, under full sail, all the sailors standing on the rigging in the uniform of their particular country, it was an amazing sight. We waved and hollered, took pictures, although the sailors were not allowed to wave back, nothing stopped the big smiles they all wore. Soon, the entire procession came to a stop, while the Tall ships lined up in proper order, sails were checked, sailors inspected, and then, we were off again, this time, the fire boats had positioned themselves in a way that as we passed by, they would spray red, white and blue water, which made a gorgeous canopy for the tall ships to sail under as they neared port. It was a spectacular sight, one I've never forgotten, and even today, thinking about it brings back the goosebumps upon goosebumps that we all experienced on that day.

Once back dockside, in port, we were all treated to tours of the individual ships, we met and spoke with the various sailors, and ascertained that they were having as much, if not more fun, than we were. Most of the personnel on these ships spoke English, albeit somewhat broken at times, and I remember especially the Argentine tall ship as being exceptionally pretty.

It took all of the 4th to visit on these ships and talk with the personnel, and it was definitely worth braving the heat of the day to experience this sort of thing. Sails lowered, anchored in port, these vessels remained beautiful and workmanship on them, the bass and wood, all shined up to perfection for the occasion.

I asked the captain on one of the South American ships if this was a regular tour for them, every year. They had first come over during our bicentennial, and every year since had made a world tour with these boats. He bowed slightly at me, smiled and said they had come this year just to ensure we had a happy and colorful July 4th, the, he wished me a Happy Independence Day.

Truly a wonderful and unforgettable 4th for us. The fireworks that night on the banks of the Savannah River were not be beaten, I still have wonderful memories, and yes, the goosebumps are still there.

Is this a great country, or what????

The Greatest Patriot

I got an email recently, of a patriotic nature, as so many of them are at this time of the year. It was thanking our troops and Veterans for their contribution to our country, and their sacrifice for our freedom. With a son who is highly decorated for his contribution during this last skirmish, I can, and most certainly do appreciate the thought.

Recently, on a trip up to the patriotic state of Virginia, I got to thinking that without our original founding fathers, even our current service personnel would not be relevant. How many times in our lifetimes have we stopped to pause and given any thought to those great patriots of the past? The ones who forged a place for us in this world, the men who sat down and worked through our Constitution and Declaration of Independence? There is a beautiful piece of property in Brookneal, Virginia, called Red Hill Estate, and it belonged to none other than our greatest orator and perhaps the best patriot this country has ever had, Patrick Henry. Gorgeous rolling hills where this man lived with his family, and 8 of his 17 children, in his later years.

We are all familiar with his "give me liberty or give me death" speech, but Henry was so much more than a great speech maker, he served 5 terms as governor of Virginia, and was elected to a 6th. He served as a representative to the House of Burgesses, and it was Patrick Henry who insisted the Bill of Rights be placed in our constitution for the benefit of further generations. Patrick henry had a deep, underlying commitment to virtue and how it influenced him over the course of his life. He was sought out by others of his generation not only for patriotic stand, but because he was a very wise man indeed. America meant more to him than life itself, and he was willing to make any sacrifice to ensure its foundation, and ultimately, her future.

The day I was there, a very nice man, dressed as Patrick himself gave the spouse and I a personal tour. Just the two of us. He talked at great length about the Henry Family, we saw the house itself, the law office, the smokehouse, lookout tower site, everything there was to see on this magnificent property. This man, aged 50 he said, spoke with great knowledge and insight into the family history, and talked in glowing terms as he escorted us to the graveyard that sits on the site. Finally, I asked him his name, as we were thanking him for a wonderful tour, and he replied that his name was Patrick Henry Jolly, the 6th great grandson of the great man himself. It was then that I noticed the family resemblance in the portraits hanging about, and this man. 6’2” he is, tall, as was Patrick Henry himself. Very tall for his generation, and after learning so much about this founding father, I realized that he stood head and shoulders above all the rest.

There’s a bumper sticker around that I see often, it says if you can see this, thank a veteran. If you know our history, thank a teacher, and if you can appreciate our history, think about and thank the patriots of yesterday, the men who made it all possible.

Big men? You betcha! Tall indeed!

Chapter III
Kinfolk and other Crazies

Old Age, I'm Killin' It

I always thought I would never get old, I was going to be the one person in the history of mankind who didn't age, never died, and would be gorgeous all my entire life! Hah! I must have been out of my mind to think that, right?

Having a grandchild with us for most the summer, I can tell you this, old age ain't for sissies! Between a park, an area lake, movies, playgrounds, wildlife preserve, and the pizza restaurant, I figure, I have about another month to live! Man, all this interaction with the grands takes effort, and stamina. I've been popping vitamins by the bottleful, to get me through this. Even my aches and pains have aches and pains! However, it's the most fun I've ever had being miserable.

Couple weeks ago, I was taking my 8-year-old granddaughter to see ***Pets 2***, and she declared that she was so happy I was an old person. Why, I asked her, "Well, because you can park anywhere, and look, we're right at the front door!" She thought that was extraordinarily terrific. I showed her the handicap license plate on my car, meaning I could park right at the front door. She wanted to where she could get one.

This child also couldn't believe that grandma would eat a pizza, kid's food, she called it. She found that amazing. Her older brother once though I was a hoot eating a bologna sandwich at a school outing of his.

As I write this, her teenaged brother is with us, and, he thinks I am awesome. Awesomely awesome, he says. He's a lot of fun too, however, at his teenager movie, I made him cover his face when a boy and girl kissed, never let it be said I corrupted my grandchild. I'm not sure, but I think he cheated and peeked. I know he cheated when we play ***Sorry***, nobody could be that lucky. Tomorrow is a cruise on an area lake, and if he doesn't fall off the boat, I'll consider myself a success at his grandparent business.

It's been a fun summer, busy, and exhausting, but oh so rewarding. One thing about old age, it is what you make of it. I'm not one to sit home and complain about my arthritis, or moan and groan over another gray hair (I have 2 now). It may kill me, but I'm having the time of my life. Soon all the grands will be gone, getting ready for back to school, moving into a new home, getting on with their lives, and, I'll be sitting here slathering my withered body with liniment! Wonderful memories, however.

Being a grandmother is the best thing I've ever done and, if I had any sense, I would have had them first. Telling that granddaughter of mine that brought a quizzical look to her face, as she told me she didn't think that was possible. I said it was, I am grandma, I can do anything I want!

Yes, sir, old age, I'm killin' it!!

Who Needs Clooney When There's Pat Boone?

Everybody's talking about George Clooney, I may as well weigh in.

I've known my share of celebrities. My dad was a book publisher, and there were always noted people drifting in and out our door. Authors, orchestra leaders, musicians – they were all a part of our lives. I've even written about some of them; John Philip Sousa, Hugh O'Brien, ray Kroc, etc., but one incident stands out in my memory.

Pat Boone was in town. It was the 50's, and his book, ***"Twixt Twelve and Twenty,"*** had just come out in the bookstores, and Pat had been invited to address a youth rally. Our church made arrangements to carpool a group of us teenagers to the high school auditorium, in order for all of us to be inspired by Pat Boone in person.

I think once you meet a celebrity, you become a fan. I don't know of anyone who's ever met a famous person and come away from the experience proclaiming how awful it was! Meeting Vaughn Monroe once, my brother and I became huge fans, even though we had not listened to him all that much previously.

Back to Pat. Our group was supposed to gather in cars, leave the church and proceed to the local high school. For some reason, we were running late, so that by the time we arrived, every seat in the auditorium had been taken and we were told that in order to see Pat, we would have to stand in the wings of the stage, just a few feet away from this teenage idol.

Now, you have to understand, in the 50's, the two biggest personalities on the world stage were Elvis and Pat Boone. Pat had hit after hit, he was on everybody's TV (never mind that we didn't have TV yet; I watched him on friends' sets), and of course I bought all his records and saw all his movies.

To be asked to stand a mere four feet away from this famous heartthrob was almost more than any mortal could stand! As he left the wings and took the stage, Pat walked right in front of me. I could have reached out and touched him! I would have, too, if I hadn't been in a catatonic state by then!

Never in my life have I gazed upon a more handsome personage, and to this day, I remain a tremendous fan of Pat Boone's.

Who needs George Clooney anyway?

I used to think that self-cleaning ovens and automatic can openers were the end all be all, and nothing could be more fantastic than that.

Do you remember, as a kid, every time a plane flew over, we'd stop and watch it awhile, marveling at the science that brought it to fruition. I never dreamed, in a million years, I'd ever fly in one of the things. It was excited to think of soaring thousands of feet in the air, with nothing below you but earth. I still feel the excitement, but not in the same way, my heart races, my palms sweat, and I have to pee. I pray the entire time that we land safely, and nobody falls out of it or it plummets thru the air like a great fireball from the sky. Hey, you get excited your way, I'll do mine! I never said I *liked* to fly, only that it excited me.

We had a neighbor family when I was a kid – they lived behind our house, and their daughter, Ann Karen, was pal of mine. Her dad bought the first Thunderbird I ever saw in my life, and of course, the first one in the entire world, as far as I was concerned. It was back in the early 50's, and her Dad wanted to take all us kids for ride in it. It was a two-seater, so, we were literally hanging off it anywhere we could grab ahold. I was sitting up on the back of the convertible top as we cruised the streets, try doing that now without a jail sentence. It was fun though, and we thought we were really special.

Ann Karen and her family were what you might call "avant garde," even back then. Her dad was an architect, and their house resembled an unfurled sheet, with a winding driveway, colored stones for a walkway, and Ann Karen was the first person I ever knew who had a telephone in her bedroom. Oh man, I lusted after that phone. Didn't have anyone to call, but still I wanted one too. How could society advance any further than having a Thunderbird and private telephone?

When America shot Alan Shepherd up into space, I was working as a laboratory technician at the local hospital, and as many employees as could fit in the place, crowded the front waiting room, watching a small screen TV, to watch it all. Mesmerized as we were, we had to go back to work, and each of us, in our own way, thought we had truly entered another realm of reality. Never, never, could we get any further than that.

Now, this, the Starman in his car, racing towards Mars and the Android belt. Who'd a thunk it!!! I saw on the news this morning too, where china has developed a flying car, tooling along at treetop level, above all the traffic. It looks like a giant drone, with a driver. Now THAT I could probably go for. Treetop level is not high, how badly could I get mangled if I fell out the thing?

I was a Science Major in college, it fascinates me, and I have always been interested in all branches of science. It excites, in a good way, so, the flying car is definitely on my bucket list. I'll let the dummy in the orbiting car have at it though, I have no desire to go to Mars or any other planet, I haven't completely conquered this one yet!!!

Favorite Country Memories

My Aunt Florence and I shared a special bond, she was the oldest of the nine siblings in my mom's family. Mama being the youngest, and although childless herself, Aunt Florence took me under her wing and treated me as she would her own child. I love her dearly.

She and my Uncle Steve had a small cottage on Green Lake, Wisconsin, back in the early 50's, that cottage enchanted me. Once I got up to the 5th grade, I spent nearly every summer up there at her place. We'd go fishing, she'd take me into town with her to the dry good's store, which I found amazing. So much merchandise, and a huge variety of things. Often she would let me pick out the petunias that she planted in her flower boxes, and I'd watch as she bought yard after yard of fabric, and maybe a few skeins of yarn while we were at. Then, we'd go into the grocery department and she'd let me choose what I wanted for our suppers at night. That store was magical to me, and being the only one around the small village (at that time) of Green Lake, it was genuine treat to go there.

Once back at Aunt Florence's cottage, I'd take a walk in the woods, picking wildflowers for her, or trying to see how many deer I could spot.

At night, I'd get to sleep on her sleeping porch at the front of the house, where I'd lie awake as long as I could, and gaze at the stars coming through the windows.

It was a quiet, peaceful time, we never did anything exciting, but I loved it, and went up there as often as I could. To this day, these memories mean so much to me, and I hold them close. How I wish all children everywhere could experience the fun and freedom of a cottage in the woods, in the country.

The Second Time Around

I'm a sucker for a good love story, I mean a good, three hanky, cry your eyes out love story. Seems I've known my share of great love stories, not the least of which was the story of my brother and his wife. They were married almost 60 years when he died a few years back. He adored her, and to her, he was her reason for being.

My British friend introduced me to a woman who married her long-lost love after both lost their spouses of many years. Those kinds of stories are the best, and, they just go to show that true love will out, if it's meant to be, it will be! Spouse and I know personally of a couple who were divorced for years, remarried others, but got back together again nearly a decade later.

The latest couple I've heard of doing this is a personal friend of mine. She left her husband 4 years ago, and has been struggling to raise their 2 children alone in the interim. It's not been easy for either of them, and as children do, they decided to meddle in their parents' lives, and lo and behold, their re-wedding was recently! Before the divorce, they had been invested twenty years together, and, that, as the wife tells me, cannot be easily dismissed.

The wonderful thing about these stories is the fact that love never dies, it may lay dormant, but it never really dies. It was Frank Sinatra who sang the words *"love's more wonderful, the second time around, just as wonderful, with both feet on the ground."* People are worth a second chance, or a third, or a 23rd. Remind you of anything? How many times have we heard how God loves us, no matter what, forgives us anything if we but ask, and offers us that 2nd, 3rd, or 23rd chance. It's one of the most magical, marvelous, and wonderful realities of our lives!

If these couples I've told you about can say to one another, "all is forgiven, come home," then why can't we say it to one another, and finally, *finally*, get along in this world? Are not we human beings worth that extra effort of forgiveness? God must think so, or He wouldn't offer it so much.

It does my heart good to hear these wonderful tales of true love, and it brings home to me the admonishment, *"love one another, as I have loved you."* If we all did this in our day to day dealings with one another, we too would have a marvelous story of love – now and forever. Our Lord expects this of us, and I for one, will try my best not to disappoint Him.

Please join me.

The Autumn of the Year, in the Winter of My Life

I resent having to grow older; it makes much more sense to start out old, and work backwards, so, that by the time our retirement arrives, we are better able to handle both the fun of leisure, and the ravages of age on our bodies. I could have faced arthritis a lot better in my 30's, than the age I am now believe me.

That being said, there are so many, many things for which I am extremely grateful nowadays. You traverse the earth today, and you see the beginning of the ravishing fall colors, enjoying the cooler days, and starlit nights. I love early fall, it absolutely revitalizes my soul.

The abundant fall harvest is truly a blessing to so many folks, and every time I see the pots of beautiful autumn colored mums, I simply swoon. Who can look on all of this and not be humbled and grateful? Any time of year is a good time, to me.

My book tour for this year is winding down, and at each stop, I see old and dear friends who have come out to say hello, and it warms my heart. I think friendships are the glue that holds us together as we age. Quite frankly, I have no idea what I would do without my friends, don't even want to think about it, they have always meant so much to me, and to this day, I sometimes pick up the phone, intending to call one of my best girlfriends and tell her something even though she passed away years ago, I miss her to this day.

Several years ago, my son dated a young woman from Lenoir, and for the years that they were there they were a team, she and I became very close; she is like a daughter to me, even though both she and my son moved on and married others, having families of their own. Patti was often a guest in our home, and I came to love our talks and phone conversations, and to rely on her friendship.

Now, I am very chauvinistic over my friends, once claimed, you are my "in" for life, and when that person disappears off my radar screen, I miss them, - terribly. Imagine my surprise the other day when I answered the phone and hear her sweet voice once again. After almost 16 years out of state, she and her husband have returned to the Lenoir area, and we picked up our phone conversation, just as if we had not been apart.

Friends mean so much to me, I am so very grateful for each and every one of them, and when one returns to me after so long an absence, well, I feel truly blessed. In this, the beautiful autumn of the year, in the winter of my life, I have my friend back. Patti's home again, and I couldn't be happier.

"Talent" for Letting Opportunity Pass Her by is Inherited from Father

I have decided that in order to stay young at heart and vital, one must try to learn something new every day. Make an effort to keep opportunity from passing you by.

Going by these guidelines, I am about fifteen years behind.

Always a day late and a dollar short, it seems, I have never been first in line when it comes to jumping on the bandwagon of fads.

I was probably the last woman on earth to wear pantsuits; my mother made me one when my children were small, thinking it would be more comfortable for me to chase three toddlers around in slacks. She was right, but I still resisted wearing pants for a long time. As a child, I knew the only people to wear jeans were the good folks on the farms, but now of course, they are a staple of my wardrobe.

Hula hoops, pet rocks and cellphones: All fads, I reasoned, and when they wore themselves out, I would be the one having the last laugh.

Hah! Several years after the fad did indeed play itself out, I thought up the idea of a pet rock cemetery.

Well, I think this trait must be hereditary, as my dad pulled the boner of all boners once about 50 years ago.

It seemed he had a friend who was an entrepreneur, and this friend approached my dad about investing in a series of restaurants where you just drove up, gave your order and could eat in the car if you liked. My father was aghast at the very idea of meal done in this way. No one, he opined, would ever do such a thing when there were fine restaurants around that one could dine in, in style, no less.

My father's friend was relentless, explaining that the menu would be posted outside and in, so customers would have a choice as to where to eat; food would be fast and nutritious and reasonably priced.

To have known my dad was to realize that this man would not only consider it beneath his dignity to eat this way, he wouldn't dream of subjecting his family to such a repast.

Our family friend was a wealthy man and he offered all of us the "ground floor" so to speak. We could invest with a minimal investment, then reap the benefits later on as these chains of fast-food restaurants took off across the country. My father would never have to work again, it was explained to him.

So sure of the complete and total folly of this venture, my dad informed Ray Kroc that he wanted no part of it, and even offered to assist the Kroc family when this foolish idea of his proved futile, as dad knew it would.

Well, it took a couple of years to get it into reality, and when Ray did open the very first McDonald's in Des Plains, IL, we were invited to attend.

Naturally, my father turned him down, but it was interesting to see this story unfold as the fast food craze took off across the country and grow into the industry it is today.

I don't know whether my dad was ever sorry about this, I never had the nerve to ask him, but I will tell you that to this day, I cringe every time I drive past a McDonald's restaurant and sigh a big sigh for what might have been.

Jan McCanless

It's Disconcerting When People Fail to Recognize You from Your Photo

Ok, let's talk about *"The Picture."* I know it's bad. When I first started writing for local newspaper, I had a picture made in the photography department and used it for several years. Then, we had our pictures taken for the church yearbook, and I liked that one better, so now, the local newspaper uses that photograph.

Trouble is, no one recognizes it as being me. I've heard all sorts of comments about that photograph, such as "Were you ill when they made it?" or "Is that really you, how long ago was it made?"

It was really a good picture until it was reproduced in the newspaper. I look embalmed in it.

A couple of months back, I was traveling through the Midwest and I told my cousin, Barb, that she would recognize me because she had seen my picture in the paper. This was especially important because it had been 20 years since we had seen each other in person, so she needed the photograph as a guide. Unfortunately, she didn't recognize me, either.

My children all tell me I should have a good photo made, and my former students ask me if I've been sick.'

You know, this sort of thing can give one a complex.

The likeness of me in another local paper is actually a very good photo. It was made on a "good hair" day when I wasn't retaining fluids. It really is a fairly good likeness.

I see photos of other columnists and I think, you know that's not a bad snapshot at all. So why had mine turned out so badly that when people look at it and look at me, they wonder who the lady in the picture is?

Erma Bombeck said that when you begin to look like your passport snapshot, it's time for a vacation. She was right.

I got out all my photo ID's to see if any of them were any better. My driver's license is terrible, like maybe I need a blood transfusion or something; my military ID isn't much better. I have sort of a "doughy" face and my hair is not good at all.

Until I can come up with something better, I guess you will just have to put up with this photo that runs with my columns. I write for another newspaper and they use the same photograph. So now, I can look terrible in more places.

It's a fact of life. Some people just do not photograph well. I used to dread having my pictures made in school because mine always looked something akin to Forrest Gump.

What started all this discussion in the first place was I was somewhere last week when somebody asked me if I was some other columnist. I definitely think it's time for Glamour Shots!

I'm As Sane as The Next Person Most of The Time

Don't get me wrong. I'm as patriotic as the next person, I love this country, and all the wonderful things she stands for – however, I have issues.

First thing is, airplanes; I'm not crazy about them, no way. This harks back to the days when I was oh, maybe 7, 8 years old, and my dad decided to take flying lessons. He did so, soloed, and even got his pilot's license. One day, he decided to take Gregg and I up in this little dinky Piper Cub he kept at the airport. I swear the thing was made out of tissue paper and rubber bands, but he swore it was safe and encouraged us to get in the blamed thing. I did so most reluctantly, Gregg, the idiot, was all agog and happy to be up in the air.

Things went well, at first – Pop was doing a good job of piloting the plane, even told us to look down at the ground and see all the farmland we were over. I did so. THEN, he decided he wanted to show us all the maneuvers he learned while in training. He took that plane up and down, up and down, then, he thought he'd fly some loop d loops. All the while, I'm peering at the ground and Gregg is shouting for him to do some more. When we finally landed, I was reeling and positively green. I threw up all the way home. To this day, I hate to fly, get deathly sick even looking at a plane, and if there is any way to get someplace by train, boat, bus, or car, I do so. I fly under protest, and I turn that fresh air thingy towards me and blast my face with fresh air. It doesn't help that I invariably get stuck in a seat next to someone who has fashioned himself to look like Adolph Hitler, or someone who feels duty bound to empty the onboard bar before takeoff.

If they can put a man on the moon, why can't they arrange it so that we can "taxi" to our destination? Not go in the air at all, just high ball it on the runway to wherever we are going. Maybe if I flew on Air Force One, with a parachute strapped to my back, and an inflatable lifeboat under my arm, I wouldn't be so apprehensive. If you know any aeronautical engineers, tell them to think about it.

I don't care for all these electronic gizmos either, and I think it's high time we went back to communicating in person with one another, writing letters, and using the Encyclopedia Britannica. Well, for instance, my computer has been off lately due to all the storms we've been having. I personally don't think it's a good idea to leave it on with lightning and thunder ripping through the area. So, I turned it on, attempted to boot it up, and stupid machine told me my user name was wrong. Now, how can that be, I only have one name!! It's a plot, I tell you, a plot to frustrate all of us known as the "greatest Generation." Sort of an electronic way to stick its tongue out at us and brag about how smart these machines are. Well, I am not amused!!

Don't EVEN mention a cell phone to me. Recently, someone gave me a new one to replace my old flip phone, which I am still learning how to use after 14 years. Anyway, this phone will take pictures that you can then send to your computers. Great, I thought, now I can use even more photographs with my articles. So, I accidentally took a selfie. How did I do that, I pondered. I turned it over and over, found some little button doo hickey, so I hit it. It took a picture of my shoe. Well, it's not a bad photo of me really. I have this maniacal look on my face, sorta like I had caught a rattle snake and didn't know how to dispose of it or let it go safely. Anyway, whenever I figure out how to use it, I may send the photo in. Meantime, you'll just have to trust me that I often times do know what I am doing – most of the time – sometimes, every once in a while.

What Is Wrong with this Picture?

I have a bad habit of not looking really good at my 3rd class mail. Most of it goes into the shredder before I notice what is being offered "for the very last time," at this new low, never before heard of price!" I decided to change my way of looking, and start reading some of it.

The other day I got one of those brochures from a leading correspondence school. Looking carefully over all the courses offered, my eye caught on the following item: LEARN AIRLINE MECHANICS BY MAIL! BE A PART OF THE COMPETITVE JOB MARKET FOR JUST MINUTES A DAY.

Well, I think I can see a problem here. I don't know about you, but as much as I hate to fly, I sure don't want to get into an airplane whose mechanic learned his craft by mail order!!

How about my cousin Diane, in northern Minnesota, who receives, on a regular basis, a catalog of Hawaiian clothing? The last time I checked, northern Minnesota was having below freezing temperatures, so, I doubt that grass skirt will offer her much warmth!

It just makes no sense, some of the things we get in the mail. My poor mother, God rest her soul, has been dead for 6 ½ years now, yet she regularly gets a Publisher's Sweepstakes entry thanking her for her recent order. Seems to me, somebody in their mail room had better check out the meaning of "recent."

I used to just hate to get calls from telemarketers, so, we got caller ID. Now, if your number doesn't show up, I don't answer the phone. The only downside to this is, I did enjoy playing "mind games" with these people, and, I do miss that. My telephone calls are all rather dull anyway, so, a bit of excitement has gone out of my life.

My niece in Wisconsin is a wonderful imitator of accents, so, she does still give the telemarketers a run for their money, it's such a pleasure to see a real expert in action!

My brother has quite a bit of acreage in Wisconsin, but he doesn't farm. However, that never stopped him from getting brochures about animal feed, fertilizer, farm equipment, and government agencies offering to stock his non-existent pond for free.

One day, he got so exasperated, he went in to see the local agriculture agent. Telling the agent that he was under the impression that the government paid some farmers to not grow certain crops, and others, to limit their production. He asked the government man to give him a list of crops he couldn't grow, and, he wouldn't grow them!

There are all kinds of things I CAN use, but I never get any brochures about them. How about the dryer we see in TV ads, where the clothes jump out of them already folded? I could use one of those. My favorite is the night the HUSBAND cooks, and, he brings the entire meal out of the oven and sets it before his beautiful wife at a beautifully appointed dining room table. Boy, I could REALLY use one of those…the oven AND the husband!

How 'bout the new car that is zipping along the highway, when it suddenly turns into a road leading into what is obviously paradise, all the while the ON STAR feature is giving out perfect directions to your destination, so that nobody has to stop at a nearby gas station and buy a map! Oh yeah, I forgot, the windows are down, the couple is dressed to the nines in what is obviously very expensive clothes, and yet, there is not a hair out of place.

Now THAT is something I'd buy from a telemarketer!

It's a Guy Thing

I wonder just how old the battle of the sexes is. I can just imagine Adam and eve pointing a finger at each other and trying to explain how "they" made them do it. If we grew up in a house with siblings, we were always trying to get the best of them, or blame something on them.

Dating was just another round of getting the jump on your dates, chasing them till they "caught" us. Once married, it is an eternal battle of wits, but it seems to me, the women are better equipped than the men when it comes to wits.

In Circle meeting the other day, we got to discussing our mates, and how frustrating they are; putting dirty socks on the floor, never knowing where the drinking glasses are kept, being totally oblivious to burned out light bulbs or litter boxes in need of cleaning.

Why is it a man can lay on the sofa, sound asleep, yet be aware of a first down on a muted television, but let the garbage bag be overflowing, and he hasn't a clue?

Do you think it's a genetic defect, or possibly a lack of training, or perhaps it's an environmental issue? All I know is, it's frustrating, and it seems to get to the acute stage when these men hit retirement. They seem to feel that since they got up and went to work every day for 30 years or so, they are now entitled to become totally obtuse.

These good church friends of mine were all expounding on the virtues of their men, trying to outdo each other with their husbands' accomplishments, yet at the same time exchanging horror stories of slothfulness on the part of their mates.

"Mine won't pick up his dirty clothes," one said.

"My husband has forgotten where I keep the dishes," another wife chime in.

"I have seen mine clean-shaven in days," offered a third.

It would appear that men can retire, women can just simply take their time going about the same chores they have always had. It has been my contention that if men could suffer just one labor pain, we would reach zero growth population immediately, and if they could somehow endure just one hot flash, I would die a happy woman.

Well, giving credit where credit is due, my spouse decided the other day that since I had been arising at 5 a.m. every day for 35 years while he worked, he would prepare breakfast for me.

"Just stay in bed," he said, "I'll do it all."

It seemed like only minutes when he hollered out to me from the kitchen, "Where do we keep the iron frying pan?"

"In the stove," I answered.

"Top or bottom?" he wanted to know. It was at this point that I thought maybe it would pay me to get up and see what he was up to.

There he was, 4 iron frying pans going, several assorted bowls filled with eggs, pancake batter, and something totally unrecognizable; measuring cups overflowing, spoons and forks everywhere.

"I'll get started in a sec," he beamed proudly, as he dragged yet another saucepan and some more utensils out of the drawer.

"Uh, can I help?" I foolishly offering. "Maybe set the table before you use all my dishes to prepare the meal with?"

"Sure," the spouse grinned impishly at me, "and while you're at it, could you butter the bread for toast, and maybe start up the coffee? Oh, and since you know where everything is, maybe you'd better get out the syrup and preserves too, and how about digging out a hot pad for me?"

Well, I have to admit the breakfast was good, and, thank goodness I have a dishwasher or I'd still be soaking that mess in all those pots and pan. Later, he wanted to how HIS breakfast had turned out.

Well, I may have to amend my statement about wits being better in women, as only a very cunning, conniving soul could mess up my kitchen so badly that I'd never want him to set foot in it again!!

What's Mine is Mine, What's Yours is Negotiable!!!

My daughter and son-in-law have been undertaking a major renovation at their place recently. Everything from new floors to paint, furniture, virtually an entire house has been remade or resurfaced. It looks beautiful too, they've done a marvelous job of it, doing practically all of it by themselves.

I was over there the other day, sitting in the living room, watching a warm and comfortable fire in the fireplace, when I look around and noticed how really beautiful the place is. It was then that it dawned on me the reason for all that beauty and warm, cozy feeling; I was looking at my own stuff!!!!

Over the years, whenever my darling, dimpled girl would visit, she always brought a shopping bag with her, and, shop she did, picking up a knick-knack here, a picture there, she literally helped herself to whatever she wanted, declaring the whole while, that, because I loved her, I would deny her nothing. Eventually, over time, she ended up with more of my belongings than I did.

Last week at church, a friend of mine was telling us about her daughter's new habit of coming over and "confiscating" a few of her parents' possessions, on the sly, or course. Seems my friend's daughter has recently graduated from college, and, moved into her own place. That would explain why my friend and her husband walked into their guest room one day, to find it completely void of furniture! Seems HER daughter made the decision to downsize her parents' things for them.

Well, as my Aunt Florence always used to say, "Kids are like that, year, they are."

I never coveted anything my parents had to that extent. I had always looked forward to having my own home, and furnishing it in my own way. Over the years, I bet I've given away a houseful of furniture to my children, collectively. Some of the things were given or willed to me, and, it's always been a particular joy to me to watch as each generation takes a family heirloom, and, makes it their own.

There was the dining room set my Aunt Florence had purchased when she remarried after my uncle died. Danish modern, it was not my style, but I kept it, knowing that it came from her, and, it came in handy displaying all my collectibles. When our daughter moved out to her own apartment, that dining room set went with her for a while, until her grandmother relocated down here following my dad's retirement. She needed the furniture, so, my daughter sent it over to grandma, and, grandma in turn, gave it to my oldest son when he struck out on his own. When he married, he and my daughter-in-law used it for a time, but I really haven't a clue where it is now. 3 generations of one family had, at one time or another, used that one suite of furniture.

During World War II, my aunt began crocheting a bedspread. It took all of the war years for her to hand make this spread, and, come VE Day, she put the finishing touches on it. I thought it the loveliest thing I had ever laid eyes on, and, I did, in fact, hope that one day it would be mine.

Now, Aunt Florence had a dog that really hated that bedspread, and, for some reason, every time it was on her bed, the dog would pull it off and drag it to a corner somewhere, only to abandon it. It was very well made, and Wags never put a hole in it, or broke a thread, he just simply didn't like it. Aunt Florence continued to use and enjoy it, eventually, she'd just shut the bedroom door and keep the dog from going in there.

When she died, I found that lovely spread, wrapped up in tissue paper, and, placed in a box on her line closet shelf – almost as if she were saving it for me. She did actually will it to me, so, it was with relish I brought it home and put it on my bed, thirty-one years ago, and, there it has remained in perfect condition1

That's the kind of thing I had hoped to leave my daughter, not necessarily my snowman Knick knacks, or my favorite casserole dish, or any of the other things she has "pilfered" from me.

Then I did notice, however, the last times she was over, she did NOT have her shopping bag with her, and, just when I though there was hope for her, she phoned and said she was coming after my kitchen hutch, as she found the perfect spot for it!!

I was worried about where I'd put the things I have in that hutch, but then, I realized, she'll probably take them too, in her shopping bag!

My Royal DNA

I come from a predominately smart family; oh, we have our usual quirky oddball (at least that's the name *they* have given me), but otherwise, we have some spectacular DNA coursing through our collective veins.

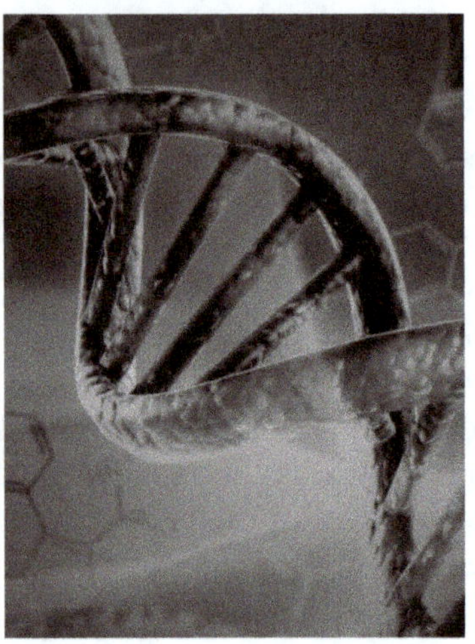

Well, for instance, there I was sitting at a church breakfast on Easter morning, and as usual, I was bragging about our famous kin, General AP Hill, of Confederate fame. You see the man next to me was a Civil War buff, he even has his own museum, so, we were sharing stories of our ancestors. Proud of old Ambrose Powell Hill, I am, and just happened to mention his esteem among his troops and the entire region. David leaned over to me and said, "You know, of course, the man died of syphilis." I was crestfallen to say the least. He could've at least waited on me to finish my meal!!!

There, there is Colonel David Gregg, kin on my mother's side, a big statue of him in Gettysburg Cemetery. I don't know any scandal about him, except, well, um – he fought for the *other side*. We don't speak too much of him naturally, and I won't tell if you don't.

AP and Colonel Gregg are not my only outstanding relatives, there is that Indian woman, Pocahontas. You see, Pocahontas married that English chap, Sir Ralph whatshisname, and, they lived happily ever after in England. Why, they even have a statue of her over there, so revered is she. Anyway, Sir Ralph was a distant cousin of the Queen's, Victoria, if I'm not mistaken, but it could have been an earlier monarch, not sure at this point, I mean, I'm still getting over the fact that Ambrose died of a social disease. I mean a thing like that can rattle ones cage! Back to Poca baby. She married this English chap, cousin of the queen's, and had children by him, and those children eventually led to myself and my brother.

Now, bear in mind, my brother isn't exactly the sort of fellow one would present to the queen, but the DNA is there, and should we take up residence in Buckingham Palace, (Buck House to those of us in the family) I could always coach him on protocol. He might, just might, look fetching in knee breeches and morning coat.

The thing is, we are kin, Elizabeth and us, and I think it only right that we be included in all this royal folderol that occurs quite frequently over there. Ascot, the coronations, etc. I have even practiced my Royal wave, it's sorta like screwing in a light bulb, and one has to plaster that fixed half smile on one's face when waving to the peons. Don't get me wrong, I love the British Royal Family, kin and all. I mean, Elizabeth and Phillip share the same wedding anniversary as the spouse and I – November 20. Every year I invite Liz and Phil (familiarity amongst family members, you know) to come across the pond and join us in celebration, but so far, they have not accepted. Probably don't know we are kin yet, but I plan on remedying that forthwith. See, I even talk like British royalty. I've known all my life about our Royal connection, but just haven't gotten around to take advantage of it, but this is the year!!!

I've been led to believe that there are over 200 rooms at Buck House, so, I can't help but think they would not miss a dozen or so of them, so, brother and I, and our assorted kinfolk can take up residence there. I mean, it would mean so much to us to live at the palace, and, um, perhaps a small stipend from the civil list.

This is the year I tell Liz and Phil, Chuck, and, all the family about our royal DNA.

Help, I've been Googled, And, I Can't Get Up!!!

People are always asking me how I choose topics to write about. I always tell them that the topics usually choose me. Here's how it works, somebody in my family, or something I might happen to see, appears to be really offbeat and perhaps, even goofy, and, it just cries out to me to write about it. For those of you out there, who wonder if all these bizarre, strange things really happen to me, let me assure you, they do. I'm a human lightning rod for the really weird, or chronically strange.

Last summer, for instance, June BC (before computer) to exact, I thought it might be fun to find out if someone could "google" me on the internet. Understandably, I asked one of my saner relatives to do it. Naturally, he was successful. Here is the jest of what he found, and, our conversation about it.

First off he found some of my columns, he told me. Then, he discovered something about me being named "Young Woman of the Year in Our County." That was a long time ago, I told him. Next up, he reads me my obituary. Whoa!!! I'm not dead, I explained, and, besides, once upon a time, there was another Janet McCanless in our part of the state.

Well, how do I know this isn't you, he inquired. Read my lips Rick, I am not dead. Besides, how can you be talking to me if I were dead???? Happens all the time, he added, where someone impersonates another person, steals their identity, and, it HAD been a while since he had seen me. Move on I told him, this is a dead issue (groan).

He went on to tell me this or that about myself, but the point being, even if you never put any item on internet, you could be there.

We concluded our conversation by him telling me to take care of myself, after all, the obituary is there, for everyone to read.

Now, remember, this cousin is one of my SANER kinfolk, I'd hate to think what my nutzoid brother, or one of my goofy kids might do with this information!

It did make me realize however, just how tenuous our hold on life might be. What with the New Year and all, I resolved right then and there to make the most of it.

Growing older is certainly not all the giggles it's cracked up to be, but I have come to terms with it, and, I sure hope, that I can age with as much dignity and grace as is possible to have.

I have also resolved to cherish every moment, even the "goofy" ones, and, learn from them, especially if circumstances don't always go my way.

Well, I guess being googled isn't so bad after all, even when my cousin Rick does it. It's kinda interesting, in a way, but what you find out about yourself can be a little daunting!

Life's funny, and, I'm sure 2020 is going to be just as full of surprises as the last several centuries have been. Hopefully, I'll be "up" for whatever lies ahead, and, I've already learned something – NEVER google yourself.

Jan McCanless

The Passing Parade

I love quirky stories, and eccentric people, they make the world spin for me. Especially nice is when my readers talk to me about an idea for a column. Shows they're reading!!! Well for instance, the other night our church organist came into choir practice and asked me if I had noticed the statue of Jesus in the front of the church. Well, yeah, I mean, of course I noticed, what about it I asked. "It has no hands," she said, somehow or other the hands are gone or have broken off." She found this fascinating, and said she thought I should write a column about it.

Other people, knowing that I write mysteries, will give me a plot line they want to see, such as the woman who told me her paper delivery person was always late, I should write a book about how everyone on the block throws something at the car as it rides down the street. "You know, to show their frustration," she said. Yes, well, I don't think I want to go there. It's humorous, to say the least, all the ideas people can come up with that I should write about. Personally, it's my belief that everyone has a story to tell, and they should take pen to paper and write it down, not me, I have my own stories to tell.

As a writer, I do a lot of pondering about things. Have you ever driven along a busy street and seen one shoe lying in the road? Now tell me, how does a person lose one shoe, and what do they do with the mate when they discover they are missing a shoe? That sort of thing just drives me nuts! I often wonder if anyone knows the difference between locked and unlocked, or open and closed. Watch sometime, as you are parked outside an establishment that is not open yet, and customers will come along, try to open the door, find it locked, but keep trying to open it. Then, they'll peer inside, as if to think that if they can see someone inside, it will no longer be closed! I myself have often tried to push open a door that clearly says pull, so, that is probably not a good illustration, but it happens a lot.

We love to go out to the park, the spouse and I, and so often I find myself chiding the ducks for trying to grab all the food I buy for them. Admonishing them to be patient and share.

Well, you get the picture. One my favorite stories about eccentrics is the one about the man who spotted me walking down the street one day and made a beeline for me. Seems he recognized me and had read a story I wrote about my dad and his love of Desoto automobiles. In the article I had described my dad's last Desoto, a long, chrome embellished red job that was just about the prettiest car I had ever seen. Well, this man stood before me, thumbs hooked through his overalls asking me where the car was, he wanted to buy it, if I'd sell it to him. It doesn't exist, I explained, or rather it did, but it was long gone by the time I had written that article for some car magazine. The gentleman pondered a while, rocking back and forth on his feet, then he asked how much I wanted for it. I explained once again that it was an article about a car, not a car in existence now. Again he thought a little while, then he told me he would give me this name and phone number, should I decide to sell the car, I was to let him have first crack at it. Giving up, I smiled and took his number and moved on. The spouse told me if he hadn't been with me, and seen for himself, he would never have believed it.

Well, as an observer of human nature, I find these types of episodes delightfully charming, and I thoroughly relish them. People, God bless them, it takes all kinds!

Getting back to the Statue of Jesus with no hands, I told our organist I didn't think I could do anything with it. It's a little odd though, seeing Jesus with His arms outstretched with no hands, but then, He doesn't really need any.

Jan McCanless

When You're Hot, You're Hot

I've mentioned so many times that my dad could not take hot weather. We lived in Florida when my brother and I were kids, and Florida is not the place to be in hot weather. Every so often, Pop would tell us he was going to the hospital to have his blood thinned. Years later, I know there is no such procedure, what he did, I think, was donate blood at the blood bank, and it made him feel lighter. Pop was one of these easily persuadable people, and if he thought his blood was being thinned, well, so be it.

One summer day, we drove down to Daytona Beach to try and cool off, and, as everyone now knows, Daytona is not the coolest place to be. However, at that time, cars were allowed to drive on the beach, just so long as you were out of there by high tide. Back in those days, they even raced cars on the beach. Well, anyway, there we were, driving along the beautiful Florida coast, and my dad found a nice section of beach to park, and out we tumbled onto the sand. Brother and I raced for the ocean, while my parents set up blankets to lay on and food to nibble on. I'm not clear on the verdict of finding a cool spot, don't know if our dad ever found it on that hot sand, but brother Gregg and I certainly enjoyed it!

Now, my dad was one of these individuals who felt nobody but he could possibly know when the right time to leave the beach was, and we sat in our wet, sandy bathing suits, watching all the other cars depart in late afternoon. The more cars that left, the better the view became for us, and the ocean is certainly lovely that time of day. It occurred to me, as I watched the water inch ever closer to our vehicle and blankets, that the beach police had warned Pop to leave before high tide came in, but for some reason, he seemed to think he knew more that than the ocean did, and still we sat, and watched.

There is a fine line involved here, you have to know the split second the water will rise, and you have to be smart enough to get the heck outta Dodge, before water invades your space. After all, the ocean had only one place to go, and it didn't need anyone's permission!

As you might have surmised, my dad lingered just a minute or two too long, and here it came, water everywhere, and before we knew it, it was halfway up our tires. Boy, did we scramble then! We all used unusual restraint to keep from saying "I told you so," and, we did make it out of there, just in time, as we were automobiling thru surf on the way off the beach.

I remember one particularly sultry night, my folks dragged their mattress to the front door, and latching the screen, they slept there all night with the front door open, trying to stay cool. Central air conditioning was unheard of back then, and only a smattering of businesses had any kind air conditioning at all. Remember those old fans that turned constantly from the ceiling? You could go into any grocery or drug store, any restaurant or hotel, and these big ceiling fans were running night and day. That was our "air conditioning."

Ever frustrated with the non-stop, uncomfortable heat of summer, my dad set out in search of a cool place to spend our summers. That's when he discovered the log cabin "resort" in the upper peninsula of Michigan, and from that moment onward, we spent all summer, every summer, at our cabin in the north woods. My dad was a publisher of textbooks, so his work ran parallel to the school year. When we were off for the summer, so was he, and we spent our days exploring the north woods, catching and eating fish, and of course, staying cool.

My brother was the bugler for his Boy Scout Troop, so, one summer, he carried his trumpet along with him up north. Remember, the term bugler, could also refer to someone blowing a trumpet or a cornet, and he was it. One evening, just at dusk, my Dad talked Gregg into blowing taps from the pier in front of our cabin, so, around 9 pm, he marched out of the end of the pier, and blew taps. The sound reverberated all over the lake area, and it was a beautiful, haunting sound that evoked peace and tranquility, and Gregg played it so well. He was ten, eleven years old at the time, and he did an excellent job. You could hear the sound of that horn for miles away, and folks all around the lake came and told us how beautiful and comforting it was. Gregg played every night of the summer that year, and a few beyond. It got so folks would look forward to hearing that lone trumpet as the day slipped quietly into evening. I can remember it as if it were yesterday. It was altogether cool, in another way.

I guess my dad struggled his entire life with the heat, and once we had central air, he rarely ventured forth during the worst heat of the day. After this past winter, I swore I would not complain about the heat ever again, and I'm not now – I am merely wishing you a cool, refreshing summer!!!

I Miss Mr. and Mrs. Dibble and O.O. Rufty's

My grocery store is gone. You know, the one I've shopped at for the past forty years or more. I sometimes wonder why grocery chains do this – buy up other perfectly good stores all the time. Banks and drug store chains do it, too. In fact, my bank was bought out not too long ago, then, was bought out again. Now, I don't know where my account is! I remember when I was a kid, and the local market, much like old grocery story here was, was bought out by the big A&P chain, and we got conveyor belts at the checkout and new buggies to push around. But the notions and hardware that old Mr. Dibble used to sell were replaced by frozen foods and prepackaged bologna. We though it the end of civilization as we know it!

As neighbors, we all were concerned for Mr. and Mrs. Dibble, the kindly couple who owned and ran the corner market. My mom could phone up there and place an order then give me a dollar. I would cut down the alley in back, through the empty lot and across the street; pick up my five slices of bologna, loaf of bread and a ½ gallon of milk; and bring the groceries and mama's change back home in about 20 minutes.

The big A&P came in, and we were all lost, wandering the aisles, looking for things in an unfamiliar place and getting acquainted with a "lady" named Jane Parker!

Soon after the big new supermarket came to town, the old Sears and Roebuck store "upgraded" their displays, and the popcorn machine was moved away from the front entrance. Remember walking into any Sears store anywhere and smelling that popcorn? It was like a trademark!

Automobile dealerships were run differently then as well. My dad and I used to drive up to the Desoto dealer in town. They all knew us. They were, after all, our neighbors, and, there would be two cars in the showroom, a black car, and a red one.

Pop most always bought the red one. Anyway, we'd walk around it, Pop would kick the tires, look under the hood, maybe ask a question or two. Then, he'd decide which one he wanted. The salesman was quite often the man who owned the dealership. He was one of probably three or four employees, and after Pop made his selection and wrote out a check for it, the manager/salesman would had the key to my dad.

My Aunt Florence talked about going to the dry goods store. Oh, that was a marvelous "emporium" that sold everything from yard goods, which my aunt always referred to as "piece goods," to penny candy, hammers and canned beans. The one she went to always had sunbonnets hanging on pegs in one corner of the store and overalls on a shelf in another corner of the store, much like from the general store did here.

I think the reason I loved the general store so much was it reminded me of that old timey dry goods store my aunt liked to visit. Well nothing stays the same does it? I predict that in time, we will have one mega-chain department store, one bank, one drugstore and, of course, only one chain of grocery store. Not only that, but they will have self-checkout, which scares me to death having to worry about scanning my own merchandise. It conjures up all sorts of horror stories for me. You know my reputation with anything mechanical. I'm liable to gum up the works for months.

I know it's coming, these mega stores and banks. I just hope they don't expect me to learn a pin number or check out my own merchandise, and, please, let there be a drive through.

I do that really well.

Jan McCanless

We Put the Fun in Dysfunctional!

I come from a predominantly quirky family. For instance, I have some "sick," male cousins who were always throwing this disgusting rubber snake into my lap, then, laughing about it. Another cousin who walked around carrying a jar of olives she ate constantly. And everyone and their dog knows about my nutzoid brother, I am always relating something he did that borders on the insane. He has passed away now, and while I miss him terribly, I know he is "up there" waiting for me, plotting some nonsense or other. He wouldn't be Gregg if he were not.

Last month I explained about my crazy mom, and this month I will tell you of one of the adventures my dad had, and its outcome. Now Pop was a rather serious, strait laced individual meticulous in his dress and demeanor. You all know how he hated hot weather, and sought out a place of relative comfort for us to spend summers at. This place was a lake in Northern Michigan, called Lake Leelanau. Beautiful area, but when we summered at our cabin up there, in the 40's and 50's, it was relatively primitive. No indoor plumbing, a well pump at the kitchen sink, one light bulb hanging from the middle of the living room, such as it was, and once every other day or so, the iceman would come and place a big chunk of ice into the wooden icebox that sat in our kitchen. Primitive, but for some reason, we loved it. We fished, hiked, enjoyed the cool air from the lake, and just generally had us a good time every summer – all summer.

Well, as it happened, the "necessary" house was down a path out our back door. You had to walk a ways to it, and in the pitch blackness of night, a flashlight was an absolute must. One evening, after supper, and just prior to bedtime, my dad took a stroll out to the "little house in back." He was gone an awful long time, finally, Mother decided someone better check on him, …naturally, she sent my big brother. He came in very soon after he had left, breathless and excited, seems a large black bear had chosen that spot, right up against the door of the place, to lay down and take a snooze. Well, guess he didn't realize that Pop was inside the facility. Anyhow, it got later and later, and still my dad was out there. Again, Mom sent brother out to see if the bear was still asleep, blocking the door to the outhouse. Yep, it was, we were told, and occasionally, my dad would stick his head out the moon shaped hole in the top of the door to check, and yes, the bear was still there, and no, he could not open the door, much less leave the thing.

What could we do? Well, we left the kitchen door unlocked for him, and all of us went to bed. That big, old bear spent the entire night curled up at the entrance to our outhouse, and it was mid-morning when my dad could finally get away. He ran down to the lake, which was just a few yards from our front door, jumped in the water, and hollered for Mama to bring him clothes, soap and a towel. I honestly did not think my dad could ever move that fast, but boy he sure did that day!

It was all over town by then, and my dad was enjoying a certain "reputation" about it all, but that is the night, my father spent the night in the outhouse.

The Duchess and Old Thing

I love the British. They have such a charming way about them, plus their quaint way of speaking. My English friends, Helene and Brian, vacationed over the summer with brother and me and our families. It was so charmingly delightful to see Helene's excitement over our wildlife, hear her rhapsodize over our food, and get plum giddy over our low prices. Yes, that's right, our low prices. Apparently, goods that are comparable to ours are either not available, or terribly expensive in England.

We weren't together long before we had devised nicknames for one another. Mine was THE DUCHESS, Helen became OLD THING, and my brother Gregg, turned into GROGGS. One of the funniest adventures we had together, concerned our cruise on Lake Michigan, and my ungraceful descent into a dinghy taking us to the yacht we had chartered.

It seems our captain had to moor his schooner out in the bay, necessitating a rubber dinghy to transport us to his boat. The day of the cruise, Helene had agonized over and over again, the fact that she had to get from the pier into this rubber boat. She was afraid, she would fall into the water, or worse yet, simply topple over headfirst into the bottom of the thing.

Piece of cake, I kept telling her. Just simply step down into the dinghy, turn around and sit, couldn't be easier. I was, after all, an "old salt," having been around boats all my life, I was not the least bit concerned, and was looking forward to the sail.

Came the afternoon of our cruise, we all excitedly hurried to the dock to meet Bruce, our captain, and, of course, the dinghy obstacle course. Brian, Helene's husband, was the first in the boat, followed by Helene. She did beautifully, gracefully stepping into the dinghy, she turned around and sat. Now came my turn. Ever the optimist, I stepped in – so far so good – turned around and sat, and promptly slid down to the bottom. Pushing myself up on my elbows, I tried again, once more sliding off to the bottom, where I decided to just stay put. I was really laughing so hard, as were we all, that I could not have gotten to my feet had I tried. So, I stayed right there, waving to my sister-in-law, and her camera. The photo you see here is of my arm, that's all you can see of me, because I'm on the bottom with all the ropes, tackle boxes, bottle water, etc.

That wouldn't have been so bad, except I landed on Helene's leg. Since there is only so much room in those rubber things, we were all arms and legs all over the place, so I really had no choice but to land on somebody.

"Duchess, you're on my leg," Helene laughed.

"I know, Old Thing, use your other one," I retorted.

Well, the fun was just starting, because we also had to get from the dinghy onto the schooner, some four feet above us as she sat in the water. I will spare you the indignity I suffered being assisted onto the deck of this boat, but once there Helene and I found very high comfy cushions to sit on while we waited for Bruce to return to the dock and retrieve my brother, sister-in-law, and the rest of our sailing party. Once all were on board, Bruce said he needed cushions for the other people, and, since we were each sitting on three apiece, could we get off and share.

What did I know – I just thought they were especially plush.

Reluctantly, we got off the cushions, Helene handing two of them to Bruce, while I attempted the same feat, and rolled to the other side of the deck. Someone grabbed me before I plunged into Lake Michigan.

Despite all these mishaps, we had a wonderful, delightful afternoon cruising around some of the islands found within the various bays of Lake Michigan. THE DUCHESS had a marvelous time; and, as for OLD THING, well, she got over it!

Just goes to show you don't have to a young "whippersnapper" to have fun these days!

Them Ain't Weeds, Them's Flowers!

I just love springtime, the beautiful weather, the green grass and trees, the flowers, it just thrills my soul and fills me with joy to see so many alive things, and all the renewal that it represents. Easter has long been my favorite holiday because of the obvious religious connotation; AND, the special time of year it occurs in.

I've long had a love affair with flowers, and have tried to infuse my yard and surroundings with fresh flowers. As I write this, my huge pots of African violets are all in bloom, gracing the ledge that surrounds my bathtub. I sit in there marveling at the beauty out my window, and enjoy those blooming violets right next to me.

Unfortunately, I seem to be the only family member who is so enamored of one of Mother Nature's more spectacular accomplishments. The kids, when they were small, seemed to aim the lawnmower every week, directly at all my cut flowers I had growing. No sooner would they bloom, than along would come the lawnmower and zap every one of them down to a small pile of attractive petals, making even the spouse convulse in laughter over my sad plight. Once, one of the boys whacked up his favorite rose bush, and he wasn't laughing then!

In desperation one time, I took little slips of paper out and taped them, one at a time, on to all the flowers in the yard, saying, "DO NOT MOW." Did it help? No.

It took me a while, but I finally caught on to the most logical solution of all, containers! I was so jubilant, you'd a thought I had invented the idea. Mama told me once the story of my brother, as a little kid, wanted to help her pull weeds, so he went into the yard, and proceeded to yank up all her flowers, and then moved on to others in the neighborhood. She said one man yelled out the window to him that "them's not weeds, them's flowers." Hmmmm, flower picking must run in the family.

Like all girls, I pressed my first corsage into a book, my wedding bouquet, it's all there, I really love flowers.

When we built our retirement home, we put it on a heavily wooded lot, no grass to mow, no weeds to pull, but I had to have my flowers, and I have 14 Dogwood trees, even a Magnolia tree. Plenty of pots with flowers everywhere. My Aunt Florence, God rest her soul, taught me to love Petunias. I think they're my favorite. SO many colors to choose from. They stand up well to heat and rain, and they are the most festive flower I can think of. Look at a pot of Petunias without smiling, you can't do it.

Well, another spring is here, all my daffodils came up early. Now I have tulips, after that iris, and day lilies will come out.

Spouse came in the house the other day wanting to know what I was going to do with all those daffodils I had blooming. Do with them? What am I supposed to do with them, I asked.

It was a moot point anyway. Soon after, the grandkids descended upon us, all wanting flowers for Mommy. Guess they must have wiped out about 45 of them in one fell swoop! Oh well, there's always next year.

Jan McCanless

He Ain't Heavy, He's My Brother

I read in the paper recently that Fidel Castro's sister has been estranged from him since 1964. That's most unfortunate, but given Castro's politics it is certainly understandable.

My brother is a jewel. In fact, if they ever have a national "Let's Celebrate Brother's Day," I'm nominating him for best bro. Now, I'm not saying that we've always gotten along. As kids we naturally had our moments. But as adults, and particularly as "seasoned" citizens, we get closer all the time. There is nothing we wouldn't do for the other one. I'll give you an example of his generosity.

Visiting him one summer, we took a drive one afternoon through the Peninsula State Park which is a lovely, huge park up in Door County, Wisconsin, which is the upper peninsula of the state. We stopped at one of the several overlooks in order to enjoy the view of Lake Michigan more fully. It was then that I noticed some concrete steps, about six of them, leading down to the overlook. Voicing my concerns about the lack of hand railings, Gregg told me to hang on to him, and throwing his arm around me, we proceeded down the steps.

It was wonderful, him holding on to me. He is such a big man, and so strong, but the only place I could really get a good grip on him was to hang on to the back of his belt; so grab hold I did, and off we went!

Down one step we went, then another, and with each step Gregg's pants sort of drooped a little, so that by the time we reached the bottom and the overlook, he could well have been described as "droopy drawers."

My sister-in-law, and our fellow vacationers, were getting more scenery than they had bargained for, which somehow amused them terribly, and they began to laugh. Well, so did everyone else in the area at the time. Gregg couldn't possibly have let go of me, I might have fallen. So he held on for dear life, I held on, and together, we made it to the bottom where he then pulled up his trousers. We then enjoyed the beautiful scenery – uh, Lake Michigan, that is.

Well, that's what one would have thought. Unfortunately, we had to then traverse the same steps going up; and, once again, I held on to the back of Gregg's belt and once more, he gave new meaning to the term "sag and drag."

By the time we had reached the top of the stops, pants dragging, we were all laughing so hard that Gregg and I would have been hard put to say just which one of us was holding up the other one!

We certainly had a good time that day, our friends from England were with us on vacation and they said they had never enjoyed the "scenery" more. You see what I mean, don't you, about my brother being the very best? What a guy!

"The state of your life is nothing more than a reflection of your state of mind." Wayne Dyer

Jan McCanless

What's in a Name

About forty years ago, I decided that I would be the exception to every rule of aging there is, AND, I would DEFINITELY NOT age. Yeah right. Even if I could turn back the clock, my name would give me away.

Have you ever notice how names occur in cycles? Women of my mother's generation were given the monikers, Ethel, Gertrude, Maude, all those good, old-fashioned names. My group came along, and we got pinned with Barbara and Diane. I remember a lot of Donna's when I was in school, and my best friend was named Ruth.

Well, if you aren't name Tiffany or Crystal or Madison, trust me, you're in the older generation.

Men, too, are subject to this phenomenon. We have lots of Edwards and Bobs, lots of Charlies, and Bills. Good, stick-to-your ribs names.

My cousin Rick and I got into an interesting conversation the other day about names in his family. It peaked, I think, when his wife was expecting their little boy, and Rick was wanting to give the child a special name. This is how he explained it to me.

"Having been a little boy during the birth of rock and roll, I wanted my son to have a little bit of the rock and roll spirit himself, and though it would be fun to give him the name of one of the early pioneers, but which one?

Bill Haley? Enough of the Bills in my family," (there were already several at that time), "I wasn't about to saddle him with having to answer to Elvis or jerry Lee his whole life. Little Richard was a bit too obvious – (Rick is, of course, Richard). Considered going with Ray Charles briefly. Then, I fell in love with the idea that he should be Buddy. Finally it fell into place when I realized the following: chuck berry is really Charles Edward Berry, and Buddy Holly's name was Charles Holly. By a cosmic coincidence, the names of my two grandfathers were Charles and Edward." (Rick and I share the Edward grandfather.) "That way I can justify the name selection to my mother! On top of that, my middle name is Charles, and, there were still more Edwards floating around the genealogical tree, including my beloved Uncle Ed," (just happens to be MY father), "and my brother, James Edward. So, I proceeded to inform my befuddled wife that this was what it just HAD to be!"

Well, if I understand my cousin correctly, his son is named after his grandfather, my father, and Rock and Rollers Chuck Berry and Buddy Holly.

Well, as I said, all the good names are coming back in fashion now. We're seeing more and more of the good, old-fashioned ones. All the grandchildren have these wonderful names, and I'm so glad. Tiffany and Sean, while lovely names, just don't resonate like the "old timey" ones do.

As for cousin Rick, I'm just very thankful he wasn't enamored of "the Big Bopper" or "Prince"…

A Little Addiction Never Hurt Anybody!

It's not easy, being the age that I am, and having to admit that I have an uncontrollable addiction. I hate to even admit such a thing. But well, I know where every Cheerwine slushy machine is in mine and surrounding counties!

I came late to this addiction, not having discovered this wonderful "ambrosia" until about three years ago. And now I am hopelessly hooked on them, having to have one or two, possibly three or four, a week!

There are much worse things to be addicted to. I don't smoke, don't drink or gamble, and I go to church every Sunday, so what's the big deal about it?

Just the other day I walked into one of "my" slushy places only to find out the machine was on the fritz. It nearly drove me crazy until I could get to another machine. That's the problem, I know where they all are, and I can get anywhere within 2 counties by way of a slushy machine! I think it should be looked on a "gift" really,

There is a convenience store just a mile or so from the house and I buy most of them at that store. Walking in the other day, the nice clerk greeted me with outstretched hand. Seems she recognized me, and knew I usually pay for my drink, then go and get the slushy. Of course, she laughed and told me it was good to see me again, and did I have a nice weekend?

Thoroughly humiliated, I told her maybe I should start wearing a disguise. But of course, she told me not to bother, she'd know it was me.

My daughter even has to pay me for babysitting by buying me a slushy. She calls it my "slush fund."

Every time I have relatives from out of state to visit me, I take them to the nearest convenience store so they too can experience this wonderful drink. And, naturally, I get myself one while I'm at it.

I had an uncle once who came here on a visit from Chicago. He had never heard of Cheerwine, and thought it some kind of afternoon dinner drink. I went ahead and let him buy several six-packs to take home with him. I mean, why disillusion the poor man?

One Christmas, I even crated up a carton of regular Cheerwine, and one diet Cheerwine to ship to my brother, knowing full well that Cheerwine in any form is better than no Cheerwine at all! Besides, pour it over some crushed ice, and it makes a very good slushy substitute until you can get to the real thing.

I used to be this way about Chinese egg rolls. Time was my daughter wouldn't take me to the "all you can eat" Chinese buffet because I'd start my meal with a plate of egg rolls. It's hard to have lunch with someone who won't even sit at the same table with you!

Think of it this way: what better way to celebrate the 4th of July than to watch the parade and fireworks while enjoying a big red slushy!

Oh, gee, I wonder if there is a 12 step program for this!

Social Media Was Not for This Mom!

I love stories about Moms, they always surprise and delight you. Moms are resilient, tough, greater than they believe, and more tender hearted than you think.

I once told my offspring that they should be glad they had me, because I was more fun than a normal mom. Whereupon one of my sons replied that he certainly would like to find out!!! Well, enough of that, this column is not about me, it's about my mom.

Now, my mom was very direct, painfully so at times. Whether she liked you or not, you found out very soon upon meeting her, and if she didn't like you, well, you had better not come around anymore. I got to thinking the other day of all this social media that is out there now. Facebook, twitter, LinkedIn, the list goes on and on. I can just imagine what my mom would have replied if someone had asked her to text them. "Say what?" She would have answered. It would have been futile. She'd look at you sternly and tell you to look at her when I spoke to her, or she to me, and put your thumbs away!!! "None of that tap tap when I'm talking to you, do you understand me?"

Thinking about watching TV, or listening to your iPad or texting during dinner, or when one of her favorite radio shows was on? Fergitaboutit! When Mom spoke, you listened, and you heard!

As old fashioned as this seems, I think communication nowadays could use a huge dose of Momism. No more complete sentences, it's more like "wr u goin?" type of thing, and it always seems as if folks have lost the art of conversation anyway, and I think that's sad. I used to love to sit in the living room and listen as my mother and various other relatives gossiped among themselves and discussed the world problems together. I learned a lot that way. Listening is as important as talking I think, and what are all these people going to do if we have a massive power outage, or thumbs go out of style?

I'm a pretty good cook, and I learned how by watching my mother, and listening to her instructions. There is always a right and a wrong way to do something, and I have always wanted to take shortcuts, and do it the easiest way possible. When it comes to preparing a decent meal, or cutting out a pattern and sewing a garment, that may not be the best way, as my mother taught me it seems, and we all take something from them with us when we lose them. We have a special day set aside to honor our moms, and whatever our memories of them, or however they may have influenced us, we need to be grateful for our moms. Maybe, like mine, yours was old fashioned, rather stern, and expected great things of you, she was still your mom, special in her own way, and worthy of remembering.

There were special aunts I had who I thought of as 2nd moms to me, and in their own way, they are special too, and grandmas of course. To all you wonderful ladies out there who are moms, have moms, grandmothers aunts, any lady who is near and dear to you.

It's Not Fun Not Getting No Respect

People who don't write for a living, don't realize that it's a job that gets no respect. I've had some funny reactions sometimes to some of my columns, and, even to me, on occasion.

Take, for instance, the other day the spouse and I were at the eye doctor's, and since our medical team is located in another county, I feel I'm safe relating this story. There I was in the waiting room, waiting on the spouse and trying to read my magazine, when two women decided to carry on a conversation across from me. They were discussing knitting, crocheting, even got into a dispute about the art of tatting. Concentrating on my magazine, I did notice that one of the women was called back to the doctor. Hoping against hope that the other lady would leave me alone, I was disappointed when she suddenly grabbed my magazine from me and asked if I had any talent.

"Talent?" I asked. "Yes, I'm a writer," I told her.

She declared that that was too bad, and began regaling me with stories about her husband and his knack for needlepoint, and I once again tried to read.

It finally hit her what I had said and she literally squealed at me that she had never met a writer before – what did I "do?" I explained that I wrote columns and magazine stories about the "passing parade," things I saw and experienced mostly; especially about people I met in the doctor's waiting rooms. I think that got to her because she got up and moved away.

Then, there was the sweet little thing I met on the street one afternoon as I was waiting on the traffic light to change from red to green at the crosswalk. Peering into my face, she got up close and declared that she was sure she knew who I was. Smiling at her, I said that was nice. Crossing at the square, she was right on my heels, finally catching me on the other side where she peered even closer at me, shook her finger under my nose, and said "I know who you are!"

By this time I was finding this person rather amusing, and burst out laughing when she finally declared, "I know you. Why you're, uh…you!"

Well, she got me there!

Writing is an interesting avocation. I can get away with a lot, so long as I change the names of the folks I encounter. The lack of respect comes from one's own family. They want to know if I'm ever going to get a "real" job. And the spouse doesn't care what my "hobby" is, so long as his dinner's on time.

Not too long ago, a reporter from the an out of town newspaper phoned me to set up an interview because I was a "real" freelance writer, and I happened to have caught their eye when I submitted a question to the ***USA Weekend*** people, and it was printed. She wanted to talk to me about my "career" as a writer.

And then, there was the time one of the lovely folks at the senior center asked me if I was the "world famous" writer.

Well, it's nice to know SOMEBODY appreciates me!

Mosquitoes, the State Bird of Wisconsin

As I write this, I'm in the North Woods of Wisconsin, visiting relatives, having attended a family wedding, and just generally, trying to have a nice vacation.

That being said, it is extremely difficult to enjoy oneself while these flying drones pester you, buzzing and humming in your ear, and just all around aggravating you. I have never seen mosquitoes like what they have up here in America's Dairyland, they are huge, annoying, and loud. I must have killed off hundreds of the little buggers by now, and when I get to heaven, I intend to have a word with Noah about this business of him taking two of everything, I mean, what was he thinking?

The weather has been very nice, quite surprising, I did not need my long johns for this trip. I'm keeping my fingers crossed for the trip home, as you all know, I don't fly well, and if the weather is the least little bit rough, I take personal umbrage!

As for the other reason for my trip, my Great niece's wedding, well, what can I say, weddings are always a joyous, happy affair, but never in my life have I seen one like this. Rachel chose to have her nuptials in a barn, everyone dressing "country," the bridesmaids wearing cowboy boots, and the good reverend, who presided, in sandals. Her brother was one of the "flower" persons, and her dad's band, entertained afterward. Talk about happy and joyous!! Big smiles all around, and when Alex, her brother walked in with his basket of flowers, we all stood up and cheered. Alex, you see, must be 30-years-old, and even his girlfriend thought him adorable.

We laughed, we smiled, we had a marvelous time, Rachel, of course was stunning, her mom looked like something out of a fashion magazine, the boots were a nice touch to her elegant gown, by the way, and I even danced with the bride's dad!

Even though I was unacquainted with half the attendees, we all felt like family on this day, and, believe me, a good time was had by all. Let's get back to this dancing business though, you have to remember that I am of the "fox trot" generation, and from what I saw the other night, all the young people are doing a kind of goose step, funky chicken type of bouncing in rhythm, everyone doing their "own thing," barely touching, and if you turn around and end up with a different partner, so much the better. I can remember about halfway through my "bounce," asking Paul what it was we were doing, and he replied that he didn't really know, just move to the beat. Well, I did, and afterward, I was ready for intensive care!!

On such occasions as these, it does not really matter who we partner with, we are all there for the same reason, to have fun, enjoy the ceremony, and wish Rachel and Rory all the happiness in the world, and I certainly do that.

No 4th of July celebration could match this family wedding for fun!

Now, I must go and find the liniment, or I'll never make it home!

Birthday, Smirthday, What's so Good about Growing Older?

I think I am going to have to trade the spouse in, or, at the very least, get him some holiday counseling! The other day I emailed my niece and asked her what her husband had done for her birthday the week before. "Well," she explained, "he gave me a romantic card, some candy, and took me out to dinner." Somehow that doesn't seem fair as the last birthday I celebrated, I was told, that to mark the occasion, I could prepare anything I liked for dinner.

What is it with these men anyway? They are always telling us not to do anything special for their birthdays, as it doesn't mean anything to them. Have you ever tried living with a man whose birthday you deliberately didn't celebrate? No, of course not, because there IS no living with a man in that situation. So, what happens when your birthday rolls around? I'll tell you what happens, that same man will remind you that he specifically told you not to celebrate his, so why should he celebrate yours? Now, somebody figure out the logic in all this.

It was not too long ago I was talking with my daughter and mentioned the fact that I thought it was so nice that her in-laws always had a party whenever any of them had a birthday. I also mentioned he fact that I had never had a birthday party, so, I think this year, she is giving me one. Just to set the record straight, it is many months until I turn another year younger, but I have to start working on the spouse now, or he won't show up.

The other day, I mentioned the card, the candy and the evening out my niece had received.

"What do you think of that?" I asked him.

"Think of what?" he inquired.

"Wizzy's birthday," he was told.

"Wizzy had a birthday?" was is only response as he continued to read the paper.

I went over the whole scenario again for him. "What do you think?" I finally said.

"That's nice, dear," was the reply I got back.

Boy, wouldn't it be nice to have someone take me to dinner, bring me a big, audacious birthday cake with ALL 36 of my candles burning; and then, he could sweep me into his arms and profess an undying love for me all the while telling me how young I look. Yeah, right.

Well, hearing me say this, the mister put down his paper, removed his bifocals, and ran a hand through his white hair.

"Okay," he said, "but it may take me a while to sweep you into my arms, I'm not as young as I used to be, you know."

His birthday always falls in June, close to Father's Day. I think this year, I'll tell him he can take his time mowing the lawn!!!

Where's Bubba When You Need Him?

I love animals, all animals, but I am especially fond of cats, dogs, fish, turtles, frogs, giraffes…well, you get the picture. I grew up with pets, the children had pets, I just love animals.

As a kid in Florida, I had a stray mutt dog, he came with the house we were renting, and his name was Tippy. A sweet natured, loveable hunk of fur, and then, I added a white cat, Fluffy. Fluffy came to us by the way of a packing case. Standing on the corner one day, a group of us kids were talking when a car pulled up the curb and tossed out a big box – full of kittens. I guess they figured with all us kids there, we'd be sympathetic and each of take one. Well, it worked, we all did, and I got the white one. Tippy didn't care, he was happy for the company and tolerated our cat pouncing on him and playing with his tail.

Big brother Gregg, was always plotting some weird activity though, and decided he would make a parachute from one of mama's good pillowcases, attach it to the cat somehow, and throw the cat off the garage roof, simply to see if it was true that cats always landed on their feet. Well, they do, and while fluffy was unhurt (we had a low-slung garage, just enough to clear the top of the car), he was fairly upset, to say the least. I had to cuddle him and get him purring again, but ever after, that cat ignored my brother. Can't say as I blame him. Don't think Mama was too happy about her nice pillowcase either.

My children were all allergic to fur bearing animals when young, so, we had turtles, a toad named Henry Kissinger, and fish. Daughter Carol decided one day she wanted a bird, and talked her dad into letting her have one. Well, she came home with a bird all right, it was a chicken, she named Angel, who, trust me, was not. Tenderhearted daddy felt sorry for a lone chicken, so, he told her to get a couple more for company. Soon our one chicken pet, grew to a flock of 8, all within the city limits, and all, according to our mayor, illegal. We got around that by naming them all, and telling the mayor and anyone else who inquired that they were pets. We had Speedy McNugget, Super McNugget, a large hen, Tweety Bird, Ugly McNugget, Dumb and Dumber. Quite a motley assortment of "pets." I don't think anyone really minded, they were for the most part quiet, until one of them laid an egg, then they would swauck their head off. Even when they wandered the neighborhood laying eggs in other yards, the neighbors were good natured about it, and I would often answer the doorbell to find a friendly neighbor standing there with a hand full of eggs, and a silly grin on their face. The chicken phase lasted only so long. The last pair we had were two large black chickens, with beautiful plumes on their heads. We were assured they were chickens, but we found at 4 the next morning that they were roosters, so, the chickens had to go before they got us all thrown off the block.

My mother always favored German Shepherds, which I think are terrific dogs. The last one she had was named Bubba, and while fierce looking, he was just a big, lap loving pussy cat. Loved fresh flowers he did, and I would often walk him through the cemetery for us to get some exercise. Well nothing would do but that Bubba had to stop and smell the flowers on the graves. We would often times stand in silence during a funeral, paying our respects to a stranger, just so bubba could get a whiff of the pretty flowers when it was all over. People must have thought we were nuts!

Bubba was a wonderful companion, and so loveable I imagine that if the circumstances had presented themselves, he would have been a wonderful watch dog, but thankfully the "bad guys" never knew how gentle he was. I think about Bubba often and hope that if there is a heaven for animals, he is there, waiting for me.

The strangest animal encounter happened to the family, yep, it was my dad again (remember the outhouse caper?), and it was up at our summer cabin. My dad, brother and I were taking a walk thru the woods when I smelled something funky – or so I thought. Nobody else seemed to smell it, but I did, and voiced my fear, loud and clear. I thought maybe a bear was stalking us. No, we continued on, and when my dad turned around at one time, he saw it – a SKUNK!! Walking along with us, a little behind, but every time we stopped, the skunk would stop. We'd start up again, and so would the skunk.

I thought the little fellow to be adorable, my dad was terrified, and said not to try and outrun it, just to ignore it. His advice? Don't make eye contact with the animal. Fortunately, the striped devil got tired of following us and sauntered off into the woods, saving us all from a tomato juice bath.

Well, these are just a few of my animal encounters over the years, now, I enjoy them through the lives of my grandchildren, animal lovers all. After all, animals are a part of God's world too!

Now, go and hug a giraffe!!

My Smart Phone – Ain't!

I don't know about you, but I am weary of gadgets. Every day there is another gadget on the market, making the previous 125 of your electronic gizmos, obsolete. Where will it stop? When will it end? I'm not a gadget person, I have a microwave oven, I have a cell phone, and an electric can opening, what more do they want of me?

Not too long ago, I used an ATM for the first time, was thrilled when it went ok, and phoned my niece to tell her about it. She burst into fits of giggles. Now, the reason she laughed is because she is one of those hot shot electronic geniuses hired by Motorola, and there isn't anything in the electronics field, that she can't operate. I hold her in the same awe as my 6-year-old grandson who comes over and sets the clock on my microwave for me. Do they have any idea how intimidating they are…I wonder?

Remember those old party line phones, where you gave the operator the name of the person you wanted to speak to, and she rang them up for you, and along the way, you could chat with everybody else on your party line. Oh gee, those were the days!!! No wonder we seniors talk about the "good old days" so much, they were a lot more fun than what's out there now! How I hate to punch in a number on that little bitty phone I have a hard time handling, only to be put on hold right away, or worse yet, given a menu to select from. I invariably hit the wrong number and end up in the shipping department, when all along, I wanted customer service. It is just soooo annoying! There outta be a law.

Now, Thanksgiving is coming up, the time of the year we are supposed to be grateful for all our blessings, and electronics. So, okay, I'm grateful for a lot of things, but the jury's still out on all the gizmos floating around.

I'm not suggesting we sit here with 2 tin cans and a length of string, but a nice, heavy, desk top dial phone would mean so much to me, it really would. I don't want a smart phone, mine would probably be dumb anyway, I don't want an iPad or iPod, or tablet, or any of those other things so popular now, and I sure don't want a kindle! I know, it's not cool, but those old timey phones and Underwood typewriters were so nice, we thought nothing could be any better. Is it too much to ask that we speak to a live person when we make a telephone call, and if I don't want to order something online, should I be ridiculed for that? Certainly not!!

I dread the day we have to order a turkey online, punch in a number to cook it, and some robot brings it to the table for us and carves it! What A NIGHTMARE! Thanksgiving is my favorite holiday, you all know that, and I'm going to do it my way, forever. As I sit here enjoying my meal, I won't even look at cable TV, nope, I recently purchased some old radio shows on disk, so, I'll listen to the radio, and enjoy every minute of it. Fibber McGee never had to worry about the connections on his laptop!

Happy Thanksgiving, ya'll!

I Like Wildlife, the Wilder the Better!

I read an article recently that posed the question, "Are we losing the Stars?" He was referring to the celestial ones, not the Hollywood type. The author's theory is that due to light pollution from industry, street lighting, and private homes, we no longer, have it dark enough to enjoy all the wonders of our solar system at night. He may be right, it is getting harder and harder to walk out into the front yard and search for the Big Dipper or any other grouping of evening "sparkers." A lot of the folks out where I live, have security street lamps that light up the place. All well and good, it would be nice to occasionally be able to gaze at the evening star without a lot of

interference, even though I would never deny these folks their lamps. Moving on, the one place I know I can be a stargazer of the first magnitude is up north in the cold country, where family members live. It's a beautiful display of the Milky Way, Orion, the Big and Little Dippers, and if conditions are just right, even catch a glimpse of the northern lights. What a show! There are no words to describe it except a big WOW!! Something else they have up there that really delights me is the wildlife. When our friends Helene and Brian were visiting from England one summer, a porcupine waddled up the road right in front of my brother's truck. Helene was beside herself, she wanted to get out and go and grab that porcupine; we told her that porcupines are not an animal that one grabs and hugs! She went nuts over chipmunks, apparently jolly olde England is lacking somewhat in the backyard variety of wild like. Well, after chewing up through our bathroom cabinets and destroying several of my better sets of towels, she can have some of my little backyard critters!

My brother and family buy huge bags of food, all to entice the wild creatures to their yard, turkeys, deer, all manner of waterfowl. Only some woods separate them from Lake Michigan, so, the wildlife up there is prolific. Sometimes watching all the animals in his yard, takes the place of other activities, as was the case on my recent trip up there. I heard quite a racket outside my bedroom window early one morning, so, peeking out and down to the ground, there was an extremely large wild, tom turkey, trying his best to impress a small flock of hens. There he was, doing his little "dance," gobbling away, tail fathers spread and fanned out, chest puffed up, really showing off for the "ladies." Finally, one hen separated herself from the rest, so, our tom moved in. Showed her his stuff, he did, and, when she was duly "impressed," she wandered off to join her girlfriends. Our little guy was not quite through, however, and continued his little "dance" and strut, until he finally decided that there was no hen around to view it all. Then, you could actually see him deflate in front of you, chest sunk back in, tail feathers no longer fanned out. He simply walked away, the rascal. The next morning, he was back again, strutting, and puffing up his chest, fanning out the feathers, but our gals were wise to him, and walked away. You go, girls! What a funny show to watch!

Deer are everywhere up there, and with Gregg's deer corn all over the yard, they use it as a sanctuary. At any given time, one can walk out his front door or peer out any window, and there are 5 or 6 of them grazing in his yard. Beautiful creatures they are, and often quite tame, thanks to Gregg's feed. One morning, I looked out and saw a couple does wading through some of the taller grass, and finally, stretching out in it, if I hadn't seen them enter the yard, I would have missed them altogether, as the only things you could see once they were lying down, were 2 small ears above the grass. I watched them for several minutes, they seemed so graceful and serene, and not the least bit afraid. Another day, I was sitting in the sun, my eyes closed, when I heard something pretty close to me, and looking up, there was a huge doe, grazing a mere few feet away. Observing her very pretty coat, and soulful eyes, it was well worth the trip up north. She looked at me, I looked at her, and she continued to eat, ignoring me completely, and me without my camera at hand!

Sea birds galore, flying low and hollering a greeting to one and all, wildlife just teems around brother's Wisconsin home. I loved walking in the early morning, observing it all, and couldn't help feeling an intruder to it.

So, getting back to my article about the disappearing stars, got me to thinking. Why all this fighting we're doing, why all the carping and denigrating of fellow political rivals, why can't we all just go out and do a little stargazing this year, quick, before the light pollution takes over, and we have nothing to look upon but illuminated buildings and highways. Take an enemy stargazing should be our motto, I guarantee once he looks upon all that magnificence that is our solar system, he'll no longer be an enemy. If you're lucky, you'll run up on a deer or a chipmunk too, possibly, even a porcupine!

Jan McCanless

And the Winner Is…

Some time ago, the woman who sits near to me in choir leaned over and said, "Jan, there is something not quite right about you." Well, what could I say, thanked her profusely. We, as Southerners, always cherish our eccentrics, and oddballs, taking great pride in everything they do. So, of course, I thanked her.

Now let's move on to some of the other "lovables" in my family, shall we? I have written books about my weird brother. The man looks like Elmer Fudd, but has the brains of Daffy Duck. You see, he was always getting us both into trouble, whether it was with his scheme to use me as his test driver in the orange crate car he made, using mom's pillow cases as parachutes when he dropped the pets off the garage roof, making tire patch cookies, whatever, it was all his scheme, and of course, his fault. The best part of it all was that I was such a little thing, it was HIM who always got the blame for everything. Well, that seems only right.

I thought I had seen every weird thing that could possibly be between brother and sister, until, that is, I went to Great Niece Rachel's wedding in June. She had a wonderful affair, very happy and friendly, had it in a barn, which my niece, her mother, made truly beautiful. It was sheer delight, and as you can see by the picture of Rachel and I, she was a gorgeous, sweet bride. Well, that's to be expected of our family. As for her brother Alex, please cast your glance at the other photo in this story, yep, that's Alex,...he was his sister's "flower person." Now, I must tell you, that in today's vernacular, Alex would be described as a "hunk" of giant magnitude. Not only that, but he is my very favorite great nephew, and a darn sweet guy to boot. However, I never expected to see him walking down the aisle in his sister's wedding, throwing rose petals along the way. I must say, he was adorable!!

Rachel is someone who we lovingly refer to as a free spirit, and was going to have her wedding, her way, and she did, and it was wonderful from beginning to end. Can't say enough good things about it. As we sat there watching her lovely bridesmaids walk the aisle, each in her own style and color of country dress, wearing their cowboy boots, I must say, it brought a tear to the eye. All sweetness and happiness, we then turned to see Alex, and another male friend of the grooms, enter, carrying their little baskets of flowers, smiling broadly, and absolutely caressing that aisle up the middle of the barn.

I'm telling you, it brought another tear to the eye! We all stood and applauded as the men entered, and they were very charming indeed.

Of course, I'm having a little fun at Alex's expense, but I know he will understand, after all, he loves me, and why shouldn't he?

My point in all this is, until now, my brother Gregg, has held the title of strangest thing ever done by one family member. Remember, this man stood in his front yard, a bucket of wet paint upended over his head, dripping paint. He also gets to play Shrek in the fall festivals held in fish Creek, well except for the coloring, there is some resemblance. So dear readers, it's all up to you. Who is the most eccentric, here you have "flower person" Alex, or…my brother (reference my books for more about Gregg). You decide.

And the winner is…

I know, it's a difficult choice.

High-Flying Adventure

I can't tell my readers anything – they'll never let me forget it!

I told everybody that I was getting a computer, after years of saying I'd never have one in the house. Then, I have to go and buy an airline ticket for myself, online yet! After saying I'd never fly!

Actually, I wanted to take the train; however, it wasn't going where I wanted to go, when I wanted to get there, so I bit the bullet and made my plans to fly to northern Wisconsin to visit my brother and his family.

The trip was going well until I got to the Greensboro airport and tried to go through security. Seems I had shipped all my luggage ahead of me, so I walked in to board a flight for 3 ½ week trip with no baggage. Apparently, the airline's suspicious of that scenario.

Then, my artificial hip set off every alarm in the place, and instead of quietly asking me to step aside for the search, they got on the speaker and made the facility-wide announcement that there was a security breach at my gate. Talk about humiliation!

I had to take off my shoes, standard procedure, and some woman with this wand-like thing takes aim at me, after I specifically told her I would willingly show her my scar. Somehow, she didn't find that amusing.

Eventually, I was allowed to board the aircraft and arrived at my brother's house up in Door County.

You would think that with all the scientific knowledge floating around NASA and other places, they could come up with some way to fly people from one place to another without going up into the air to do it. I mean, how hard could it be?

Twenty-four days later, I had to repeat the process and return to Greensboro. It had been 16 years since I was in the Chicago O'Hare airport, and let me tell you, it isn't for the faint of heart. Just trying to exit a restroom in the place takes a maximum effort to keep from becoming lost.

The day I flew home, there were thunderstorms throughout the Midwest, so we were delayed in our takeoff by 45 minutes. Not an easy thing to endure when you are already contemplating exiting the aircraft in a screaming fit. I took comfort in seeing that our pilots were at least voting age and looked as if they knew what they were doing.

The flight was bumpy, up and down due to all those storms, and I wasn't able to see anything but clouds until about 10 minutes out of Greensboro.

I had missed my beloved mountains, which I'd been able to look at during the flight out. I was unable to see the beautiful Ohio River that meanders through the wonderful state of Ohio, I missed all the corn and wheat fields of southern Illinois and the smokestacks over Gary, Indiana.

The first thing I was able to see clearly on my return trip was the gorgeous Carolina blue sky. It's a blue unlike any I've seen anywhere, and it looked mighty good to me! I was home and eternally grateful to have made the trip safely.

I don't care what my readers tell me now, I'm ready for them. It's great to be home, and the trip wasn't so bad, all things considered.

Would I do it again? NOT ON YOUR LIFE!

Family Reunion

I was eight years old when my family moved to Florida, so by now, am thoroughly "southernized." My parents, however, had their roots firmly planted in the Midwest; so, wanting to reconnect to my large and scattered family, I had to travel to the nation's midsection to do so. It's not often I've been able to visit at length with my widely scattered cousins, but recently I decided that that was exactly what I had to do.

When you have lived in a region as long as I have, it's almost culture shock to travel to other areas and "mingle" with the masses. Vacations usually found my family and me touring points of interest throughout the South so an extended visit to Chicago and Wisconsin was high adventure.

Somewhere in southern Indiana, I left the soft, dulcet tones of the southern drawl behind and began getting my ears accustomed to the flat, hard sounds of the mid-westerner. North Carolinians do things at a slower pace than northerner's, too, and having a brisk sit or doing nothing very slowly, is second nature to us.

My Northern cousins moved faster, stepped livelier, and left me in the dust whenever we went anywhere. What's the rush, I wanted to know. A nice stroll gets you there almost as quickly, I reasoned. And it gives you time to take in the "passing parade."

Grocery shopping with my cousin Barb was altogether a new adventure for me. As I browsed the numerous shelves and wide aisles of her HUGE Jewel supermarket, I would often find her several aisles over, hurriedly placing items in her buggy, as I lagged behind marveling at all the strange sounding names on all the "foreign" looking foods on the store shelves.

Checking out of this Chicago mega-store, I wondered where all the "gangsters" were that one hears about in this city. The checker informed me, with a broad smile that they were probably waiting for me in the parking lot.

Eventually I got accustomed to the fast pace: the hurried too-busy-to-shop demeanor of the strangers I passed. I even got so I could understand the ice cream vendors when they barked, "youwanjimmiesonat?" with jimmies being the small, colored candies that northerners seem to want to put on everything they eat.

My family reunion was great fun, as I reconnected to my cousins I hadn't seen in 50 years; meeting their grandchildren and realizing that family ties are very strong. No matter how many years have gone by, or how great the distance between your homes, it only takes being together a short while to reaffirm the gene pool.

While you are young and raising a family, you don't have the money to travel great distances, and, when the family is grown and gone, and you have the money, often enough you don't have the time or energy. But however you accomplish it, family reunions are worth the effort. With our blended societies across the country, traveling gets easier and more comfortable all the time. Seeing how the "other half lives" can be great fun, and a real eye opener.

I don't know if I could ever get used to the fast pace, or the cuisine, so much different to this old Southern palate, but I'm really glad I went. Gladder still be back home.

Now, would you please pass the grits!

Days of Perch and Sunshine

When I was about 12, my Aunt Florence and Uncle Steve retired from the Evanston, Illinois, home to a small cottage in Green Lake, Wisconsin. Nothing was more pleasing to me than spending time up there with them during my summer vacations.

(Picture is Jan being hugged by her Aunt Florence, Jan shows off her morning's handiwork in Green Lake, WI, in 1955.)

Fishing was the mainstay of my visits. I'd go out nearly every morning with Uncle Steve and Uncle Homer, who also lived nearby, in Homer's boat, dangling worms in the warm sunshine. We almost always caught something. I recall a time when Uncle Steve brought up a huge catfish, the first one I had ever seen, and it fascinated me. He tossed it back, though, explaining that catfish weren't keepers, at least not in that part of the country. What we were after, he said, were perch or sunfish.

One special day, I caught two perch. I couldn't wait to get back to have my picture taken with those fish and my favorite aunt. I even cleaned them myself!

Everyone Needs an Aunt Florence

My Aunt Florence was one in a million. She had unconditional, unlimited love for all her nieces and nephews. But my brother and I were the youngest, so we felt that we had a special place in her heart. We spent almost as much time at her house as did at our own.

She was our source of comfort, and her home was a refuge. She put up with our antics as long as I knew her. We'd phone and ask if her refrigerator was running, and when she said yes, we'd tell her to go and catch it. No matter how corny the joke, she indulged us and shared in our laughter. She called us the Katzenjammer Kids.

My mom's oldest sibling, Aunt Florence had a motherly way with everybody. Usually attired in a freshly laundered housedress and clean apron, she wore the title of homemaker as a badge of honor. And I considered it an honor to help her clean.

Each spring and fall we'd take down the priscillas from the windows, launder them, starch them heavily and hang them on curtain stretchers in front of the open dining room windows. They dried clean and stiff, and when she put them back up, they looked and smelled wonderful.

She also loved animals and always had a dog or two around the house. When Scrappy, our pet parakeet, got lost in our house once, Aunt Florence brought over Wags, her collie, to help us find it. And sure enough, Wags quickly sniffed out the lost bird, who'd gotten stuck on the floor behind the refrigerator.

Aunt Florence and Uncle Steve never had a lot of money, but no one was ever turned away from her door or her dining table. She could stretch a meal to accommodate any number of relatives in need of a good hot dinner. Periodically, one sister or another lived above them in the tiny apartment that they rented or loaned out. If you needed a place to stay, it was yours.

This photo of Aunt Florence and me was taken in 1955 on the dock at their retirement place in Green Lake, Wisconsin, where I frequently spent my summers drowning worms and enjoying our time together.

When I married, I gave her special status at my reception, and she showered me with gifts. Many seemed simple and humble, like a paring knife. But it was a knife she chose with great care, because she knew I would use it constantly.

Later on, each of my babies received one of Aunt Florence's exquisitely knitted ensembles, lovingly wrapped and shipped to wherever we were living at the time.

Today I look at the gorgeous crocheted bedspread that she spent four years making for me, and I miss her all over again. If I could, I'd give an Aunt Florence bedspread to each and every person I thought deserved one.

The Bucket for My List Has a Hole in It

The photo you see of the grubby old man, who bears a strong resemblance to the Unabomber, is my cousin Rick. I have often told you of my more "eccentric" relatives, but I fail to tell you sometimes of the more normal ones. Well, not today either! As always, there's a story to tell you.

A bucket list…everybody has one. Mine? Well, I think my bucket has a hole in it, I have not accomplished anything I have on mine, especially that one about seeing the pyramids at dusk, or climbing the Eiffel Tower. Just haven't found the time. But Rick? Well now, that's a horse of a different feather.

One day I received an email from him about his cross-country trip traversing Route 66, along with dozens of photos and a very well written narrative. It was more than a little interesting – he saw things along the highway, straight out of the 50's; visited Las Vegas, California, and all sorts of interesting places, looked at the native wildlife (the native Californians were of particular interest), and the most fascinating eating places I think I've ever seen. By the way, why is it men are always interested in the eating places? Doesn't anyone ever feed the beasts? I digress.

Rick dabbles on the fringe of show business, and has been known to be an actor a time or two, so it was not surprising to see his photo on the stage at the Oscars. No doubt, he gave a terrific acceptance speech to the cleaning crew. He was also at the Nixon library, and had his picture made sitting behind the desk in the replicated oval office. Now THAT I find great! I mean, I could get some major mileage from that one, not to mention giving my children heart failure looking at it.

He started at his home in Chicago, made a circuitous route thru the south, Midwest, far west, up to Minnesota to see more relatives, and home again to Chicago. I mean it was a dream trip, and I would have loved to have made it with him.

Him with his long hair and beard, driving a rusticating relic of a car, must have been quite a sight, but I give him credit, he did it! He did what many of only dream of doing – driving Route 66 and seeing the country. AND, the country saw him!

It took him a month, he stuck to his budget, and did what a lot of us, a lot older, never would have done. I like that in a person, but then, I have…um, shall I say, "different" relatives.

I enjoy travel, but as I've aged, I have modified my bucket list somewhat. My travel friend Camille and I are talking now of seeing Key West next year, we go someplace every year, you know, and Key West sounds doable to me. Not sure yet about canoeing the Everglades or waving a flag from the top of the Statue of Liberty, but I'm working on it! It is, after all, springtime and time to get outdoors and enjoy the sunshine and fresh air. These days, I'm content to sit on my deck and read, but I'm getting there, don't push me!

For those of you contemplating doing something bizarre or out of the everyday, go for it! No time like the present. Who knows, you might run into cousin Rick, and if you do, don't be scared. Just tell him hi from me, and smile as you wave goodbye to him! He may not look it, but he's really harmless. Go Rick!!

Piano Teacher, Composer, Inventor, Band Leader – He Did It All

I got a lot of feedback on my column of Ray Kroc's friendship with my dad. My friend in California didn't realize that Daddy had been a publisher and hobnobbed with the well-known and the up-and-comers.

It's true. We always seemed to have an author or two floating around the house. The best part of all this was the fact that my dad would be given books to preview before they were published for the general public. I even wrote some of the reviews for these same publishers. It was just a natural occurrence to have folks like Ray Kroc, author Adela Rogers St. John and a few others visit on a regular basis.

Of all the "characters" who were a part of our lives, Lee Williams certainly stands out. Lee was a musician and at one time, an orchestra leader. Very creative, he was the inventor of the clock radio. He also was our family's piano teacher, coming by the house on a weekly schedule to teach all of us to play. My parents saw Lee and his wife, Thelma, on a social level. Over the years, we came to know this twosome quite well.

Once, during a conversation with my dad, he made mention of a song he had written a few years before which he thought was very good. In fact, Lee had tried his hand at getting radio shows and various big-name bands interested in playing it.

For some reason, this particular melody just wasn't catching on and he, being a down-and-out orchestra leader, was in need of funds. The only natural thing for him to do was to sell his copyright of it in order to raise money.

Timing is everything, my dad, explained – the right tune, at the right time, in the right place. It was the same in publishing.

As luck would have it as soon as Lee sold his copyright, the song hit big and to this day is played and sung wherever the "old-timers" gather.

The song? It is a little ditty titled ***"Melancholy Baby."***

And now, as they say, you know the rest of the story.

Sharing Fishing Stories Injects Joy and Laughter into Our Lives

One of the things I am most grateful for in this world is the friendship with many vast and interesting people.

Two of these friends are rather new to my life, we met over the Internet via my brother. It seems these good friends share a love of fishing with my dear sibling, and over the course of several months now, we have been sharing fish stories.

I make no excuses for my love of fishing. However, try as I might, I can't catch anything that remotely resembles a fish! My lures have brought up boots, seaweed, and other lures and, in one instance, just as I cast my line out, a duck lifted off from the lake, right onto my hook. The noise coming from this poor fowl was deafening as I reeled him in so I could release him from my hook. It turned out well, as it was only a wing feather caught, but he was secure enough that he couldn't get away. Soon he was on his way flying across the lake, while my children collapsed into peals of laughter watching the whole sorry episode unfold.

Well, I thought that was the ultimate fish story until I heard of my friend Helene's experience. Seems her husband, along with my brother, were fishing on Lake Michigan one day. It was chilly and quite breezy, so as the men cast out over the lake, the wind brought my friend Brian's hook back toward him and hooked him right on the seat of his trousers. It was only as he tried to reel in he realized he was his own "catch." He hollered for his wife to unhook him. She struggled against the wind, turning this way and that, only to realize she had "wound" them up in his fishing line.

Soon they were both hollering for assistance as the wind buffeted them back and forth and they inched closer to the edge of the pier.

It would be a really good story if I could tell you they tumbled over the edge and were bobbing about tied together as they made their way to the shore. I don't think it happened that way at all. They did eventually free themselves but the sight of them tied, poor Brian with a fishhook in his pants, was enough hilarity even with them getting themselves untangled.

Oftentimes life is funnier than fiction and the sometimes awkward situation we find ourselves in can either frustrate and anger us or we can be amused by them, recognize them for the great good fun they are and laugh over them for years to come with our friends. I try to choose the latter.

Just another reason to cherish my friends and family: They bring laughter and joy into my life. The spouse and I are blessed to have many such incidents in our journey through what, at times, can be a very difficult trip.

Thank God for good friends. They expand our world. In this upcoming season of gratitude and joy, may you have many, many joyful times with family and friends.

Chapter IV
Brain Drippings

Cats are Great People

About 10 years ago, the spouse and I became the proud parents of some cats. They were neighborhood strays that had come around one cold, blustery day, and, well, you know, I felt sorry for them, so, the next thing I knew, they were up at the local vet place being groomed and vaccinated. All in all it has worked out well, I think.

Pets, if you can afford them, are kinda neat, and in retirement, they are a lot of company and comfort to you. I try to remember that every morning at 3, when one of ours decides to walk across our heads. We did have 4 at one time, but we lost 2 of them, so we are left with a 20lb Maine coon cat, and a misfit mutt of a cat who gets away with most anything he wants to. Truly a free spirit, our "little" cat was an undersized runt who had been on his own, in the wild, for 18 months or so. He was not well, and, it took us quite a while to get him into shape. Now, he rules the roost, and, also that 20 lb. cat who was here first.

Animals have always been a part of my life, I had several cats as a child, and, my parents always had a German Shepherd dog. I remember, as a youngster, going over to see my Aunt Mable quite a lot. Aunt Mable had a very large Persian cat who always ran whenever anyone came to the door, so, I never really got to play with it, or even pet it. Her cat was not people friendly. In fact, I didn't even know it was a cat for many years, all I ever saw of it was a glimpse of a tail before it ran behind her dining room sideboard. She must have enjoyed the animal though.

Had another aunt who had several cats, and, she had trained her cats to use the bathroom, instead of a litter box. That was a sight to see, let me tell you.

Most of my relatives, in fact, owned pets, and, it was from them, that I got my love of animals, which was passed along to my children. One of our favorites, was a pet rabbit the children had for 9 years. She was litter box trained, and lived in the house with us. She caused quite a stir whenever the doorbell rang, as our bunny would invariably hop over to the door to see who was calling. Delivery men would be stopped in their tracks by this rabbit. One even asked me if it was a real rabbit. I told him no, I wound it up every morning, and let it hop around!

The grandchildren love my cats, but at the first sign of their car in the drive, the cats head for under the bed and "refuge" from the storm of Tonka trucks, doll carriages, and hot wheels zooming through the house. My grandson, in fact, is convinced the animals live under my bed. He will even tell you that Maw Maw's cats are old, and live under the bed!

Well, I have figured out why animals and "seasoned" citizens get along so well. Besides the aforementioned companionship, they listen to you, never argue, and put up with all our complaining about aches and pains. They accept you for what you are, never try to change you, and, they are great fun to come home to. Wouldn't it be nice if human friends did the same?

I Don't Do High Fashion Well

Today I got one of those offbeat high fashion catalogs in the mail. You know the kind, blouses cut down to "here,' skirts up to "there," and, coats that resemble some kinds of wearable blanket. High fashion, it says, and, always, it's the very last catalog you'll get from them, until the next one, of course! I know women who actually wear that stuff, and, they spend the entire time pulling the blouse up, and, the skirt down. Not me, if my shoes are tied and match one another, that's good enough for me!!!!

I have always admired one of my aunt's, she's an artist, professional one, and, she has always had such flair with her clothes and jewelry. She's one of these people who literally sweeps into a room. Can you remember the last time I swept into a room? Well, me neither!

My daughter has been especially critical, over the years, of my wardrobe. I wear a lot of very comfortable clothes that may not be the height of fashion, but I like them, so, why shouldn't I wear them?

I recall one time in particular we were going someplace and my daughter informed me that I was an embarrassment to her because I was wearing polyester. Well, at the time, polyester was the big thing. Remember how everything was made out of it, even men's suits and sport clothes. In the 70's it was all the rage, and, oh, those leisure suits!! I guess the polyester era must have lasted a good ten years or more. Thank goodness the natural fibers, like cotton, are popular now. I wear a lot of cotton, and, I'm especially fond of cotton shirts.

Cotton t-shirts are my thing, and, if they have an animal on them, so much the better. I have one in particular I really like, it's got the Budweiser lizards on it, and, the writing underneath them says, "We could've been huge."

The last time I went up north to visit my brother and family, I bought all the women folk a pretty t-shirt with hummingbirds on it. We looked like a bunch of summer camp counselors when we went anywhere together while wearing them. It was kinda fun, seeing all these ahem, middle aged women wearing their hummingbird shirts. I don't see a thing wrong with it, but the daughter, she gets all upset over this kind of thing. Maybe it was just the fact I wore the Budweiser shirt to a church function that upset her. At least no one had the temerity to question me about it.

Well, all this takes place only in the comforts of my home, or those of a relative, maybe shopping or running errands too, but when I go to church or am out in the public, I try to look nice.

I really did wear mismatched shoes one time, it was when I was teaching, and in a hurry one morning, I grabbed two different colored loafers. They were the same style, so it was an easy mistake to make, and my students though it great fun, my children, however spent the day walking with their heads down. Yeah, like nobody else ever does that!!

The kindest thing my female child ever said to me was the day we were going to lunch together, and, I took great care in my appearance. Meeting her at the restaurant, she proclaimed that I wasn't half bad once I got color coordinated.

Sweet child!!!

Where Did All the Bargains Go?

I'm a catalog freak, I'll look at all of them that come to the house, and, we have many that come to the house on any given day. I read them all, do some comparison pricing, then, I go and try to find the same thing at Walmart.

The other day a catalog came that had mostly furniture in it, and, as I was browsing through it, I noticed that there was a nice chair on sale for around $300, and, the matching ottoman was a bargain, so they said, at $199. Now, this sort of thing really gets my dander up, time was, if you bought a chair from a furniture store, they'd give you the matching ottoman. They were a set, buy one, get the other. Not anymore!

I went with Mama once to purchase some curtains for the front room, remember when our living rooms were called front rooms, or parlors? Well, I was just a kid, but off we went to get these new curtains. Finding what she wanted, the salesman rang up the sale, then, he gave my mother the hardware required to hang them, the rod, the hooks, whatever was required. He just put them in the bag. It was just something the merchants did as a courtesy for their customers.

Bargains like that are hard to find nowadays, and, when was the last time a clerk just gave you something like the hardware required to hang a curtain rod?

My Mama was a funny lady when it came to bargains, I have seen her drive 10 miles out of the way just to save a nickel off the price of an item. Bless her heart, she thought she was being very wise in her shopping.

The spouse of the house is the one who is a real bargain shopper, and a gadget freak to boot. We have 2 kinds of pizza cutters at the house, several different sized and shaped beverage openers, and a lifetime supply of small appliance covers, all purchased because they were on sale. If one is good, 6 is better is his theory. I had an uncle like that once, literally shopped himself out of the house when he ran out room for all his purchases.

What is it with Americans and their bargains? I've known people who will pay outrageous prices for things, or go out of their way to buy something, simply because they thought they were getting a bargain, or better yet, getting something for nothing.

My cousin, Diane, who gets up close and personal with her catalogs too, gets a kick out of the "last chance" opportunities that come her way. Last chance to get this or that before the price goes up, or, worse yet, you STOP GETTING THEIR CATALOG!!!! I must admit, I am a sucker for those ads, and, have been known to buy something just to keep getting those catalogs of high-end decorator "do dads." Oh, I'm so ashamed.

Cruising on the Mississippi Queen this past December, I had packed clothing items that were much too warm for the 80's temperatures we were having on the southern river, so, I had to go to the gift shop and purchase some lighter shirts to wear. Boy, don't you HATE when that happens????

There I was, in the gift shop of our steamboat, looking over all the discounted merchandise, when I found a pair of earrings, they had marked down to $15.00. Naturally, I felt guilty buying them, because I was, after all, supposed to be looking at some lighter weight clothes to wear on the boat, and for some of our shore excursions.

Just my luck, they had marked the shirts down by more than $5.00, so, of course I bought two of them!! Mama'd be proud!

Happiness is not having what you want, but wanting what you have…

Or so they say. I must agree with whoever "they" are. If you want to be truly happy, and content in this life, then you must be happy and content with what you have.

I asked my adult Sunday school class one day to tell me what happens when you get what you think you want. The answer of course is, that you want something else. It's a never-ending cycle.

This particular time of year, especially, I begin to think of all the blessings we have, and privileges we enjoy in this country. When you give it serious consideration, it is astounding!! No one comes along and tells you what job you must have, where or if, you may go to church, what restaurant will be open for your patronage, how you must get to school or work, and the list goes on and on. For the most part, we enjoy freedoms unparalleled in other countries.

As I get older, I am finding myself with less and less patience for the folks who continually scream about having to stand for the flag and national anthem; I kinda resent the fact that there are lots and lots of people riding "free" in this great land of ours, while the rest of us work so they can do so, then, complaining about it. My son spent 26 years in the military, fought in two wars, so, everyone could enjoy the freedoms of this land. While he was ensuring that you have all the rights you are entitled to, he earned a purple heart, the Navy Cross, and numerous other medals in service to America. Please don't denigrate that service by refusing to stand for the anthem, or not honoring our flag.

Not happy with our country? Go watch a 4th of July parade, and I dare you not to get goosebumps when the military marches by, or the children riding on a float wave a flag at you. There is nothing more American than a good old-fashioned parade, and the time we spend honoring and appreciating our wonderful US of A. Something to be happy about.

Watch a fireworks display of the 4th, and remember your history. Our forefathers worked, marched, and fought for our freedoms, in much harsher conditions that any of us experience today, and a lot of them died quite young, just so we could enjoy our good life unencumbered by despots and dictators who want to remove it from us. Something else to be happy for.

Not honor our country and be grateful for what we have here in America? Who could possibly do such a thing?

God bless America!

Lemon Squeeze

There once was a religious young woman who went to Confession. Upon entering the confessional, she said, "Forgive me, Father, for I have sinned."

The priest said, "Confess your sins and be forgiven."

The young woman said, "Last night my boyfriend made mad passionate love to me seven times."

The priest thought long and hard and then said, "Squeeze seven lemons into a glass and then drink the juice."

The young woman asked, "Will this cleanse me of my sins?"

The priest said, "No, but it will wipe that smile off of your face."

***

Looks of Disappointment

A man just waking up from anesthesia after surgery, and his wife was sitting by his side. His eyes fluttered open and he said, "You're beautiful." Then he fell asleep again. His wife had never heard him say that before, so she stayed by his side. A few minutes later his eyes fluttered open and he said, "You're cute."

The wife was disappointed because instead of "beautiful," it was now "cute." She asked, "What happened to beautiful?"

The man replied, "The drugs are wearing off."

***

Catholic Dog

Muldoon lived alone in the Irish countryside with only a pet dog for company. One day the dog died, and Muldoon went to the parish priest and asked, "Father, my dog is dead. Could ya' be sayin' a mass for the poor creature?"

Father Patrick replied, "I'm afraid not; we cannot have services for an animal in the church. But there are some Baptists down the lane, and there's no tellin' what they believe. Maybe they'll do something for creature."

Muldoon said, “I’ll go right away Father. Do ya’ think $5,000 is enough to donate to them for the service?”

Father Patrick exclaimed, “Sweet Mary, Mother of Jesus! Why didn’t ya tell me the dog was Catholic?”

***

Donation

Father O’Malley answers the phone. “Hello, is this Father O’Malley?”

“It is!”

“This is the IRS. Can you help us?”

“I can!”

“Do you know a Ted Houlihan?”

“I do!”

“Is he a member of your congregation?”

“He is!”

“Did he donate $10,000 to the church?”

“He will.”

***

Pest Control

A woman was having a passionate affair with an Irish Inspector from a pest-control company. One afternoon they were carrying on in the bedroom together when her husband arrived home unexpectedly.

“Quick,” said the woman to the lover, “into the closet!” and she pushed him in the closet, start naked.

The husband, however, became suspicious and after a search of the bedroom discovered the man in the closet.

“Who are you?” He asked him.

“I’m an inspector from Bugs-B-Gone,” said the exterminator.

“What are you doing in there?” The husband asked.

“I’m investigating a complaint about an infestation of moths,” the man replied.

“And where are your clothes?” Asked the husband.

The man looked down at himself and said, “Those little bastards!”

***

Marriage Humor

Wife: "What are you doing?"
Husband "Nothing."
Wife: "Nothing…? You've been reading our marriage certificate for an hour."
Husband: "I was looking for the expiration date."

***

Wife: "Do you want dinner?"
Husband: "Sure! What are my choices?"
Wife: "Yes or No."

***

Girl: "When we get married, I want to share all your worries, troubles and lighten your burden."
Boy: "It's very kind of you, Darling, but I don't have any worries or troubles."
Girl: "Well that's because we aren't married yet."

***

Son: "Mum, when I was on the bus with Dad this morning, he told me to give up my seat to a lady."
Mom: "Well, you have done the right thing."
Son: "But mum, I was sitting on daddy's lap."

***

A newly married man asked his wife, "Would you have married me if my father hadn't left me a fortune?"
"Honey," the woman replied sweetly, "I'd have married you, NO MATTER WHO LEFT YOU A FORTUNE!"

***

A wife asked her husband: "What do you like most in me, my pretty face or my sexy body?

He looked at her from head to toe and replied: "I like your sense of humor!"

***

A man was sitting reading his papers when his wife hit him round the head with a frying pan.

"What was that for?" The man asked.

The wife replied "That was for the piece of paper with the name Jenny on it that I found in your pants pocket."

The man then said "When I was at the races last week Jenny was the name of the horse I bet on."

The wife apologized and went on with the housework.

Three days later the man is watching TV when his wife bashes him on the head with an ever bigger frying pan, knocking him unconscious. Upon re-gaining consciousness, the man asked why she had hit again.

Wife replied "You horse phoned."

The Most Joyous Day of the Year

I've heard it said that April is Mother Nature's apology for March. That's certainly true this year – wow, what a winter!

I sat in my den, during these 70+ degree days and watched on the news as the northeast and Midwest were blasted with cold, ice and snow. My brother and his family are residents of northern Wisconsin, and he has had a lot of snow this year, but he loves it. I like being able to exit my home on occasion during the winter, so I don't wish to live in that environment, but by the same token, he finds the sub-tropical temperatures down here stifling. Well, to each his own, I guess. We here in North Carolina, just have found this winter pretty amazing, and, um…different.

One thing about April, it's a great leveler, nearly everyone has pretty days in April, the flowers come out, the trees leaf out, grass turns green, and all kinds of wonderful, exciting things occur in our environment, AND, when Easter comes in April, we get a bonus!!

It's mind boggling to think of the past 2,000 years and contemplate the events leading up to, and the actual Resurrection itself. What a miraculous gift we have been given, and there is nothing on earth to equal the joy of the Resurrection.

When I was a child, I naturally though of Easter as the time for chocolate bunnies, new shoes, and prettily decorated baskets. It took me awhile to grow up and realize the true meaning of Easter, and to appreciate all that the holiday means. When I think about Easter, I think about renewal, all things fresh and new, and, the life that Our Master lived, all leading up to his greatest of all miracles.

It's a miracle for us as well, and we are given a "reprieve" thru the Easter story. We can start over, secure in the knowledge that death has been overcome, that no matter our sins or transgressions, we are forgiven, and granted eternal life through Him who paid our debt, and died our death. No greater sacrifice or love has ever, now will ever exist. It's breathtaking, and very humbling.

As you move through the Lenten Season, on towards Easter, contemplate all that the day means to us, especially here in this country. We have a great many blessings in America, not the least of which is the right to worship as we please, where we please, and, when we please. The Resurrection has many meanings, but for me, it reemphasizes the fact that I am a saved child of God, with a Savior who loves me very much.

I'll never look at a cross the same way again! Blessings to you, and Happy Easter!!!

I've heard young people claim, so often, that us "seasoned" citizens live in the past, that the past is all we talk about. I don't think so. I think what we miss more than anything is constancy in our lives; a beloved doctor retires, a bank merger with another, a department store closes. All these changes cause us upset, as we have to reset our psyches then to accept and adjust to uncommon changes in our lives. On top of that, we are expected to learn how to use a host of electronic devices we were not raised knowing how to operate, and yes, it's frustrating. I sometimes look at my computer and think to myself that life is too short to tolerate these glitches the machines can make. I talk to mine, even yell at it, demanding that it do what I want it to do. I even threaten it with a hammer. So, do we yearn for the good old days??? In a way, yes, but what we yearn for most of all, is a simpler lifestyle that is not available in today's world.

At the grocery store the other day, the cashier was trying to adjust that funny looking machine right there by the check out. You know, the one that will ask you to enter a phone number or ask you if you want change back. She couldn't get it to work, and Lord knows I couldn't, nor did I care!!!

While we waited on the manager (a "youngster," younger than the shoes I was wearing), I told her how it used to be when my dad decided to get a new car. This was something he did every 6 months, always with the same Desoto dealer, and I would very often accompany him to the dealership. So, my dad would walk around the showroom, decide on a car, and he and the salesman would then retire to the office to discuss the deal. "How much is the car?" My dad would ask, he was quoted a price, and then he would ask the salesman "how much will you give me for my car?" The last question was always, "will you take a check?"

Pop would make out the check, and together, we'd go out to the parking lot and empty out the glove box of our car, check the trunk for anything, and just make sure we weren't leaving any belongings behind. Then, we'd walk around to the other side where the new car was waiting for us, put all our belongings in the new glove box, and drive off. At most, the entire thing took an hour. Have you bought a car lately? How long did it take you just to sign the papers on it, an hour, 2 hours? Of course, that was only after the all afternoon haggling had been completed, and it always got to me when the salesman said in his sonorous voice, "well, I'll have to check with our sales manager about this deal, you are virtually stealing this car at this price." I always imagined he took the time to use the restroom while we sit there sweating bulletins hoping this magnificent deal of a car didn't get away from us. Then the guy would come back and tell us how went to bat for us and really pushed his boss to accept our offer. Then, he would apologetically hand over the keys, AFTER we signed 4,832 papers on the car. Doncha love it!!

You see, this is what frustrates us, the complications of any transaction we make. Why can't we just walk into a place, hand over our check and walk out with the merchandise? So, do we miss the good old days? Well, I guess you could say we do in a way. I miss the simplicity of the times more than anything, because I do love the modern kitchens and washing machines that practically do everything for you. But what I hate is having to wait while some confounded machine tells me my user name is incorrect, and I should open an account before I leave a message on that website. I don't want to open an account, I just want to leave a message!! I'm tired of filling out the same forms over and over again, every time I go to the doctor for something, and seeing a different face each time. Frustrating.

I should be in charge, I'm not, but I should be!! If I were, things would be so different believe me, and it would be against the law to have to wait more than 15 minutes to transact any business or see any doctor!! My dad had the right idea, he was self-employed, but he reasoned his time was as valuable as anyone's, so, if he waited more than 30 minutes for anything, he'd send *them* a bill.

Hey it works for me!!

A Time for Transition

I have always looked at March as a time of transition. Winter is not quite through with us, and spring hasn't made an appearance yet. It's an in between time really. What has lain dormant for so long is now awakening, natures renaissance.

There is a lot going on during March, it's the time of Lent, for one thing, time to contemplate putting away the old and getting out the new. If you're like me, you might even be thinking about doing some potting and gardening.

I have recently lost someone near and very dear to me, so, this March, during all the transition from one season to the next, I am giving serious thought to all the changes going on in my life. No longer young, but not yet old, it has been a difficult winter to for me, but I am looking ahead to spring.

Spring brings with it warmer, nicer weather, budding of trees and shrubs, and the first peek at flowers. A true renewal of the earth, and along with all of that I am thinking of how to continue on with my various activities, show reverence for the Lenten Season, and remember my friend. Spring may be the best time of year for that, it brings God's promise home to us, that tomorrow will be brighter, lovelier, and better than today. Mother Nature will move on, doing what she does best, renewing the earth and brining new life to fruition. How can we not follow her lead? Spring is literally a new beginning for us, welcoming us to the wonders of nature, as they gradually unfold around us. Spring delights and surprises us as we walk the land, noticing new sprouts, listening to the returning birds, as they go about their next building with glorious chirping.

A couple weeks ago, I noticed that 2 of my Daffodils had opened up in full bloom, and I had several buds among the rest of them. It worried me to see them blooming so soon, and I didn't want to think of them getting frost bitten and dying too early. They are still there, with more opening up every day, but now I smile when I see them, marveling at their tenacity in the face of some really cold weather, and praising them for giving me a sign of early spring and hope. The beautiful, yellow Daffodils, a bit of sunshine on these drab, still winter days. I know the promise of spring is still ahead, and when it finally gets here, how delighted we all will be. Warmth, sunshine, and God's glorious earth, how could it possibly get any better?

Birth Control for Grandma

The doctor that had been seeing an 80-year-old woman for most of her life finally retired. At her next checkup, the new doctor told her to bring a list of all the medicines that had been prescribed for her.

As the doctor was looking through these, his eyes grew wide as he realized Grandma had a prescription for birth control pills.

"Mrs. Smith, do you realize these are BIRTH CONTROL pills?"

"Yes, they help me sleep at night."

"Mrs. Smith, I assure you there is absolutely NOTHING in these pills that could possibly help you sleep!"

She reached and patted the young Doctor's knee. "Yes, dear, I know that. But every morning, I grind one up and mix it in the glass of orange juice that my 16-year-old granddaughter drinks and believe me, it definitely helps me sleep at night."

You got love Grandmas!

Biology Exam

Students in an advanced Biology Class were taking their mid-term exam. The last question was, “Name seven advantages of Mother’s Milk. The question was worth 70 points or none at all.

One student, was hard put to think of seven advantages. He wrote:

1. It is a perfect formula for the child.
2. It provides immunity against several diseases.
3. It is always the right temperature.
4. It is inexpensive.
5. It bonds the child to mother, and vice versa.
6. It is always available as need.

And then the student was stuck. Finally, in desperation, just before the bell rang indicating the end of the test, he wrote:

7. It comes in two attractive containers and its high enough off the ground where the cat can’t get it.

He got an A.

Wise Italian Grandfather

An old Italian man in Brooklyn is dying. He calls his grandson to his bedside, "Guido, I wan' you lissina to me. I wan' you to take-a chrome plated...38 revolver so you will always remember me."

"But grandpa, I really don't like guns. How about you leave me your Rolex watch instead?"

"You lissina me, boy! Somma day you gonna be runna da business, you gonna have a beautiful wife, lotsa money, a big-a home and maybe a couple of bambinos.

"Somma day you gonna come-a home and maybe finda you wife inna bed with another man. Whatta you gonna do then point at your watch and say times up!"

***

An Honest Diagnosis

A man told his doctor that he wasn't able to do all the things around the house that he used to do.

When the examination was complete, he said, "Now, Doc, I can take it. Tell me in plain English what is wrong with me."

"Well, in plain English," the doctor replied, "you're just lazy."

"Okay," said the man. "Now give me the medical term so I can tell my wife."

***

A Ride in the Taxi

A woman and her twelve-year-old son were riding in a taxi in Detroit. It was raining and all the prostitutes were standing under awnings.

"Mom," said the boy, "What are all those women doing?"

"They're waiting for their husbands to get off work," she replied.

The taxi driver turns around and says, "Geez lady, why don't you tell him the Truth? They're hookers, boy! They have sex with men for money."

The little boy's eyes get wide and he says, "Is that true Mom?"

His mother, glaring hard at the drive, answers "Yes."

After a few minutes, the kid asks, "Mom, if those women have babies, what happens to them?"

She said, "Most of them become taxi drivers."

***

Some Thoughts

1. I didn't make it to the gym today. That makes five years in a row.

2. I decided to change calling the bathroom the John and renamed it the Jim. I feel so much better saying – I went to the Jim this morning.

3. Last year I joined a support group for procrastinators. We haven't met yet.

4. I don't need anger management. I need people to stop irritating me!

5. When I was a child I thought Nap Times was a punishment…now, as a grown up, it just feels like a small vacation.

6. My people skills are just fine. It's my tolerance of idiots that needs working on.

7. If God wanted me to touch my toes, he would've put them on my knees.

8. The kids text me "plz" which is shorter than please. I text back "no" which is shorter than "yes."

9. I'm going to retire and live off of my savings. Not sure what I'll do the second week.

10. Even duct tape can't fix stupid…but it can muffle the sound!

11. Why do I have to press one for English when you're just gonna transfer me to someone I can't understand anyway?

12. Of course I talk to myself. Sometimes I need expert advice.

***

Quotable Quotes

"What lies behind us and what lies before us and what lies before us are tiny matters compared to what lies within us." Ralph Waldo Emerson

It Couldn't Be Done

Somebody said that it couldn't be done, but he with a chuckle replied that "maybe it couldn't," but he would be one who wouldn't say so till he tried.

So he buckled right in with the trace of a grin on his face. If he worried he hid it. He started to sing as he tackled the thing that couldn't be done – and he did it.

Somebody scoffed: "Oh, you'll never do that; at least no one has ever done it." But he took off his coat and he took off his hat, and the first thing we knew he'd begun it. With a lift of his chin and a bit of a grin, without any doubting or quiddity, he started to sing as he tackled the thing that couldn't be done, and he did it.

There are thousands to tell you it cannot be done, there are thousands to point out to you, one by one, the dangers that wait to assail you. But just buckle in with a bit of a grin, just take off your coat and go to it. Just start to sing as you tackle the thing that cannot be done, and you'll do it.

Only by God

Spring and all of nature's splendor is upon us. It puts me in a mood to admire and appreciate all that nature provides for us. This essay appeared recently in our church newsletter, and it address just such an issue. Written by my friend, Lou Ann, I am happy to share it with you here.

If you consider an eagle's majestic strength, then a hummingbird's tiny fragility, yet both of soft features and hollow bones, then, you must admit they were designed only by God.

If you consider the mammoth baleen whale straining sea water for the minute plankton and algae, then, you must admit they were designed only by God.

If you consider the colors of the sunrise and sunset, and the infinite array of iris, tulips and roses, then, you must admit they were designed only by God.

If you consider all the tastes of apples, peanuts and chocolate, then the smells of tangerines, popcorn and coconut, then, you must admit they were designed only by God.

If you consider the intricate delicacy of snowflakes and the ordinariness of a raindrop, yet both have awesome power when they multiply and join, then you must admit they were designed only by God.

If you consider simple things beside, under, and over you, yet study it and find how complex, then, you must admit they were designed only by God.

Thank God for Eccentricity

My good friend Evelyn caught me up at the Senior Center the other day and told me how much she enjoyed my writing. I told her the same thing about hers. Then, she said she felt as if she already knew my brother, based on the things I write about him. Well, I had to laugh, as NOBODY can figure out my brother. He's one of those undefinable people that families tolerate because he's kin! Sweet, but what we here in the South call, "off the wall." I will say this, he makes life interesting.

Now eccentricity seems to run in the family. Many say that I am eccentric. Be that as it may, I got to thinking the other day about how much we take everything, including our uniqueness, for granted. Everybody's different, we all look at things in our own way, and have our own perspectives about life. My brother, for instance, thinks nothing in life is as wonderful or worth any effort, except fishing. I love to write, to sew, to be creative.

In this, the month of Thanksgiving, I think we should all make a pact to cherish our own special uniqueness, to hold dear to us those things that makes up the fabric of our lives. So what if my brother is a little on the "goofy" side, he is what makes life wonderful for me.

I don't think anything makes us appreciate what we have quite like tough times, and, while we here at home put up with this war, our slow economy, etc., we need to especially find something for which to be thankful.

My family will gather again this year, and, we will once more give thanks for our blessings, not the least of which will be one another, and all that makes up each one of us.

My favorite time of year an I sincerely hope you enjoy it and are blessed beyond expectations.

Happy Thanksgiving!

***

Pull an Honest Load

I found this wonderful poem that describes how we all should be, and I'd love to share it with you.

A horse can't pull while kicking – this fact I merely mention
And, he can't kick while pulling – which is my chief contention
Let's imitate the good old horse, and lead a life that's fitting:
Just pull an honest load, and then there'll be no time for kicking!

Author Unknown

Forget Plastic Surgery – Staying Young Is All About Attitude

It always amuses me to see the lengths people, celebrities especially will go to stay young – or so they think.

Do you know the amount of money spent annually on face lifts, tummy tucks and other procedures of that ilk? I don't either, but it must be a bunch.

Nobody, but nobody, is leaving this life alive, but the way some people spend money to retain their looks, you would think they plan on living forever. One Sunday recently, my pastor even preached on that very subject. Well, like everybody, I have my own theories about staying fit and young.

Attitude is everything. You have a bad attitude about things and you are going to be unhappy and sicker than others.

Religious faith plays into it, as well. It's been proven scientifically that the faithful live longer, happier lives, as do married folk.

I think the biggest factor is friendship. When you can interact with friends, either face-to-face or on the phone, it can make your day.

Not too many weeks ago, I picked up the phone and heard a distinctive British accent. It had to be my email friend, Helene, calling from England. What a joy to connect to someone half a world away.

We were going to have a good old "chin wag" my friend said. "Chin wag" being the quaint term applied to a conversation between two friends. I just love the British and their wonderful turns of phrase. We spent close to two hours on the cross-Atlantic phone discussing everything and everybody in the world.

My friends make my world turn for me, and I consider many, many family members as good friends. Every day I look forward to connecting by email to as many of them as I can. We are there for one another. We talk about everything.

I am very grateful that on cold, bleak days I can always be cheered up by "visiting" with good friends and scattered family members.

You can't beat the clock. You can't stay young, but you can sure feel good, get a good cheering up and maybe even feel younger by enjoying friendships and cherishing a few good buddies.

As I write this, I was interrupted by my friend, Kathy, calling from her home in Las Vegas. Spending 20 minutes talking to her sure made me feel great.

The wrinkles are still there. I'm not any younger. I just feel terrific. So go ahead, spend part of your day having a good "chin wag." You'll be better for it and it's a lot cheaper than plastic surgery.

Candy for a Wordsmith

For all the lovers of words:

•A bicycle can't stand alone because it is two-tired.

•What's the definition of a will? It's a dead giveaway.

•Time flies like an arrow. Fruit flies like a banana.

•A backward poet writes inverse.

•In democracy, it's your vote that count. In feudalism, it's your counts that votes.

•A chicken crossing the road is poultry in motion.

•If you don't pay your exorcist you get repossessed.

•With her marriage she got a new name and a dress.

•Show me a piano falling down a mine shaft and I'll show you A flat major.

•When a clock is hungry it goes back four seconds.

•The man who fell into an upholstery machine is fully recovered.

•A grenade thrown into a kitchen in France would result in Linoleum Blownapart.

•You feel stuck with your debt if you can't budge it.

•Local Area Network in Australia: The LAN down under.

•He often broke into song because he couldn't find the key.

•Every calendar's days are numbered.

•A lot of money is tainted. "Taint yours" and "Taint mine."

•A boiled egg in the morning is hard to beat.

•He had a photographic memory which was never developed.

•A plateau is a high form of flattery.

•The short fortune-teller who escaped from prison was a small medium at large.

•Those who get too big for their britches will be exposed in the end.

•When you've seen one shopping center, you've seen a mall.

•Those who jump off a Paris bridge are in Seine.

•When an actress saw her first strands of gray hair she thought she'd dye.

•Bakers trade bread recipes on a knead to know basis.

•Santa's helpers are subordinate clauses.

•Acupuncture is a jab well done.

Those Were the Days...Remember?

Couple weekends ago, the spouse and I decided to take a Sunday afternoon drive. Remember those? When my brother and I were kids, our dad would very often take us to ride on Sunday afternoon. Quite a feat for him, since he traveled during the week anyway, more driving was not on his agenda, but that's what we did "back then."

Sundays were special days, we dressed up to go to church, and stayed dressed in our Sunday best for the rest of the day. Playing was out, it was, after all, Sunday, so, we could read a book, listen to the radio, or maybe the family would go visiting, greet visitors to our home, sit on the front porch, or if we were lucky, take in a picture show.

Based on what I've observed over the years, no one has a "Sunday best" anymore, and if they do, they don't seem to want to wear it to church, and it has become like any other day, just another day of shopping the mall, "hangin' " out, or taking in a fast food restaurant. Not that I'm criticizing, mind you, only taking note of how we have changed in our society. Anyway, back to our Sunday drive.

We live in a particularly lovely area of the state I think, a lot of rural farms around, and beautiful homes to admire along the way. We started out, driving slowly so as not to miss anything. First one driver after another ran up on our bumper, honked, shook their fist or worse yet, made obscene gestures to us. We'd pull over to allow them to pass, but it didn't seem to improve their mood any.

Time was when the Sunday afternoon drive was a great time to be together as a family, converse with one another, and get to see some interesting sites along the way. Brother and I used to keep a tally of the tractors, the hay bales, the blue or red trucks, and the horses we'd pass along the way. Perhaps I'm being a "Pollyanna," but I miss those times, the closeness of family, we just don't seem to have that anymore in this country, and the Sunday afternoon drive has become obsolete. Like corsets and wearing hats to church.

Well, the leisurely drive on a pretty weekend afternoon may have gone by the wayside, but we thoroughly enjoyed it. Gave us a chance to reconnect with the countryside, gave us the opportunity to see the leaves as they slowly began to lose their summer green, and certainly made us slow down for the afternoon. We even stopped for ice cream!!!

If you are one of those folks on the merry go round of a busy life, too occupied to see the wonderful, beautiful world around you, I highly recommend a relaxing afternoon drive. Sunday or any day. We need more of that in this country, it's good for the soul, gets you back to nature, and lets you appreciate all the fascinating things you might see along the way. You needn't go far, just go! This season of Thanksgiving is a great time to get out and see the world around you, and give thanks.

Eternal Truths

They are called eternal truths, those little bon mots of wisdom we find all over the place, at the bottom of a newsletter page, in the Readers' Digest, they're everywhere. Sometimes they are funny, but often times, they are just a phrase or a saying that reaches out and speaks to us. Well, for instance, here's an eternal truth: put wire coat hangers in a dark closet, and when you go back to get one, there will be more of them there than what you originally put in the closet. It is my contention that wire coat hangers multiply in dark spaces. Not only that, but they are duty bound to get hung up on one another. Have you ever seen two or three that were locked together? It's almost impossible to get them apart with any ease at all. That's what coat hangers do. Did you know that once over the hill, you pick up speed? That is not only an eternal truth, it's a sure thing. Here are some more for your funny bone.

I love cooking with wine, sometimes I even put it in the food.

If it weren't for stress, I'd have no energy at all.

Whatever hits the fan will not be evenly distributed.

Everyone has a photographic memory, some just don't have film.

Experience is a wonderful thing, it enables you to recognize a mistake when you make it again.

By the time you can make ends meet, they move the ends.

Learn from the mistakes of others, you can't live long enough to make them all yourself.

If the shoe fits, buy it in every color.

If you are too open-minded, your brains will fall out.

Going to church doesn't make you a Christian, any more than standing in a garage makes you a car.

Bills travel at twice the speed of checks.

Some days are a total waste of make-up.

A balanced diet is a cookie in each hand.

Middle-age is when broadness of the mind, and narrowness of the waist, change places.

Opportunities always look bigger going than coming.

Junk is something you've kept for years and throw away three weeks before you need it.

I know God won't give me more than I can handle, but I just wish He didn't trust me so much!

Eternal
Truth

Here's an Idea That's Just Too Good to Be True – Act Now Before It's Too Late

I have decided that one of the things that will keep a person young is to come up with one good idea a day. Something that will really help humanity and clean up our world.

I came by this when I opened what must have been a pound of junk mail with all kinds of offers simply too good to refuse according to the accompanying flyers.

Why is it every hair-brained scheme that offers to separate me from my hard-earned money is an "offer too good to pass up?" Notice how these things always have a time limit. You must act now, the brochure advises, or someone else will reap all the benefits that would otherwise be yours.

Have you ever stopped to consider just how much it costs to send these schemes out to every living, breathing being in the universe? It must be a lot. No wonder they want you to send money, you gotta pay for all that postage.

I end up tossing most of my mail in the trash can. I simply can't afford to save all that money. I would end up saving myself right into the poor house.

Magazines, now that's another story. Mine come with all kinds of inserts. Once you pull them out, you are left with about 25 pages of articles, sometime even less. I think of all of the money it takes the magazine people to mail them out. If they removed all those cardboard-like inserts, they could quite probably cut their postage in half.

Now back to my plan of coming up with an original idea every day. Obviously, I'm too late for the hula hoop or the electric can opener, but I do have an idea to get rid of all that junk mail and those frustrating magazine inserts.

Once a year, maybe sometime in the fall, companies would be allowed to send their junk mail and the whole country could spend the day making a bonfire from it. After it gets to burning really well, we could gather up all the dried kudzu and toss it on the fire, thereby killing three birds with one rock. Don't you see, the ad people would be satisfied since they get to send out all their mail; we get to burn it and get rid of kudzu all at the same time.

Personally, I think it's a peachy keen idea. Now if I could just come up with a patent on a riding vacuum cleaner, I could really clean up.

Love That New Car Feeling But I Wonder What This Button Is For?

We are not extravagant people, but occasionally, the spouse and I purchase a new car. Boy don't you love the smell and feel of a new car? Buying a new automobile is a lot of work nowadays, all kinds of papers to sign, deals to make – it can take a whole day just to drive it off the car lot. Let's face it, it's a real pain.

As a kid, I used to accompany my dad sometimes when he bought a new car which was just about every six months. He traveled for a living, and six months was about all his cars could take.

We'd go down to the Desoto dealership – that was when Desoto's shared showroom space with Plymouths – and we'd pick out a new car, mostly red, with lots of chrome, and Pop would write out a check for the amount. We'd leave the old car and drive off in the new. Simple as that.

Then there was my Uncle George, who drove Packard's. He liked the Packard; there was always so much shiny chrome, and the headlights were just huge. His favorite was a big silver one, with whitewall tires. Man, you could see Uncle George coming in that car a block away.

He actually drove it very little. Uncle George was a Chicago City cabbie, so he drove his taxi everywhere and left that gorgeous automobile in the garage out behind his house. Didn't want to get it dirty, he said.

Now, for those of you who are uninformed, we washed our own cars back then – the drive-through car wash hadn't been invented yet. Uncle George was basically lazy, so he wasn't about to wash someone else's dirt off *his* car!

Cars were more fun back then. They weren't used as much as they are today, and with fewer people on the road, it was certainly more pleasurable to drive around than it is today.

Pop's Desoto's had what was called "push button" drive. The dashboard was all buttons, and you literally pushed in the one you wanted: R for reverse, D for drive, etc. No manual transmission for my father. He liked his comfort. I remember being fascinated at the automatic seat. He would push a button and the front seat would either glide forward or backward, just as smooth as anything.

Well, cars today are still featuring all the buttons, gadgets, bells and whistles that you care to pay for. The only trouble is, now I am a participant. I can no longer sit there idly watching while someone else does all the button pushing. I actually have to do it myself. That's where the problem starts.

I'm one of those people who does not, as a rule, read the directions for anything. I struggle along, trying to figure it out for myself, resigning to read instructions as a last resort, like after something is broken. Then I read, trying to comprehend how to fix it. It should come as no surprise then, that as I am driving along in this aforementioned new car, I may want to turn on the windshield wipers or the lights, but inadvertently I turn on the rear window defroster, which also defrosts the rear view mirrors, I might add.

Sometimes the windshield wipers come on when I am trying to adjust the radio. I never could tune a radio, but that's another story. Bottom line, if you see me in my new car, which is black, by the way, and, I'm driving along, windshield wipers working just fine on a sunny day, and the gas cap opening and closing, have a little compassion, won't you?

Sooner or later, I'll figure everything out, and then I won't be a hazard anymore. Whatever you do, *don't* tell my kids. They are still dealing with the issue of me having a driver's license.

Ford Motor Co. Is Not the Only One With A Better Idea

I have a niece who is an absolute whiz at all things mechanical, another one who is a genius Realtor; a sister-in-law who's brilliant at a computer and a son who's a military genius. You realize that I come from a predominantly smart family. Now, before you chime in asking what happened to me, hear me out.

There's always a better way to do things, and I'm basically convinced that the auto makers could do a lot more to prevent accidents. Naming their cars, for instance. Accidents are no laughing matter, of course, but I do think more thought should be put into the names these cars are burdened with, and maybe we could slow everyone down. I'll give you an example.

When you buy a car with a name like Dart, it brings to mind something really fast. Have you ever seen anyone throw a slow dart? How 'bout the Acura? That sounds like something you "aim" at another person. Then, there's the Cougar, the Mustang, the Intrepid. They all sound fast and invincible. That can be misleading when you're driving a two-ton "guided missile" on the road.

My idea is to slow everyone down by word association. For instance, give teenagers a car with a name like Sedate or Fogey, which would just beg them to drive under the speed limit.

My dad was the type of individual who felt he should be the one to say when his children could drive, not the state of Georgia. I was terribly disadvantaged anyway, because when we lived in Florida, at that time you could get a driver's license at age 14, provided you passed the test. Naturally, my brother passed it; plus, he was very tall, so no trouble seeing over the steering wheel for him.

Soon after that, we moved to Georgia, and the age limit was 16, unless, of course, you had my dad for a father. I remember my dad taking me to the empty parking lot at the shopping center – they weren't called "malls" back then – and I practiced steering around the marked parking spaces while he controlled the brakes and speed. Back in the dark ages, when I was a teenager, there was no driver's education; you simply took you chances that you could pass the test when it came to your time with the examiner.

When the time came for me to get a license, I was almost 18, and out of high school, a point of infinite humiliation to me at the time.

My father was driving a wide track, huge station wagon then that resembled nothing if not an armored tank.

I couldn't tell you to this day how I passed my driving test in that big automobile. But I did, probably because the Georgia State Examiner felt sorry for me – my father insisted on peeping around the doorway and watching me while I took the written portion. After the road test, the trooper said I had passed, but warned me to be careful driving that big car.

Was he kidding? I could barely see over the steering wheel! The best part about that car was it was so huge and so heavy, not very easily maneuvered either, that you couldn't help but drive slowly in it. Well, see, that's my point. We need to give these cars big, cumbersome names, like Big Bertha or Pile Driver. I guarantee it will slow everybody down to a crawl, and that can't be bad, can it?

Ford isn't the only one with a better idea.

Believe Me, "Golden Years" Are Not for Sissies

I don't know about you, but I really thought growing older would be more fun. As I get up close and personal with the family physician, I wonder when the "golden years" are going to start.

Every day there's a new ailment or wrinkle. Only when I am with the grandchildren do I feel young, and then, as soon as they leave, old age creeps in again.

I have given serious thought to a complete body makeover, but I don't think there is a clinic anywhere that can handle it. So I am stuck here on Earth in this body, with this life.

Whatever the numbers, old age doesn't have to be all gloom and doom. I try every day to learn something new. For instance, one of my daughters-in-law showed me a new way to fold bath towels so they would fit better in my linen closet. Doesn't really grab you, does it?

Ok, how about this? There are all kinds of interesting people and places out there, and the sooner we get on with the business of making their acquaintance, the better off we will be. Nothing makes one feel better than to get out and about to meet and greet.

Walking along Main Street one day, a "seasoned" gentleman stopped me and told me how much he enjoyed my writing. Thanking him, I attempted to move on and relish the compliment he had just given me.

Not so fast – he wanted to chat. In particular, he was interested in a story I wrote once for a magazine, concerning an old Desoto my dad drove. Was it still drivable, the old fella wanted to know? I tried to explain that it was just a story about a car. There was no longer any car.

"Do you want to sell it?" He inquired.

No car, I explained. There was a car, but no longer. It was simply a story I wrote about a car that is no longer in existence.

Not to be undone, he wanted to know how much I wanted for the car. Now this might have frustrated someone else, but I find this sort of exchange very amusing. He was a cute old guy, a little stubborn and obtuse, but hey, we've all been there, right?

I couldn't help but laugh at the old guy, so sincere and all, as I tried, once again to explain that I had written a story about a formerly existent automobile. His face just beamed at me as he insisted on giving me his name and telephone number in case I decided to sell the car.

As I walked away laughing, I was grateful for my "seasoned citizen" fan, all my fans, and grateful too that for some reason, speaking with that gentleman put a spring in my step. Old age may not be for sissies, but when you think of the alternative, it ain't so bad after all!

I Could Stay Young Forever, If It Weren't for Missing the Good Stuff

It isn't that I mind aging so much, if I just didn't have to get older to do it! Let's face it, aging isn't all it's made out to be. I don't have a million-dollar retirement; I can't cruise the Mediterranean; and, I don't have a condo on the Cote D'Azure to make my retirement a life of ease.

What I do have is a lot of memories of many of life's truly wonderful things that made day to day living so much more enjoyable. I miss, for instance, walking into the corner drugstore when everyone knew my name, and asking for "fountain Coke." You know, the kind made with Coke syrup and carbonated water. Then, I could walk to the neighborhood market where the butcher would custom cut my meat order, and then wrap it in that really neat butcher paper and label it. Mama would take the meat home, and stow it away in our tiny freezer compartment, no rewrapping necessary.

I miss the milkman, too. I'd meet him at the door every morning, and give him my order, and send back the "empties." There was just something so comforting in hearing that old milk truck making its way through the early morning hours, and I never met a milkman who wasn't just the friendliest person you'd ever meet.

Store clerks all knew us, knew the family, and never hesitated to inquire after one or the other's health. Boy, those were the days, weren't they?

My family was friends with the local Judge, Saegar, was his name. A big, barrel-chested guy who never knew a stranger. I can't tell you if he was really a judge, or maybe just a magistrate, but everybody called him Judge Saegar, Alex Saegar. We went to one of his office weddings one night, very late. The bride's father toted a gun, too, I want you to know.

One of the more colorful characters that dotted my childhood was the family insurance man, Clarence Coakley. Another gentleman of size, he'd call on all of us once a month to pick up our premium money. He knew all of mama's family, sold all nine siblings their insurance, and even handled grandma and grandpa's insurance. That's the way it was back then, you had entire families for clients.

Mr. Coakley was a tall, distinguished looking fella, with pretty, curly gray hair; and he would park his old car in the middle of the block and walk to each client's house – stopping for coffee, and maybe a slice of homemade cake along the way.

Mr. Coakley would oftentimes collect Mama's insurance money at the same time as he'd get my Aunt Florence's. Seems we were over there a lot, and, it simply saved time. We'd all sit on my aunt's big, overstuffed horsehair sofa and living room chairs and visit for a while, while Mr. Coakley took out his insurance book and marked off my aunt and uncle and my parents. As was the case so often in those days, Aunt Florence sometimes didn't have her monthly premium money, so Mr. Coakley would tell her not to worry, he'd just get it the next month. Then, he'd thank her for the coffee and cake, tip his hat, and be on his way to the next house.

I miss all that. I miss being able to twist, wearing poodle skirts and bobby sox, and, I miss not being able to wear high heeled shoes anymore.

Well, one thing I have learned. Life's too short to sit around pining for the good old days. We've got to be flexible, "go with the flow," and, be able to cope in this modern push button world. Besides, when you think of the alternative, growing older isn't so bad after all.

Women are Heaven – Sent, Men are from Nowhere!

I don't know what it is about men, but they are born clueless, and then get worse! Lately, it seems, all I've heard are horror stories from one woman after another, telling me how inept their husbands are. I think it's a genetic flaw, myself.

Most men find themselves incapable of following simple instructions from their wives. Take my son-in-law, for instance. He is the world's best son-in-law and I love him dearly, but I feel sorry for him living with my daughter because I know she has a certain way of doing everything. Helping her with the laundry one day, he – against – her strict orders – put one of her best sweaters in the dryer. Naturally, it came out looking as if it had been custom made for their three-year old daughter.

Now, this is exactly what I mean. Most men either don't listen to their wives, or fail to hear them altogether. Recently, during all this muggy weather we've been having, my adored one failed to hear me ask if he would help me around the house. He did put down his newspaper long enough to tell me I was working entirely too hard, and it was difficult for him to watch me. Then, he asked me to take whatever I was working on into the other room! Hmmm, I wonder under what statutes murder is legal in this state?

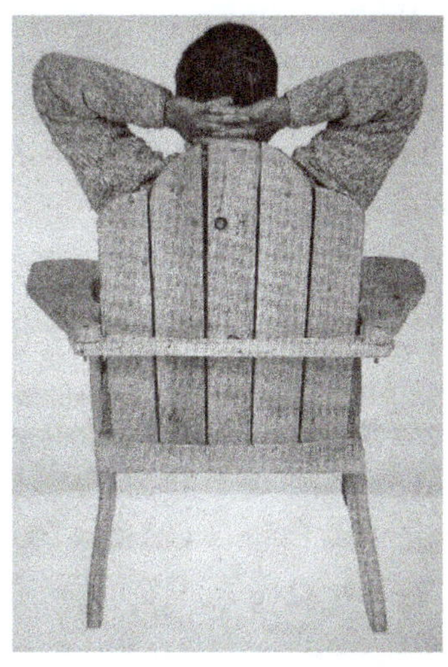

There is one exception to this rule, however, and many's the time it was my brother. For instance, one evening many, many years ago, he was entrusted with my care while our parents went out for the evening. Being bored, he phoned them and asked if could make some cookies for the two of us. My mother, thinking to discourage him, said, "Just one or two."

For anyone else, this would have been the end of it, but not MY sibling. First, he dug out Mama's recipe for chocolate chip cookies, HIS favorite. Then, he proceeded to gather the ingredients, but couldn't find the mixing bowls. Not to be the least bit daunted, he realized he had to climb atop our kitchen table to reach the bowls for mixing up the cookie dough. Naturally, when he did, he hung a little too long onto the cupboard door, and it came crashing to the floor, my sweet brother on top of it.

We conspired to move the door out of the way, and proceeded with our baking. Remembering Mom's admonition to only bake one or two of them, he rolled out the dough into 3 giant sized cookies, which he then slid into the oven.

You can well imagine the mess my parents came home to later that night. HOWEVER, Gregg followed instructions, and the cookies really turned out to be pretty tasty. Mother dubbed them Tire Patch cookies, because she said they were big enough to patch truck tires. She wasn't really happy about the torn cupboard door, however.

I thought about this story the other day, when I asked my brother to do something for me, and he actually did it! He said he wasn't busy anyway. He was sitting in the living room thinking about going fishing, all the while watching my sister-in-law, Bev, bent over working in the garden. He had been wondering if she would be finished in time to fix lunch!

I rest my case!

If You're as Old as You Look, I'm Done For

There is the old saw that says a woman is as old as she feels, a man as old as he looks, and a child as old as they are treated. Basically, I feel rather youngish. In fact, I tell everyone that I am only 11 years old, when in reality, I'm only 2 years younger than my oldest child!

We all like to think we're young and invincible, able to leap tall buildings in a single bound. But the most perfect thought about age was given by a lady in our church who, upon the occasion of her 100th birthday, declared that she regretted that her life was HALF OVER! Imagine half over at 100! Now, you gotta admire that kind of spunk!

Remember, as children, we though that our 40-year-old teachers were ANCIENT. I had an aunt who was a school teacher back in the 40's and 50's, and I recall prefacing all remarks about her by saying my OLD MAID school teacher aunt. It was just assumed, back then, that school teachers were old maids: a very quaint and antiquated terminology in today's world. Truth is, women and men marry much later nowadays, and I've known women who even put off child bearing until their mid-forties.

Back to age, I do know that age is relevant in today's world, and you are only as old as you feel, which put me in mind to repeat that I'm still only 11 years old.

It got me to thinking though, about all the things that make us feel young. My mother had a red dress back in the 50's that had a very full, pleated skirt, and every time she wore it out in the evening, I would ask her to twirl for me. "Twirl, Mama," I can remember saying, just as if it were yesterday. Mama would twirl in the thing, the skirt billowing out, and she told me that always made her feel like a young lady again.

My brother loves to fish, and declares that fishing away on the pier, or out in a boat, makes him feel really young. And, when he catches a big fish, as he is want to do, he feels invincible.

I don't know why, but the smell of bread baking makes me wax nostalgic for the good old days when I was really, truly young. Guess the smell reminds me of the homes I used to visit, where the mothers in residence always had something baking in the oven.

Next, I went to my closet, to see if anything hanging in there reminded me of being young. My leather boots do, of course. And this one outfit I wear and wear, that has a long paisley skirt and a loose-fitting black top to it. I get lots of compliments when I wear that outfit. I guess that's why I wear it. It hides a great many figure flaws as well, thereby enabling me to pretend I still have that size 10 shape the spouse was so crazy about.

The other day, I tried that twirling thing my mom used to do – put me on the floor with a 30-minute dizzy spell! Mary Tyler Moore used to twirl her hat in the opening of her old TV show. Don't know how she stayed on her feet doing that!

Anyway, once over my dizziness, it was back in my lounge chair, feet up, cat on my lap, snoozing. I didn't feel any younger, but I did feel better, and that goes a long way towards feeling youthful. Don't you think?

...And, Another Thing!

How can we celebrate the New Year, when I'm not finished with the old one yet? I have unresolved issues, and I can't let it go at that. Actually, I'm compiling a list of things I want to discuss when I get to heaven, I'm up to three pages now.

For instance, as I write this, we are expecting a harsh winter storm, and for the life of me, I can't figure out why everyone is running around like Chicken Little. I have a daughter-in-law who is from Nebraska, and she fails to see the reasoning behind the rush to buy milk, bread, and toilet paper every time a snowflake threatens us. My own daughter answered her that it was "tradition" in the South to do so. For now, that satisfies her. Don't know how long I can hold her off though. I mean, this is serious!

...And, another thing, Christmas decorations go up here immediately after Thanksgiving, if not before, and come down Christmas Day. Makes no sense to me. For one thing, it kinda takes the edge off the celebration of Thanksgiving, AND my birthday, and Christmas doesn't officially end until Epiphany, somewhere around the 6th of January. Just saying, but I would like to have answers to these puzzlements. The year spouse and I lived in Boston when first married was interesting, because on walks around the neighborhood, I noticed Christmas wreaths still hanging until almost Easter. Now, that's another thing!

The woman who was my godmother was French. A war bride from WWII, and she railed and railed against her American daughter-in-law for putting money in the bank, then writing checks against it. She thought that idea ridiculous. Her theory was that you're going to spend it anyway, so, why not cash the check, keep the money in your pocket, them when you needed it, it was right there. Hmmm, not sure I buy into that, but to each his own right?

The BIG question I have for my heavenly friends when I get there, and rest assure, I WILL get there, is this. Why must it be only the woman who bears the children, and suffers menopause? Why can't God, in His Wisdom, share the responsibility somewhat. I mean, look at it this way. The world is overpopulated as it is, let men have a share in the labor and birth process, and you will see zero population growth in no time flat! As for menopause, imagine 150,000 soldiers on the front line, all having hot flashes and mood swings. Talk about a short war!

Well, these are just a few of my gripes. I failed to mention my all-time bugaboo though, why is there only one shoe in the road! Why not two? What, somebody gets mad and throws out one shoe? How can you lose one shoe? This is something I have pondered for decades, and no one seems to have an answer for me. That's ok, I'll add it to my list.

...And another thing. Have the happiest, most blessed New Year's ever, my friends!!

Remember These?

I got to reminiscing the other day with friend, and there were so many things we both miss in our lives. The old-fashioned curtain stretchers that my Aunt Florence was so fond of, for one thing. She used to set them up on the days she spring cleaned, and they were all over the house, but to this day, the smell of bleach makes me wax nostalgic for it. You could smell those bleached curtains for a block away as they dried on the stretchers.

Another thing I miss is the old wringer washing machine, not because it was easy, certainly, but because I was so fascinated by the sheer act of using it. I thought it was a marvelous invention, and watching my mom run clothes through that wringer was a real treat…until the day I tried it and ran my entire arm through it!

A lot of what we consider today, to be "old timey" are what made up our home entertainment consumption. I mean, who needs Wi-Fi or a "tablet" when they had all this good stuff around the house??

Remember the clothesline? There was a sort of ritual to using one, and it was always done in the same manner. Housewives were judged on how well they managed the clothesline, and what was put on it more or less told the neighborhood what was going on in your life. The following are some thoughts on this subject, enjoy.

Mom's Clothesline

We had a long wooden pole (clothes pole) that was used to push the clotheslines up so that longer items (sheets/pants/etc.) didn't brush the ground and get dirty. I can hear my mother now…

The Basic Rules for Clotheslines:

(If you don't even know what clotheslines are, better skip this.)

1.You had to hang the socks by the toes…NOT the top.

2.You hung pants by the BOTTOM/cuffs…NOT the waistbands.

3.You had to WASH the clothesline(s) before hanging any clothes – walk the entire length of each line with a damp cloth around the lines.

4.You had to hang the clothes in a certain order, and always hang "whites" with "whites," and hang them first.

5.You NEVER hung a shirt by the shoulders – always by the tail. That would the neighbors think?

6.Wash day on a Monday! NEVER hang clothes on the weekend, or on Sunday, for Heaven's sake!

7.Hang the sheet and towels on the OUTSIDE lines so you could hide your "unmentionables" in the middle (perverts & busybodies, y'know!)

8.It didn't matter if it was sub-zero weather…clothes would "freeze-dry."

9.ALWAYS gather the clothes pins when taking down dry clothes! Pins left on the lines were "tacky!"

10.If you were efficient, you would line the clothes up so that each item did not need two clothes pins, but shared one of the clothes pins with the next washed item.

11.Clothes off of the line before dinner time, neatly folded in the clothes basket, and ready to be ironed.

12.IRONED??!! Well, that's a whole OTHER subject!

And now a Poem...

A clothesline was a news forecast, To neighbors passing by,
There were no secrets you could keep, when clothes were hung to dry.
It also was a friendly link, for neighbors always knew
If company had stopped on by, To spend a night or two.

For then you'd see the "fancy sheets," And towels upon the line;
You'd see the "company tablecloths," With intricate designs
The line announced a baby's birth, from folks who lived inside,
As brand new infant clothes were hung, So carefully with pride!

The ages of the children could, so readily be known
By watching how the sizes changed, you'd know how much they'd grown!
It also told when illness struck, as extra sheets were hung;
Then nightclothes, and a bathrobe too, haphazardly were strung.

It also said, "On vacation now," When lines hung limp and bare.
It told, "We're back!" when full lines sagged; With not an inch to spare!
New folks in town were scorned upon, If wash was dingy and gray,
As neighbors carefully raised their brows, And looked the other way.

But clothesline now are of the past, For dryers make work much less.
Now what goes on inside a home, Is anybody's guess!
I really miss that way of life, It was a friendly sign
When neighbors knew each other best...By what hung on the line.

Jan's Plan

Having just come off the holiday season, I have to wonder once again, if we aren't overdoing just a "tad," a lot of holidays in this country. Now, I know, a lot of folks complained about the shortened Christmas season this year, due in large part, to Thanksgiving being so late, but I gotta ask you, was it really short? Think about it, we start hearing carols and seeing decorations in the stores along about Labor Day, and they continue until the big day. Along comes Halloween, and we no sooner figure out what we're going to "be," when the Christmas brouhaha begins again, in earnest this time. December 26th, and the Valentine's go on sale, along with all the St. Patrick's paraphernalia, and as soon as Valentine's is over, here come the plastic Easter bunnies and candied eggs. A body could get whiplash watching the speed of all this!

Well, I have a better idea, and here's my plan. Labor Day ushers in the fall season, nothing about back to school, Halloween or anything else until the day after, then, we'll concern ourselves with the goblins and spooks. Touting Thanksgiving will start on November 1st, and the day after, it can begin to look and sound a lot like Christmas. How'm I doing so far?

February 1st ushers in the Valentine stuff, and March 1st begins the St. Patty's Day rush. Easter varies, so, any time after say, March 10th, we can look forward to that, and of course, along comes pretty little May and Mother's Day!!! 4th of July will not be discussed until at least midway through June, and then, we can enjoy a nice respite until Labor Day, when it all starts all over again. Well, there is more to this than simply the holidays, and the avoidance of burnout from them, it would also require a change in the sports schedule. As it stands now, basketball often times slips over into very cold weather, I mean, how can you sit in the stands and enjoy a hot dog when there is frost on the ground? Not only that, but my favorite sport, horse racing, is almost skipped over entirely, and we simply can't have that, so, again, here's my plan for better enjoyment of the seasons.

January 1st through March we can have basketball. April 1st begins baseball and runs maybe until October 1st. Golf, tennis, swimming and fishing can go from May 1st until September, and then, we can have football and maybe ice hockey through Christmas. Horse racing can be any time!!! Well, there you have it, my plan for the greater enjoyment of sports and holidays. We can reserve January for all misc. winter sports, such as ice skating, skiing, whatever your fancy is. But you see, the object of my plan is to insure no one gets overburdened with watching the same sport, day after day, and there will be a shortened season for everything, thus making our pleasure over sports much better. Holidays won't overlap, and nobody will get tired of any of them, and all this happiness and pleasure can only lead to lower crime rates, less stress, more overall happiness, and world peace.

Now, let's move on to world peace, I have a plan for that as well. I am tired of war, aren't you? I guess there will always be some nutcake out there who wants to take over the world and have himself a little dynasty, but let's be practical here; we all have to inhabit this world, we all have to make our own way in it, and we all have to get along somehow or we'll blow ourselves to bits. Besides, I don't look good doing the goose step march or wearing a burka. Not an attractive look for me. So, here's my plan – any talk of war, and we gather up all the dictators and wannabes, take them to a spa and dump them in a hot tub, with a little soothing music, maybe a nice glass of wine, and perhaps some heavy hors d'oeuvres. Let them soak and "wallow" for a while, get them out, dry them off and whisk them immediately in for a massage. If after all this pampering and spoiling, they still speak of war, it will be proven beyond doubt that they are not human, and we can shoot them off into outer space for an eternity. On the other hand, most of them will be so mellow and relaxed, they'll agree to anything, and war won't be one of them.

There you have it, my plan for a much more satisfactory life, and a world at peace. Personally, I think it's a peachy keen idea, all of it, and if I could ever get in to see some of these world leaders, I'd explain it to them, but they refuse to return my calls.

Since this if the first part of February, I can officially wish you all a Happy Valentine's Day, and I want you to give serious thought to my plan, I haven't heard of a better one, have you?

You Know You're Getting Old When...

You hear all the time about how bad it is to grow old, you can't remember anything, or names, or faces, but I say, think of the alternative, and growing old isn't so bad!

One of the best things to reminisce about is Halloween, when we were kids, remember? We used to throw a sheet over ourselves, and go as ghosts, meet up with a bunch of other kids, and we'd go in packs from one house to another, collecting all the goodies we could. We'd drag our sack full of candy and treats behind us, knocking on one door after another, and some of the adults even tried to scare us somewhat as we trudged through the night. Mom and Dad didn't worry about us, we really had nothing and no one to fear, all the neighbors looked out for us anyway, and quite often, we ended up just having the best time of our lives. My cousin, Shari, and I were always in competition to see who could get the most "stuff" in their bag. We'd bring a bagful home, dump it out, and head out again.

When my own children came along, nothing would do but what they had to have store bought costumes, no homemade gear for them! I dressed them in identical Devil suits, which I felt was very appropriate! They still went around the neighborhood, but I went with them, or I drove them over to their dad's office and let them trick or treat all the employees.

We used to love it when one of our "customers" would drop a few nickels or dimes in our sack, and one man in my old neighborhood would pass out quarters, oh, that was big stuff! My Aunt Florence used to make the world's greatest Popcorn balls that she gave out, and my brother and I would try to hit her door several times during the evening, as they were truly delicious.

Nowadays, with all the emphasis on healthy snacks, I try to remember that and give sugar free gum, rolls of pennies, or some other "good for them" treat. Well, you can imagine how well that goes over.

Well, times have really changed haven't they? I used to appreciate a good ghost story or tale of some ogre monster lurking around the block, waiting to grab one of the children. Gee whiz, we aren't even allowed to do that anymore! Whoever it is who is taking the fun out of all these holidays, stop it now!

In lieu of not being able to scare the daylights out of some unsuspecting young person this year, I have come up with a few funnies to share with my fellow seasoned citizens, so, now, you can still get a chuckle by reading the following:

- •You look forward to a dull evening
- •You sit in a rocking chair and can't get it started
- •You turn out the light for economic, rather than romantic reasons
- •Your knees buckle but your belt won't
- •Calling long distance wears you out
- •Your back goes out more than you do.

Who says we can't still have a laugh! Enjoy, and have a Happy Halloween!

When My Brain Turns to Mush Just Send Me on a Cruise

I have told my children that when my brain turns to mush, and I dribble my soup, just to take me out to a field somewhere and leave me there. The problem now is, convincing them to wait until that time arrives. I think they already have a place picked out for me, and I am afraid to eat in front of them now, I spill something, and I am outta here!

Got a flyer the other day from the American Cruise lines, they are the ones who operate the river boat cruises in this country, up through Nova Scotia, and all points in between. Some of them are paddlewheel boats, some river barges, but they run a nice ship. We have taken two of their Mississippi Cruises, and now we are in some club, called the Eagle Society. This means, we are entitled to some discounts on future cruises and we get a special reception on each cruise, just us and the captain.

Well, I can heartily recommend them, and on our last cruise, we met some very interesting folks. One woman especially, was so gracious, and stately, really tall, elegant woman with a regal bearing. I found out she was a philharmonic orchestra conductor when the spouse asked her which Beatles' song she liked the best. The look on her face was priceless, but she was very gracious about it when she told him that particular group was not in her repertoire. At that time, I slunk over to the corner of the lounge and nursed my iced tea, anonymously!

Then, there was the very nice couple who owned a ranch out in Montana, in reality, it takes up half the state, but I didn't know that either until the spouse asked him if he had ever ridden a bull. Again, I slunk off and nursed my wounds with that one.

Actually, the book signing I did on board was quite successful, and you have to admire the taste these good people had, after all, they bought my book! The point I'm trying to make is, cruising is wonderful, and I know of a woman who is now living on board one of those monster cruise ships that travels between mainland America and the Caribbean Islands. She picks up her mail in every port of call, gets her food and entertainment on board, has access to health care, and laundry facilities, I mean, what more could you want? I kind of like the idea of resting on the top deck, a nice, frothy drink in my hand, big sun hat over my face, and some adorable, buffed young man coming up to me and asking me to the shipboard dance that evening. Yeah, right!

I was planning on spending my golden years at a fancy hotel with room service and free wake up call, but now that I think about it, a cruise sounds even better. Won't tell the kids where they can find me either, lest they have a spot reserved for me at Shady Pines, and certainly won't tell my spouse, he might embarrass me again, but it's definitely worth looking into, I think.

With any luck, the captain will take a shine to me, and let me drive the boat – provided there is not a sand bar within miles of me. Sure as the world, I would find it!

Ok, so, that's my plan, and you are welcome to come along and join me. We'll have fun, as we sail into our sunset years together. Bon Voyage!

Jan's Proverbs

It's better to walk alone, than with a crowd going the wrong way.

You cannot hang out with negative people, and expect to live a positive life.

Be with someone who makes you happy.

Never lose hope, you never know what tomorrow may bring.

One of the hardest decisions you'll ever make in life is whether to walk away or try harder.

If you are depressed, you are living in the past, if you're anxious, you are living in the future, and, if you are at peace, you are living in the present.

Music is what feelings sound like.

The mind replays what the heart can't delete.

You know why it's hard to be happy? We can't let go of what makes us sad.

A pretty face is nothing if you have an ugly heart.

We are not human beings on a spiritual journey, we are spiritual beings on a human journey.

When nothing goes right -go left.

Be thankful for the bad things in life, for they opened your eyes to the good things you weren't paying attention to.

The October of Our Years

I hear people all the time talking about the autumn of their years, or the springtime of life. Well, that sounds good, but I refuse to grow older, I'm still 11 years old at heart, even though my body is telling me I'm 34. My 50 years old son looks at me like I am crazy when I say things like that, but I'm serious!!! You're only as old as you feel, and, you can talk yourself into anything.

This summer, when I was entertaining grandchildren, I was everywhere, we went here, there, movies, parks, lakes, etc., and I had a ball!!!! When Trevor and I got to a nearby lake, there was a giant-sized checker game in the waiting room/diner of the area's paddle wheel boat, so, he and I played a game. I skunked him!!!!! Take no prisoners is my motto, and if you're going to play, play to win, so, I did.

Staying active, both physically and mentally, is the key to staying young. When I was physically able, I got out and played ball with the grands, even took a turn on the swings at the park with them. Can't do it anymore, but by golly, I can still beat em at Monopoly, checkers, whatever, and still delight in doing so. Nothing keeps you young quite like grandchildren, and the only thing more wonderful than my grandchildren are YOUR grandchildren, so, enjoy!!!

I love the saying about not covering up wrinkles or hiding age, because you want others to see that the road has not always been smooth or easy. I want folks to know I've been 'out there working my way through this life like everyone else, riding the wave of ups and downs, finally sliding into the grave with a martini in one hand and a box of chocolates in the other, shouting “Woo wee, what a ride!!!”

October is my favorite autumn month, so, if you are, like me, in the autumn of your years, enjoy, and hang on, shouting “woo wee! What a ride!!!!!”

Save Your Sanity, Don't Look in the Mirror

I don't know when it happened, or even why it happened, but for some reason, I have aged. You know, when you are a kid, you'd look at an old person, and say, "Man, I'm never going to look like that!!" Hey, stuff happens!!!

Here I am, 34-years-old, with 9 grandchildren who happen to think I am awesome, and I look in the mirror, and I see my mother. Now, don't get me wrong. My Mom was a nice person, but that doesn't mean I want to look like her. Everything I have either leaks, dries up, or sounds like Rice Krispies whenever I move. My joints hurt, I'm wearing orthopedic shoes, bifocals, and a back brace. My body makes noises like a coffee pot, and my energy level, after 11 am, hits the basement. Isn't there some kind of law against this sort of thing?

I remember how happy I was, when, at 17, I was taken for 25, and could go practically anywhere I wanted on my looks. Don't think I didn't take advantage of it too, because I did. Now, my own grandchildren want to help me out of my chair.

I remember once, when I was teaching school, and this particular day happened to be my birthday. I admonished my children not to say anything about it to their high school buddies, I even threatened them. Of course, you know what happened, they blabbed it all over school. One student walked into my classroom, and congratulated me on my birthday. Then, he asked me how old I was. At this time, I think I was 44 years old, and smiling, I asked him how old he thought I was. "Well," he said "you don't look a day over 65." I informed him that up until that day, he was passing the course, but of course, I said, things change.

My own dear, sister-in-law said she would hate to be young again, and especially if she had to date again, "all those painful high heel shoes, and holding your stomach in, not for me", she said. Yeah, I guess that is a bummer

Well, when I was younger, times were quieter then, no electronic gizmos to interrupt your thinking. No computers to frustrate you, we even had coffeepots where you brewed the stuff on top of the stove, remember those? .I had just conquered the new kind of coffee maker, with those little cups of grounds, when something else came on the market. Whew!! I get tired just trying to keep up!

I look at my grandchildren, and wonder about all the innovations that will be coming in their lifetime, why, my granddaughters will probably grocery shop on another planet, for Pete's sake!! Well, so long as they continue to think of me as awesome, I reckon I can put up with the gurgling, coffee pot sounds, the sore joints, the social life consisting of doctors' appointments, and, good friends slipping away into assisted living. All part of being 34 I guess.

Sitting on my deck, taking my fiber pills may not be everyone's cup of tea, but not sure I'm ready for the alternative either.

Believe in Yourself

Jan McCanless, author of the Beryl's Cove Mysteries and numerous other publications, knows the hard work that goes into writing researching books and articles. In addition to the Beryl's Cove Mystery series and other books, she is a freelance columnist for the Salisbury Post, a regulator contributor to Senior Savvy, The Saturday Evening Post, Sophie Woman's Magazine and a host of other periodicals. In her book ***The In$ and Out$ of Making Money*** from Writing, McCanless encourages writers to believe in themselves and in their works so that they can benefit from all of their efforts poured into their manuscripts.

"If you can't believe in your writing, how can you possibly expect anyone else to believe in it? Think about this, if you've gotten so far as to get something published, then there must be something redemptive about your writing. Shore up your self-confidence, and go forth and promote," advises McCanless. She encourages authors to pour their energy into selling the books they have written while still devoting time to researching and writing new books.

Her career as a novelist started with an idea that kept popping into her thoughts as she tried to focus on her job as a newspaper columnist. She had never written fiction, but she decided to jot down her ideas for a book before moving forward with her journalism career. Thankfully, McCanless didn't stop writing after she put her thoughts on paper. "I never dreamed my notes would turn into a book, then nine books, much less having all of them become bestseller. I am currently on book number 14, the ninth in the mystery series."

McCanless knows that writing a bestseller requires more than just jotting down notes. She advises writers to take time to do their research. "Your facts have to be correct," she states. "My second mystery was entitled ***The Case of the Doomed Diplomat***, and the action takes place in Las Vegas and Nellis Air Force Base, neither of which I knew anything about. So, I used my Nevada friends, the Internet, my Air Force son, whatever I could to research the area."

"You have to be accurate in anything that is of a factual nature. My latest book, ***Murder in Midair***, required me to learn a lot about British Airways, so I again researched everything I could about their planes, the construction of them, speed, altitude at which they fly, anything I could find out about the planes. The airline involved was true to life, it was just the characters and the action that were fiction. Beryl's Cove is a fictional place, but I still have to know quite a bit about the Outer Banks area of North Carolina in order to be credible."

McCanless also knows that strong characters are needed to keep readers returning to her books. "As for my characters, I'm a great people watcher; people fascinate me, and I enjoy making up some of my more nefarious residents of Beryl's Cove. Plus, I come from a large family, and several composites of family members have ended up in the books. Since they are unable to pinpoint which ones, they can't sue me!"

She reminds writers to keep the characters real and remember that everybody is flawed in some way. "My point is to take a person, make them vulnerable, then expand on the vulnerability. Writing about bad guys is the easiest part of fiction – just let all your hostilities and frustrations bubble up into a person, and voila, you have a bad guy. With all the stuff going on in the world today, it isn't hard to find something to write about when it comes to adding in the more smarmy characters. I simply have fun with it, if murder can be considered fun, and I'm proud to say, no one gets killed off who doesn't deserve it."

Readers will be glad to know that McCanless has no plans of slowing down her writing career any time soon. "Along with teaching writing seminars, I am continuing my magazine and newspaper columns – six national periodicals and two newspapers. It keeps me busy and off the street. My next book is entitled ***Murder for the Profit***, and it should be out next year. I am having great fun with it."

She tells her seminar students to believe in themselves and stick with the writing process. "Know your subject, do your research, and write it well."

"Vitality shows in not only the ability to persist but the ability to start over."

—F. Scott Fitzgerald

Chapter V
Happy Endings

The Greatest Valentine Story Ever Told

I don't think there is anyone anywhere who hasn't at some time, rhapsodized over the story line of Casablanca. Who among us hasn't yearned for a Rick or Ilsa in our lives – some long lost love that we thought we'd never see again, but pined for every day of our lives? We are all romantics at heart. And, on this Valentine's Day, I'd love to share with you – in their own words – the story of my friends, Carole and Claude. They live in a beautiful chalet home high in the French Alps. You will never hear a more heartwarming love story than theirs.

"It was the floods of 1959 that brought my father, sister, brother and me to the French Alps, as my father was the Chief Mining Expert in the company that was rebuilding the road that ran into the Queyras Valley. My father had rented a flat in a house just outside the village and Claude and his family were our neighbors. It was June, 1961, when we arrived. And I was 14 years old, having just finished school. We all became great friends, and Claude and I fell in love. He was 18, and was working in his father's building business. At the time they were building a house between theirs and ours, which meant we saw each other frequently.

In October of that year, I went back to live with my mother in England. Early in 1962, Claude went to do his two years' army service and it was then that we began writing to each other. I was at college then. During the summer holidays I would come back to visit my family and see Claude.

The last time I saw him was in September 1964. We made plans and talked of getting married. But early in 1965, he wrote to tell me that he had met another girl, and was getting married. I didn't reply to his letter. I was just totally distraught as he was my first love; and, at that time, I thought he would be last and only love.

My sorrow turned to anger and I burned every one of his letters and got on with my life. It took me a very long time to get over the betrayal; but I married and was lucky enough to travel extensively with my husband, a journalist. Every time we flew over the Alps, I did wonder how Claude was and what he was doing but that was all. My son was born and all was perfect until 1998, when I suddenly became a widow. I was working for a Sports Car Club from home and my social life was pretty full. But somehow, the emptiness lay very heavy on my heart.

On the 22nd of December, I received a letter that was to change my life. It was from Claude, telling me he was widowed, and wanted to see me again. The shock was huge, and out of curiosity, more than anything, I rang him.

It seemed he had been trying to find me and it was through a postcard I had sent to his mother some 40 years before that he finally managed to trace me. All my anger came back at being dumped back in '65, and it took another six months before I agreed to meet him outside a metro station in Paris in May 2002. When I arrived, he was there, with his back to me. I was nervous, but then he turned around and gave me a smile that lit up the sky. We both had aged and we had both been marked by life, but I would have recognized that smile and those twinkling eyes anywhere.

After that he came to England and I visited him in Guiles Tre with my son. Throughout our many letters in 2001-2003 we got to know each other again and it was obvious that the bond we had forged in 1961 was still there and had never really gone away.

In June 2004, Claude and I were married. It took us 40 years to fulfill the plans we had made that September in 1964, and now we're like two old slippers, comfy and snug together.

Everyone has one big love in their lives. Now I know that Claude was, and always will be, mine."

You couldn't make up this stuff. Great story, isn't it?

Happy Valentine's Day to all you lovers out there!

Jan McCanless

The Most Beautiful Girl in the World

It's nice every so often to hear of a happily ever after story, and this one is, I think, exceptional.

She was 15, he was her teacher, but forbidden as it was, the attraction was there. He couldn't get her out of his mind, she was beautiful, and such a good student.

They began to date, student and pupil, going places they didn't think other students would be. It was a different time back then; he asked permission to date her, and received the parental yes.

The war interrupted everything, and he enlisted in the Navy, and went, leaving her behind, but still, she was on his mind. The most beautiful girl he had ever seen, he told her. When his tour of duty was up, he returned home, to North Carolina, and the girl he left behind.

After her graduation, they married, and began their family. He realized he could not support a family on the teacher’s salary back then, so, he left teaching and went to work for the government's postal department. Soon, there were 3 little mouths to feed, and they were happy. Her brown eyes still sparkle when she tells me about it, and to this day, you can still discern her beauty pageant looks, and not a day goes by he does not tell her she is the most beautiful girl in the world.

Married now for over 60 years, I asked her what the secret to a successful marriage was. As they tend to one another, and help each other to get around, she smiles and says, “Be kind to one another, tell your spouse you love them, every day, and don't sweat the small stuff”.

Good advice under any circumstances.

Are they living happily ever after? After three children, one grandchild, and one great grandchild, you bet!